Contents

Contents

Name _____

Strategy Workshop

As you listen to the story "The Pumpkin Runner," by Marsha Diane Arnold, you will stop from time to time to do some activities on these practice pages. These activities will help you think about different strategies that can help you read better. After completing each activity, you will discuss what you've written with your classmates and talk about how to use these strategies.

Remember, strategies can help you become a better reader. Good readers

- use strategies whenever they read

- use different strategies before, during, and after reading

- think about how strategies will help them

Name _____

Strategy I: Predict/Infer

Use this strategy before and during reading to help make predictions about what happens next or what you're going to learn.

Here's how to use the Predict/Infer strategy:

1. Think about the title, the illustrations, and what you have read so far.
2. Tell what you think will happen next—or what you will learn. Thinking about what you already know about the topic may help.
3. Try to figure out things the author does not say directly.

Listen as your teacher begins "The Pumpkin Runner." When your teacher stops, complete the activity to show that you understand how to predict what you think might happen in the story.

Think about the story and respond to the question below.

What do you think might happen in the story?

_____

_____

_____

_____

As you continue listening to the story, think about whether your prediction was right. You might want to change your prediction or write a new one below.

_____

_____

_____

_____

_____

Name _____

Strategy 2: Phonics/Decoding

Use this strategy during reading when you come across a word you don't know.

Here's how to use the Phonics/Decoding strategy:
1. Look carefully at the word.
2. Look for word parts that you know and think about the sounds for the letters.
3. Blend the sounds to read the word.
4. Ask yourself if this is a word you know and whether the word makes sense in the sentence.
5. If not, ask yourself what else you can try. Should you look in a dictionary?

Listen as your teacher continues to read the story. When your teacher stops, use the Phonics/Decoding strategy.

Now write down the steps you used to decode the word *hundred*.

_____

_____

_____

_____

_____

_____

_____

_____

_____

_____

Remember to use this strategy whenever you are reading and come across a word that you don't know.

Name _____

Strategy 3: Monitor/Clarify

Use this strategy during reading whenever you're confused about what you are reading.

Here's how to use the Monitor/Clarify strategy:
- Ask yourself if what you're reading makes sense—or if you are learning what you need to learn.
- If you don't understand something, reread, use the illustrations, or read ahead to see if that helps.

Listen as your teacher continues to read the story. When your teacher stops, complete the activity to show that you understand how to figure out why Joshua tells the man to give Aunt Millie a map of the course.

Think about the story and respond below.

1. What do you know about Joshua?

_____

_____

_____

_____

2. Can you tell from listening to the story why Joshua talks about checking his herd? Why or why not?

_____

_____

_____

_____

3. How can you find out why Joshua isn't talking about training?

_____

_____

_____

Name _____

Strategy 4: Question

Use this strategy during and after reading to ask questions about important ideas in the story.

Here's how to use the Question strategy:

- Ask yourself questions about important ideas in the story.
- Ask yourself if you can answer these questions.
- If you can't answer the questions, reread and look for answers in the text. Thinking about what you already know and what you've read in the story may help you.

Listen as your teacher continues to read the story. When your teacher stops, complete the activity to show that you understand how to ask yourself questions about important ideas in the story.

Think about the story and respond below.

Write a question you might ask yourself at this point in the story.

_____

_____

_____

_____

_____

_____

_____

_____

_____

If you can't answer your question now, think about it while you listen to the rest of the story.

Name _____

Strategy 5: Evaluate

Use this strategy during and after reading to help you form an opinion about what you read.

Here's how to use the Evaluate strategy:
- Think about how the author makes the story come alive and makes you want to read it.
- Think about what was entertaining, informative, or useful about the selection.
- Think about how you reacted to the story—how well you understood the selection and whether you enjoyed reading it.

Listen as your teacher continues to read the story. When your teacher stops, complete the activity to show that you are thinking of how you feel about what you are reading and why you feel that way.

Think about the story and respond below.

1. Tell whether or not you think this story is entertaining and why.

_____

_____

_____

2. Is the writing clear and easy to understand?

_____

_____

_____

3. This is an adventurous fiction story. Did the author make the characters believable and interesting?

_____

_____

Name _____

Strategy 6: Summarize

Use this strategy after reading to summarize what you read.

Here's how to use the Summarize strategy:
- Think about the characters.
- Think about where the story takes place.
- Think about the problem in the story and how the characters solve it.
- Think about what happens in the beginning, middle, and end of the story.

Think about the story you just listened to. Complete the activity to show that you understand how to identify important story parts that will help you summarize the story.

Think about the story and respond to the questions below:

1. Who is the main character?

_____

_____

_____

2. Where does the story take place?

_____

_____

_____

3. What is the problem and how is it resolved?

_____

_____

_____

_____

Now use this information to summarize the story for a partner.

Name _____

Think About Journeys

What kinds of journeys do you know about? Use the space below to jot down all kinds of journeys.

Journeys I've taken	Journeys taken by people I know	Journeys from books, the movies, or TV

Choose one of the journeys above that was really important to the person who took it, and answer the following questions:

Who took the journey?

_____

Where did that person go and why?

_____

_____

How or why was that experience important?

_____

_____

_____

Name _____

Challenges Along the Way

As you read, complete the chart below for each story.

	What problems or challenges do the characters face on their journey?	Why is the journey important to the characters?
Akiak		
Grandfather's Journey		
Finding the Titanic		
By the Shores of Silver Lake		

2   Theme 1: **Journeys**

Name _____

Cold Words

Match each word to its definition by writing the letter on the line beside the word. Then answer the questions that follow.

____ blizzard

____ checkpoint

____ courageous

____ experienced

____ musher

____ rugged

a. the driver of a dogsled team

b. having a rough, uneven surface

c. a very heavy snowstorm with strong winds

d. a place along a route where vehicles or travelers are counted

e. having skill or knowledge from doing something in the past

f. brave

1. How would a **blizzard** affect driving conditions?

_____

_____

2. What have you done that is **courageous**?

_____

_____

3. Why does a **musher** have to love animals?

_____

_____

4. Why do **experienced** drivers make fewer mistakes?

_____

_____

5. Why is a **checkpoint** a good thing to have in a long race?

_____

_____

Name _____

Story Map

Main Characters

_____

Setting

_____

Problem Facing Characters (page 37)

_____

_____

Step One (page 39)

_____

_____

Step Two (page 40)

_____

Step Three (page 42)

_____

Solution (pages 49–50)

_____

_____

Name _____

Hero of the Trail

Complete the information for the TV special based on *Akiak*.

TV Sports Special

Title character: _____

Brief description: _____

_____

Second main character: _____

Brief description: _____

_____

Background about the Iditarod: _____

_____

_____

Organization of story: _____

_____

Summary: _____

_____

_____

_____

_____

_____

_____

_____

_____

_____

Name _____

Universal Knowledge

Read the story. Then complete the chart on the following page.

Saving the Solar System!

Justin stood back, turned on the switch, and watched the planets begin to move. He had worked for months creating a motorized model of the solar system to enter in the science fair. And today was the day. He carried the model out to the car, where his mother was waiting.

Justin tried to get the model into the car without damaging any parts. It didn't fit! "Mom!" Justin almost shouted. "Please! Let's ask Mrs. Kravitz from next door if she'll help with her minivan."

Justin explained his problem to Mrs. Kravitz, who smiled and said, "I'd be honored to help save the universe!"

When they finally reached school, Justin removed the model from the minivan, thanked Mrs. Kravitz, and carried in his project. He took his assigned place and then realized that there was no electrical outlet close enough to plug in his model. And the judging was about to start!

Justin spotted the janitor, Mr. Jackson. Justin asked if he might borrow an extension cord. Mr. Jackson smiled as he handed the cord to Justin and said, "I'm happy to do anything to help the universe."

Justin thanked Mr. Jackson, quickly attached the extension cord, and finally plugged in his model. Just as the judges were stepping up to his area, Justin flipped the switch. The planets slowly began to move, just as they should. Justin sighed with relief. The solar system had been saved.

Name _____

Universal Knowledge

**Complete this Problem-Solution Frame for the story
"Saving the Solar System."**

The Problems That Justin Faces and the Solutions He Finds
Problem 1: _____   _____
Solution 1: _____   _____   _____
Problem 2: _____   _____
Solution 2: _____   _____

If you had been Justin, what would you have done in advance to
avoid the problems he faced on the day of the science fair?

_____

_____

What might Justin have done if Mrs. Kravitz and her minivan were
unable to transport his project?

_____

_____

Name _____

Adding *-er* and *-est* to Adjectives

Add *-er* to an adjective to compare two people, places, or things:

Willy's team of dogs is fast**er** than the other team.

Add *-est* to an adjective to compare three or more people, places, or things:

Mick's team is fast**est** of all.

Read each sentence. Change the adjective in parentheses to the correct form as you write it in the puzzle. Remember the spelling rules!

Across

1. People believed Akiak was the (brave) sled dog of all.
3. After the race, Mick was the (happy) musher in Alaska.
4. A dog's undercoat is (fine) than its outer coat.
7. Huskies are not the (friendly) breed of dogs.

Down

2. The ice is (thin) at the edge of the lake than in the middle.
3. The snowfall is (heavy) today than yesterday.
4. Isn't that the (fat) Husky puppy you've ever seen?
5. The cocoa is (hot) than the tea.
6. The sky on the first day was (blue) than a robin's egg.

Name _____

The /ă/, /ā/, /ĕ/, and /ē/ Sounds

Remember that the /ă/ sound is usually spelled *a* followed by a consonant sound. When you hear the /ā/ sound, think of the patterns *a-consonant-e*, *ai*, and *ay*.

　　　　　/ă/ p**a**st　　　/ā/ s**a**fe, g**ai**n, gr**ay**

Remember that the /ĕ/ sound is usually spelled *e* followed by a consonant sound. When you hear the /ē/ sound, think of the patterns *ea* and *ee*.

　　　　　/ĕ/ k**e**pt　　　/ē/ cr**ea**m, sw**ee**t

► In the starred words *break* and *steak*, *ea* spells the /ā/ sound, not the /ē/ sound.

► In the starred words *field* and *chief*, the /ē/ sound is spelled *ie*.

Write each Spelling Word under its vowel sound.

Spelling Words

1. gain
2. cream
3. sweet
4. safe
5. past
6. reach
7. kept
8. gray
9. field*
10. break*
11. east
12. shape
13. steep
14. pray
15. pain
16. glass
17. west
18. cheap
19. steak*
20. chief*

/ă/ Sound	/ĕ/ Sound
_____	_____
_____	_____

/ā/ Sound	/ē/ Sound
_____	_____
_____	_____
_____	_____
_____	_____
_____	_____
_____	_____

Name _____

Spelling Spree

Finding Words Write the Spelling Word hidden in each word below.

1. painting _____

2. reshapes _____

3. cheapest _____

4. screams _____

5. again _____

6. preacher _____

7. sprayer _____

8. pasture _____

Familiar Phrases Write the Spelling Word that completes each phrase.

9. grill a _____

10. found _____ and sound

11. tastes as _____ as honey

12. a big _____ of milk

13. the _____ of police

14. _____ a secret

15. a _____ of wheat

Spelling Words

1. gain
2. cream
3. sweet
4. safe
5. past
6. reach
7. kept
8. gray
9. field*
10. break*
11. east
12. shape
13. steep
14. pray
15. pain
16. glass
17. west
18. cheap
19. steak*
20. chief*

Proofreading and Writing

Proofreading Circle the five misspelled Spelling Words in this weather report. Then write each word correctly.

The weather for this week's Iditarod will start off cold and grae. Then a storm front from the wast will bring snow to the area. The snow will be very heavy to the est, up in the mountains. If you're traveling in that area, play it safe! Watch out for ice on the steap hills. We should get a braek in the weather later in the week. The clouds will move away, the sun will return, and the temperature will warm up to just below freezing!

Spelling Words

1. gain
2. cream
3. sweet
4. safe
5. past
6. reach
7. kept
8. gray
9. field*
10. break*
11. east
12. shape
13. steep
14. pray
15. pain
16. glass
17. west
18. cheap
19. steak*
20. chief*

1. _____
2. _____
3. _____
4. _____
5. _____

✏️ **Write an Explanation** The Iditarod is a difficult race that requires skill, courage, and lots of training. Do you like snowstorms and sledding? Have you ever trained a dog? Would you like to race in the Iditarod? Why or why not?

On a separate piece of paper, write a paragraph explaining why you would or would not like to take part in the race. Use Spelling Words from the list.

Multiple-Meaning Words

> **de•scent** (dĭ sĕnt´) *noun* **1.** Movement from a higher place to a lower one: *the descent of an elevator.* **2.** Downward slope or inclination: *a staircase with a steep descent.* **3.** Ancestry or birth: *That family is of Russian descent.* **4.** A sudden attack: *The bird's descent on the worm was swift.*

For each sentence, choose the correct definition of the underlined word and write its number on the line.

1. The hill's <u>descent</u> was not very steep, so we reached the bottom easily. _____

2. Many people of Inuit <u>descent</u> live in Alaska. _____

3. The explorers had a difficult <u>descent</u> down the rocky mountain. _____

4. The hungry dogs made a quick <u>descent</u> on the food. _____

> **ref•uge** (rĕf´ ūj) *noun* **1.** Shelter or protection from danger: *The frightened cat took refuge under the bed.* **2.** A place providing shelter or protection: *There are many animals in the wildlife refuge.* **3.** A source of comfort or relief: *Listening to music is her refuge when she's feeling sad.*

For each underlined word, choose the correct definition and write its number on the line at the end of the sentence.

5. The injured elephant was sent to a <u>refuge</u> for sick animals. _____

6. During the blizzard, the lost dog found <u>refuge</u> behind a snowdrift. _____

7. After losing the game, the team took <u>refuge</u> in knowing that they played their best. _____

8. The huge tree provided a <u>refuge</u> for the bird's nest. _____

Name _____

Finding Kinds of Sentences

Rewrite each sentence on the lines below, adding the correct end mark. Then write what type of sentence it is.

1. The trail is very long and difficult

   _____

   _____

2. Did Akiak ever win a race before

   _____

   _____

3. How many teams began the race

   _____

   _____

4. What a smart lead dog she is

   _____

   _____

5. Hold on to the dog, please

   _____

   _____

Name _____

Sentences About Alaska

**Read the facts below about Alaska, and use the facts to write
five sentences. Write at least one command, one question, one
statement, and one exclamation.**

Facts

- became 49th state in 1959
- largest state of all
- Mt. McKinley: highest mountain
  in North America
- Yukon River: 2,000 miles long
- many active volcanoes
- midsummer sun shines all night
- capital is Juneau
- Iditarod race in March each year

1. _____
   _____

2. _____
   _____

3. _____
   _____

4. _____
   _____

5. _____
   _____

Name _____

Capitalizing and Punctuating Sentences

**Careful writers capitalize the first word of every sentence
and make sure that each sentence has the right end mark.
Read the sentences below. Rewrite each sentence,
adding capital letters and end marks where needed.
Then write what kind of sentence each is.**

1. this race was the first one for some dogs

   This race was the First one for some dogs.

2. did you ever see the Iditarod race

   Did you ever see the Iditarod race.

3. how fast the sled dogs run

   How Fast the sled dogs run?

4. watch the lead dog of the sled team

   Watch

5. which team won the race

   _____

Name _____

Planning Chart

Use this chart to help you plan your news article.

Topic of news article: _____

Who?	What?
_____	_____
_____	_____
_____	_____
_____	_____
When?	**Where?**
_____	_____
_____	_____
_____	_____
_____	_____
Why?	**How?**
_____	_____
_____	_____
_____	_____
_____	_____

Name _____

Adding Details

From the details given below, choose the detail that you think adds the right information to each sentence and write it in the blank provided.

Through icy water and confusing trails	fifty-eight
a maze of	deep, wet
wait out the storm	From Anchorage to Nome,

1. _____ ,
   the sled dog teams battled wind, snow, and steep, rugged trails.

2. The race began and one by one, the _____
   teams took off.

3. _____ ,
   Akiak never got lost, but always found the safest and fastest way.

4. Akiak was limping because the
   _____
   snow had made one of her paws sore.

5. Akiak burrowed into a snowdrift to _____
   _____ .

6. Halfway to the checkpoint, Mick's team came upon
   _____ snowmobile tracks.

Name _____

Revising Your Personal Narrative

Reread your story. What do you need to make it better? Use this page to help you decide. Put a checkmark in the box for each sentence that describes your personal narrative.

Rings the Bell!

☐ The beginning catches the reader's interest.

☐ The story is told in sequence and is easy to follow.

☐ Everything in my story is important to the topic.

☐ The sentences flow smoothly and don't repeat unnecessary information.

☐ There are almost no mistakes.

Getting Stronger

☐ The beginning could be more interesting.

☐ The sequence of events isn't always clear.

☐ There are some things that I could take out that don't relate to the story topic.

☐ I could combine some sentences to make this flow more smoothly.

☐ There are a few mistakes.

Try Harder

☐ The beginning is boring.

☐ Events are out of order and confusing to the reader.

☐ A lot of the story doesn't relate to the main topic.

☐ There are a lot of mistakes.

Name _____

Varying Sentences

Change these paragraphs in the spaces provided. Each paragraph should have at least one example of each type of sentence: declarative, interrogative, command, and exclamatory.

Balloon Bread
No Sentence Variation

My mom and I made bread. We mixed warm water and flour. We added yeast. We let the dough rise. The dough kept rising and rising. We baked the bread. It came out way too light and fluffy — like a balloon. We put in too much yeast. Better luck next time.

Balloon Bread
Sentence Variation

_____

_____

_____

Junk Food
No Sentence Variation

Am I unusual? Why don't I like junk food? Why do I lose my appetite at fast food places? Do you like junk food? Does it make you sick? Do you think it's unhealthy? If so, then why do you eat it? And why does everyone else like it so much? Why am I so confused?

Junk Food
Sentence Variation

_____

_____

_____

Name _____

Spelling Words

Words Often Misspelled Look for familiar spelling patterns to help you remember how to spell the Spelling Words on this page. Think carefully about the parts that you find hard to spell in each word.

Write the missing letters and apostrophes in the Spelling Words below.

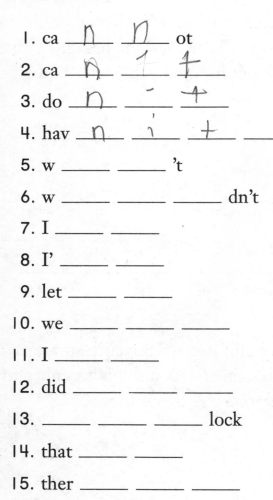

1. ca _n_ _n_ ot
2. ca _n_ _1_ _t_
3. do _n_ _–_ _t_
4. hav _n_ _i_ _t_ ___
5. w ____ ____ 't
6. w ____ ____ ____ dn't
7. I ____ ____
8. I' ____ ____
9. let ____ ____
10. we ____ ____ ____
11. I ____ ____
12. did ____ ____ ____
13. ____ ____ ____ lock
14. that ____ ____
15. ther ____ ____ ____

Spelling Words
1. cannot
2. can't
3. don't
4. haven't
5. won't
6. wouldn't
7. I'd
8. I'll
9. let's
10. we're
11. I'm
12. didn't
13. o'clock
14. that's
15. there's

Study List On a separate piece of paper, write each Spelling Word. Check your spelling against the words on the list.

Name _____

Spelling Spree

Write the Spelling Word that fits each clue.

1. If you're talking about your future, you might use this contraction. _____

2-3. This contraction and this word both say you're not able to do something. _____

4. A group of people talking about themselves might use this contraction. _____

5. This contraction tells you things not to do. _____

6. This contraction can tell time. _____

7. This contraction is the past tense of *doesn't*. _____

8. This contraction is a quick way to say you don't have something. _____

9. "I will not" can also be said "I _____."

Find a Rhyme **Write a Spelling Word that rhymes with the underlined word. Be sure it makes sense.**

10. _____ trying to find words that <u>rhyme</u>.

11. Ina <u>couldn't</u> pay attention to the movie because Ben _____ leave her alone.

12. If my ankle wasn't hurting me, _____ try to <u>ride</u> that horse.

13. My sister said _____ a kid in her class who eats four <u>pears</u> for lunch every day.

14. Well, _____ see who <u>gets</u> to the end of the block the quickest.

15. I think _____ the girl who <u>bats</u> from both sides of the plate.

Spelling Words

1. cannot
2. can't
3. don't
4. haven't
5. won't
6. wouldn't
7. I'd
8. I'll
9. let's
10. we're
11. I'm
12. didn't
13. o'clock
14. that's
15. there's

did not = didn't
I will = I'll
of the clock = o'clock

Theme 1: **Journeys**   21

Name _____

Proofreading and Writing

Proofreading Circle the five misspelled Spelling Words in this advertisement. Then write each word correctly.

Spelling Words
1. cannot
2. can't
3. don't
4. haven't
5. won't
6. wouldn't
7. I'd
8. I'll
9. let's
10. we're
11. I'm
12. didn't
13. o'clock
14. that's
15. there's

Think you dont have enough money to take a journey? Think again! With Express Airlines' new sale fares, you ca'nt afford not to travel! We've got flights going all over the country, at prices you won't believe. You can leave any time between six oclock in the morning and midnight. And we'ere proud to offer the best service of any airline out there. So you see, theres no reason not to fly with us!

1. _____

2. _____

3. _____

4. _____

5. _____

Journey Sentences Suppose you were going on a journey to a place where they spoke a foreign language. What are some things you might want to know how to say once you got there?

On a separate piece of paper, write five sentences you would want to know for your journey. Use Spelling Words from the list.

Name _____

Traveling Words

Write the words next to their definitions. Unscramble the circled letters to answer the question that follows.

Vocabulary

bewildered	homeland	longed
marveled	reminded	surrounded

1. country you were born in

2. wanted very much

3. became filled with wonder

4. puzzled greatly

5. made someone remember

6. put all around

What is a word for someone who takes a trip?

c t

Name _____

Word Web

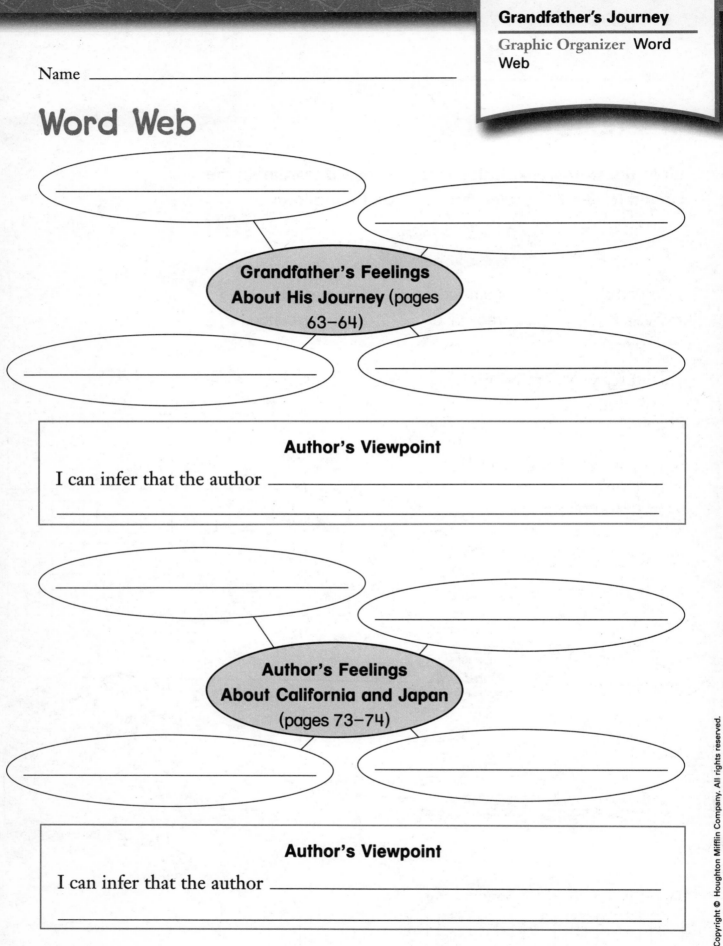

Grandfather's Feelings
About His Journey (pages
63–64)

Author's Viewpoint

I can infer that the author _____

_____

Author's Feelings
About California and Japan
(pages 73–74)

Author's Viewpoint

I can infer that the author _____

_____

Name _____

Grandfather's Diary

Help grandfather write his diary by filling in the blanks.

Entry 1—The Pacific Ocean is huge. Once we left Japan, we did

not see land again _____

Entry 2—America is as big as the ocean, and there is much to see.

I am excited and delighted by _____

_____

_____

_____

Entry 3—My favorite place is California because it has _____

_____

Entry 4—I returned to Japan to _____ and then

settled in _____

Entry 5—I miss my _____ and

homeland, so when my daughter is nearly grown, I take my family

_____

Name _____

A Moving View

Read the story. Then answer the questions on the following page.

Saying Good-bye, Saying Hello

"Hurry up, Anna! We've got a long drive ahead of us! We've got to get started now!" Recently, all my father seemed to do was shout. All I did was mope and complain. It only seemed fair because we were moving away from our home and from the friends I loved. As our car pulled away from the curb, I waved weakly at Andrea and Kelly. They were my very best friends in the whole world. And even though they promised to write every day, I knew our friendship might never be the same.

On the long drive from Indiana to New Mexico, my father talked and talked and talked about how happy we were going to be in our new home near my grandparents. But I didn't care. All I could think of was losing my whole life.

When I opened my eyes, the gentle desert sunlight smiled hello to me. We turned down a dirt road and out of a sand-colored house came running my grandparents and many other smiling relatives. My cousin Sunita pulled me away from the crowd and told me that we would be going to the same school and might even be in the same class. She also told me her favorite jokes, and I started laughing really hard.

I thought to myself, "Maybe I only left a part of my life behind. Maybe this next part will also be wonderful."

Name _____

A Moving View continued

Answer these questions that refer to the story "Saying Good-bye, Saying Hello."

What phrases does the narrator use to describe moving from Indiana?

_____

What can you infer about the narrator's feelings toward Indiana?

_____

_____

What phrases describe the narrator's experience in New Mexico?

_____

How does the narrator feel about New Mexico?

_____

_____

What is the author's purpose in writing this story?

_____

_____

Name _____

Suffixes *-ly* and *-y*

Add *-ly* or *-y* to a base word to mean "in the manner of."

high/high**ly**   rain/rain**y**

When a base word ends in a consonant and *y*, change the *y* to *i* before adding *-ly*.

speed**y**/speed**ily**   eas**y**/eas**ily**

When a base word ends in a short vowel and a consonant, double the consonant before adding *-y*.

fog/fog**gy**   tin/tin**ny**

Choose one of the pictures to write about in a short paragraph. Add *-y* or *-ly* to at least four of the words under the picture. Use them in your paragraph.

| chill | happy | quick | salt | | sad | merry | luck | sun |
| final | fog | sudden | weary | | silk | lone | hungry | soft |

_____

_____

_____

_____

Name Oswaldo

The /ĭ/, /ī/, /ŏ/, and /ō/ Sounds

Remember that the /ĭ/ sound is often spelled *i* followed by a consonant sound. When you hear the /ī/ sound, think of the patterns *i-consonant-e*, *igh*, and *i*.

> /ĭ/ st**i**ll /ī/ cr**i**me, fl**igh**t, gr**i**nd

▶ In the starred words *build* and *built*, the /ĭ/ sound is spelled *ui*.

Remember that the /ŏ/ sound is usually spelled *o* followed by a consonant sound. When you hear the /ō/ sound, think of the patterns *o-consonant-e*, *oa*, *ow*, and *o*.

> /ŏ/ **o**dd /ō/ wr**o**te, c**oa**st, sn**ow**, g**o**ld

Write each Spelling Word under its vowel sound.

Spelling Words

1. snow
2. grind
3. still
4. coast
5. odd
6. crime
7. gold
8. wrote
9. flight
10. build*
11. broke
12. blind
13. folk
14. grown
15. shock
16. ripe
17. coal
18. inch
19. sigh
20. built*

/ĭ/ Sound

still
build
inch
built

/ŏ/ Sound

coal

/ō/ Sound

/ī/ Sound

grind
crime
ripe
flight
blind

Name _____

Spelling Spree

Letter Math **Write a Spelling Word by adding and subtracting letters from the words below.**

Example: sm + poke − p = *smoke*

1. s + high − h = _____

2. b + quilt − q = _____

3. c + goal − g = _____

4. gr + blown − bl = _____

5. r + swipe − sw = _____

6. f + yolk − y = _____

7. cr + slime − sl = _____

Inside Switch **Change one letter on the inside of each word to make a Spelling Word. Write the words.**

Example: drip *drop*

8. grand _____

9. shack _____

10. blond _____

11. itch _____

12. old _____

13. brake _____

14. stall _____

15. write _____

Spelling Words

1. snow
2. grind
3. still
4. coast
5. odd
6. crime
7. gold
8. wrote
9. flight
10. build*
11. broke
12. blind
13. folk
14. grown
15. shock
16. ripe
17. coal
18. inch
19. sigh
20. built*

Name _____

Proofreading and Writing

Proofreading Circle the five misspelled Spelling Words in the tour schedule. Then write each word correctly.

California Dream Tour!

Day 1: Your plane lands in Los Angeles. Tour this famous city. Then ride along the area's beautiful cost.

Day 2: Spend a relaxing day on the beach at Santa Monica. Sun, surf, or bild your own sandcastle.

Day 3: Ride by bus to Yosemite National Park. Play in the sno on the mountains, then rest up at the lodge.

Day 4: Visit Sacramento. Explore the spot where golde was discovered in 1848. Pan for any of the precious metal that might still be left in the mountain streams.

Day 5: Take a bus to beautiful San Francisco and catch your flite home.

1. _____ 4. _____

2. _____ 5. _____

3. _____

Spelling Words

1. snow
2. grind
3. still
4. coast
5. odd
6. crime
7. gold
8. wrote
9. flight
10. build*
11. broke
12. blind
13. folk
14. grown
15. shock
16. ripe
17. coal
18. inch
19. sigh
20. built*

Write a Contest Entry A local travel agency is having a contest. First prize is a trip to anywhere in the United States. Where would you go if you had the opportunity? Would it be San Francisco? The Rocky Mountains? The Florida Everglades?

On a separate piece of paper, write a paragraph telling where you would go if you won the contest and why you want to go there. Use Spelling Words from the list.

Name Oswaldo

What's the Order?

Put each group of words in alphabetical order. Write the words on the lines provided.

week
war
where
warbler
when

_____
_____
_____
_____
_____

towering
travel
thought
there
trip

_____
_____
_____
_____
_____

steamship
seacoast
strong
songbird
sunlight

_____
_____
_____
_____
_____

Name _____

Identifying Subjects and Predicates

Copy each sentence and draw a vertical line between the complete subject and the complete predicate of each sentence. Then circle the simple subject and underline the simple predicate.

1. Grandfather met many different people in his travels.

   Grandfather met many different people in his travels.

2. The seacoast of California appealed to him.

   _____

3. The young man found a bride in Japan.

   _____

4. The two people made their home in San Francisco.

   _____

5. Memories of Japan filled Grandfather's mind.

   _____

Name _____

Connecting Subjects and Predicates

Draw a line connecting each subject in Column I with the predicate in Column 2 that makes the most sense. Put the two sentence parts together and write the whole sentence on the lines below. Then circle the simple subject and underline the simple predicate of each sentence you wrote.

Column 1	**Column 2**
I. The old man	a. went back home with him.
2. Songbirds	b. laughed with him.
3. The man's family	c. reminded him of Japan.
4. His old friends	d. married a man in Japan.
5. The couple's daughter	e. remembered his homeland fondly.

I. _____

2. _____

3. _____

4. _____

5. _____

Name _____

Sentence Combining

Use the joining word in parentheses to combine each pair of sentences
below with a compound subject or a compound predicate.
Write the new sentence. Then circle the compound part in
your new sentence and write whether it is a compound
subject or a compound predicate.

1. The grandfather talked with his grandson.

   The grandfather told stories about California. (and)

   _____

   _____

2. Grandfather raised songbirds.

   Grandfather loved their songs. (and)

   _____

   _____

3. Warblers were his favorite birds.

   Silvereyes were his favorite birds. (and)

   _____

   _____

4. Bombs fell.

   Bombs ruined many homes. (and)

   _____

   _____

5. The old man lost a home.

   His family lost a home. (and)

   _____

   _____

 Theme 1: **Journeys**   35

Name _____

What Are My Thoughts?

Title of Story _____

Response Journal

Use the questions below to write your responses to the story.

How do I feel about the events of the story?

_____

_____

How do I feel about the main character?

_____

_____

What do I like best about the story? What do I like least?

_____

_____

What do I think will happen next in the story?

_____

_____

What puzzles me about the story?

_____

_____

Which character in the story is most like me? Why?

_____

_____

What else would I like to say about the story?

_____

_____

_____

Name _____

Giving Examples

Improve each of the following response journal entries by adding examples based on *Grandfather's Journey*. Write your examples on the lines provided.

1. If I were to travel in a foreign country, I would like to do and see many things.

   _____

   _____

   _____

2. If I lived in a foreign country, I would miss many things about the United States.

   _____

   _____

   _____

3. When I was the age of the small boy in the story, I too had a favorite thing to do on a weekend with my family.

   _____

   _____

   _____

4. Some things puzzle me about the people in the story.

   _____

   _____

   _____

5. I have some class project ideas related to Japan.

   _____

   _____

Name _____

Seaworthy Words

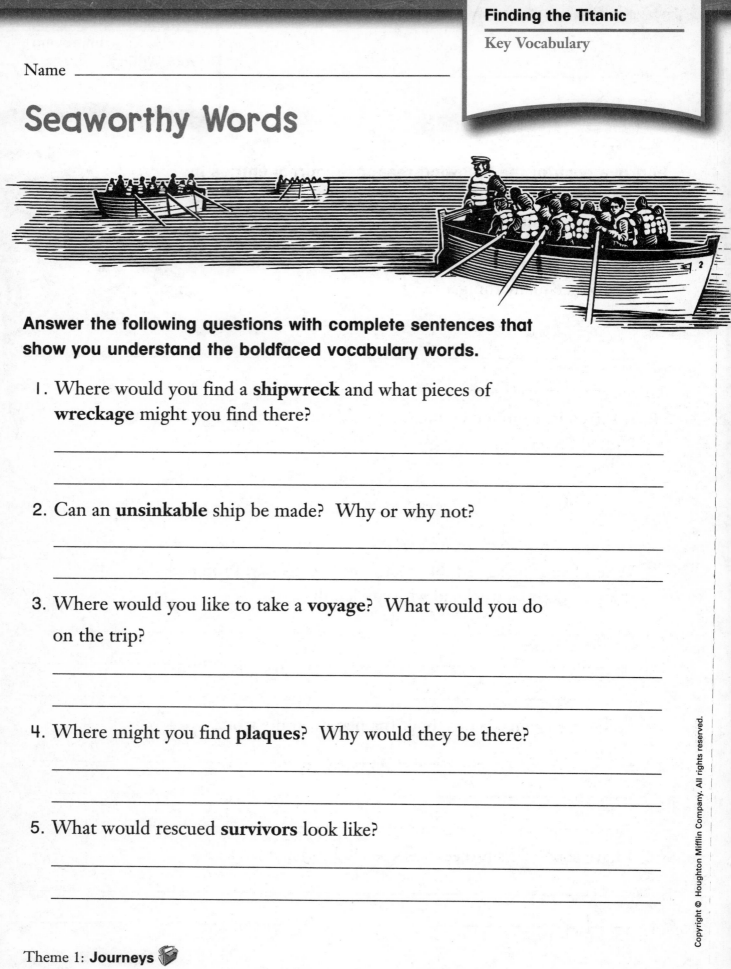

Answer the following questions with complete sentences that show you understand the boldfaced vocabulary words.

1. Where would you find a **shipwreck** and what pieces of **wreckage** might you find there?

   _____

   _____

2. Can an **unsinkable** ship be made? Why or why not?

   _____

   _____

3. Where would you like to take a **voyage**? What would you do on the trip?

   _____

   _____

4. Where might you find **plaques**? Why would they be there?

   _____

   _____

5. What would rescued **survivors** look like?

   _____

   _____

Name _____

Organizational Outline

I. Chapter One

A. Main Idea: _____

_____

B. What the pictures show: _____

_____

II. Chapter Two

A. Main Idea: _____

_____

B. What the pictures show: _____

_____

III. Chapter Three

A. Main Idea: _____

_____

B. What the pictures show: _____

_____

IV. Chapter Four

A. Main Idea: _____

_____

B. What the pictures show: _____

_____

V. Chapter Six

A. Main Idea: _____

_____

B. What the pictures show: _____

_____

Name _____

Time Goes On

Complete the sentences about the time line. Then answer the question below.

1910

April 10, 1912 The *Titanic*, a brand new luxury liner as tall as an

_____, set sail from Southampton,

England.

April 15, 1912 The *Titanic* crashed into an _____.

Many people were still on board when the giant ship _____.

1950

August 25, 1985 The *Titanic* lay _____

on the ocean floor, too deep for any diver, but the *Argo*, an

_____ equipped with a video camera,

searched and found the *Titanic*.

August 31, 1985 The first piece of the *Titanic* found by the

cameras was a _____ used to drive the

ship's engines.

1980

1985

July 13, 1986 The robot, _____,

1990

photographed the shiny chandelier that hung over the Grand

Staircase.

How is it possible that the *Titanic* could not be found

for seventy-five years but can now be seen and photographed?

_____

_____

40   Theme 1: **Journeys**

Name _____

Organizing the Wreckage

Read the article. Then answer the questions on the following page.

Why Did the *Lusitania* Sink?

1. Exploring the Wreck

Dr. Robert Ballard, the explorer who discovered the *Titanic*, decided to look for the *Lusitania*. He wanted to find out what caused the huge explosion onboard the ship. He also wanted to know why it sank so quickly. Using high-technology submarines and robots, his crew explored the wreck. What they found was a huge hole in the ship's bow. The hole was right where there were compartments used to store coal, which fueled the ship. And to their amazement, the hole looked like it was blasted from the inside out!

2. Setting Sail

On May 7, 1915, the British ocean liner *Lusitania* was sailing off the coast of Ireland. It was on its way from New York to England. In Europe, World War I was being fought, but no one thought that a submarine would sink an ocean liner filled with passengers. On that day, however, a submarine launched a torpedo toward the *Lusitania*. When the torpedo struck the ship, there was a huge explosion. The ship sank in less than 20 minutes, and many passengers and crew lost their lives.

Time Line: The Wreck of the *Lusitania*

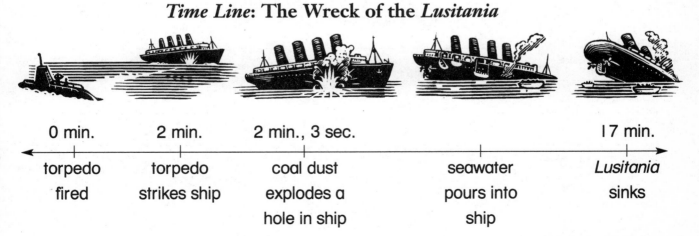

0 min.	2 min.	2 min., 3 sec.		17 min.
torpedo fired	torpedo strikes ship	coal dust explodes a hole in ship	seawater pours into ship	*Lusitania* sinks

Name _____

Organizing the Wreckage

continued

Answer the following questions about the sinking of the *Lusitania*.

1. What are this article's special features?

   _____

2. What is the purpose of the visual aid?

   _____

   _____

3. How well does this visual aid work? Explain your answer.

   _____

   _____

4. What would you do to better organize this article? Explain
   your answer.

   _____

   _____

   _____

   _____

   _____

Name _____

Syllabication

All words contain **syllables**, which are smaller parts you hear when you say a word out loud. For example, the name *Titanic* contains three syllables: /tī - TAN - ĭlkl/. Some long words such as *thought* have only one syllable.

dreamed	largest	passenger
dreamed (one)	larg-est (two)	pas-sen-ger (three)

Use what you've learned about syllabication to break each word into syllables. Rewrite the word to show the syllables. (The first one is done for you.) Then arrange the words with three syllables to make an exciting newspaper headline from 1985.

OCEAN DAILY TIMES

_____ _____

_____ _____ !

1. cabin   **cab-in**

2. explore   _____

3. signals   _____

4. underneath   _____

5. huge   _____

6. bigger   _____

7. Atlantic   _____

8. iceberg   _____

9. discovered   _____

10. sinking   _____

11. straight   _____

12. Titanic   _____

Name _____

The /ŭ/, /yo͞o/, and /o͞o/ Sounds

Remember that the /ŭ/ sound is usually spelled *u* followed by a consonant sound. When you hear the /yo͞o/ or the /o͞o/ sound, think of the patterns *u*-consonant-*e*, *ew*, *ue*, and *ui*.

/ŭ/ br**u**sh   /yo͞o/ and /o͞o/ **tube**, **few**, **true**, **juice**

► In the starred word *done*, the /ŭ/ sound is spelled *o*. In the starred word *truth*, the /o͞o/ sound is spelled *u*.

Write each Spelling Word under its vowel sound.

Spelling Words

1. brush
2. juice
3. fruit
4. tube
5. lunch
6. crumb
7. few
8. true
9. truth*
10. done*
11. suit
12. pump
13. due
14. dull
15. tune
16. blew
17. trunk
18. sum
19. glue
20. threw

/ŭ/ Sound	/yo͞o/ or /o͞o/ Sound
_____	_____
_____	_____
_____	_____
_____	_____
_____	_____
_____	_____
_____	_____
_____	_____
	_____
	_____
	_____

Name _____

Spelling Spree

Word Search **Write the Spelling Word that is hidden in each sentence.**

Example: We found shelter in a small grass <u>hut</u>. *shut*

1. Don't trip over the cable wire.
2. The two sisters sang a duet.
3. Beth reworded her opening paragraph.
4. You can fill that tub easily with a garden hose.
5. The snowstorm was not unexpected.
6. The frisky lamb rushed to the pasture.
7. The explorers found a small uncharted island.
8. That ruthless villain must be punished!

1. _____   5. _____
2. _____   6. _____
3. _____   7. _____
4. _____   8. _____

Alphabet Puzzler **Write the Spelling Word that would appear alphabetically between each pair of words below.**

9. forest, _____, gate

10. castle, _____, cute

11. trumpet, _____, trust

12. garden, _____, hard

13. duke, _____, dusty

14. jam, _____, justice

15. robot, _____, suitcase

Spelling Words

1. brush
2. juice
3. fruit
4. tube
5. lunch
6. crumb
7. few
8. true
9. truth*
10. done*
11. suit
12. pump
13. due
14. dull
15. tune
16. blew
17. trunk
18. sum
19. glue
20. threw

Name _____

Proofreading and Writing

Proofreading Circle the five misspelled
Spelling Words in this interview. Then write
each word correctly on the lines below.

Reporter: I'm writing a story about the
Titanic. Can you answer a fue questions?

Scientist: I'll try. Do you mind if I eat lunch while
we talk?

Reporter: No, I don't mind at all. Tell me, is it troo
that the ship broke in two before it sank?

Scientist: Yes, that is correct. After the impact the crew
tried to pomp the water out, but it was no use. The
iceberg had dun too much damage.

Reporter: Can you som up for us what you've learned
from the Titanic?

Scientist: There's no such thing as an unsinkable ship.

1. _____   4. _____

2. _____   5. _____

3. _____

Spelling Words

1. brush
2. juice
3. fruit
4. tube
5. lunch
6. crumb
7. few
8. true
9. truth*
10. done*
11. suit
12. pump
13. due
14. dull
15. tune
16. blew
17. trunk
18. sum
19. glue
20. threw

Write a Story Have you ever wondered what you would do
in an unfamiliar or dangerous situation? Write the beginning
of an adventure story. The setting could be anywhere—an
underwater cave or a galaxy far, far away.

**On a separate sheet of paper, write the opening paragraph for
your story. Use Spelling Words from the list.**

Name _____

Find a Better Word

In each sentence, replace the underlined word with a better word or words. Choose your word or words from the thesaurus entries below and write them on the line. Remember that more than one word may be correct in some cases.

1. **bottom:** base, floor, depths, foot, ground
   Many ships have sunk to the <u>bottom</u> of the ocean as a result
   of accidents or storms at sea.

   _____

2. **group:** band, body, crew, crowd, gang, heap
   There was a large <u>group</u> of people on the dock waving good-bye
   to the passengers.

   _____

3. **recovery:** bailout, release, rescue, salvage
   In the distance the survivors could see the <u>recovery</u> ship.

   _____

4. **hard:** stable, solid, sound, stout, sturdy, tough
   The <u>hard</u> deck of the ship felt good beneath her feet.

   _____

5. **dangerous:** adventurous, bad, perilous, risky, serious
   Alvin's first trip to video the wreckage was <u>dangerous</u>.

   _____

Name _____

Connecting Compound Sentences

Underline the two sentences that have been combined in the compound sentences below. Then circle the conjunction that joins them.

1. The *Titanic* had nine decks, and it was as tall as an eleven-story building.

2. The Becker family boarded the ship, and a steward helped them to find their room.

3. Ruth took the elevator to the lowest level, and she found a swimming pool there.

4. Ruth wanted to go on deck, but the weather was too cold.

5. The ship was traveling fast, but ice could slow it down.

Name _____

Compound Sentences in a Letter

Read this student's letter to a friend. On the lines below, write compound sentences.

Dear Sylvia,

    I just read about the sinking of the *Titanic*. The author of the piece is a scientist. His name is Robert Ballard, and he explores the oceans. Ballard has found undersea mountains, but he is also interested in sunken ships. He searched the Atlantic Ocean for the *Titanic*, and his crew finally found it. The ship was on its first trip to the United States in 1912. It was supposed to be unsinkable, but it hit an iceberg. The iceberg tore a hole in the hull of the ship, and the ship sank.

        Your friend,

        Janice

_____

_____

_____

_____

_____

_____

_____

_____

Name _____

Writing Compound Sentences

Good writers often combine two sentences with related ideas into a compound sentence. Read the following pairs of sentences. Then rewrite each pair by combining the sentences into a single compound sentence, adding one of the joining words *and* or *but*. Punctuate the sentences correctly.

1. The three-man crew climbed into the tiny submarine. It slowly went down to the ocean floor.

   _____

   _____

2. The captain looked out the window. A black wall of steel appeared.

   _____

   _____

3. He looked for the yellow letters "Titanic." They were covered over with rust.

   _____

   _____

4. The little robot was steered into a hole in the deck. Soon its camera was taking pictures of the wreck.

   _____

   _____

Name _____

Writing an Answer to a Question

For each question, write the answer on the lines provided. Write the start of the answer on the first answer line. Write the rest of the answer on the other answer lines. The first one is done for you.

Question: Would you enjoy a camping trip?
Start of answer: Turn question into statement
I would enjoy a camping trip because _____

Rest of answer: Facts that complete the statement and answer the question asked.
I enjoy outdoor activities such as hiking, rafting, and walking in the forest. ___

Question: Would you enjoy a train trip?
Start of answer: Turn question into statement

_____ because

Rest of answer: Facts that complete the statement and answer the question asked.

_____

_____

_____

Question: Would you enjoy a trip on an ocean liner?
Start of answer: Turn question into statement

_____ because

Rest of answer: Facts that complete the statement and answer the question asked.

_____

_____

_____

Name _____

Writing Complete Sentences

Incomplete sentences can sink your writing, so make sure you know them when you see them! Mark each of these items as follows: If it is an incomplete sentence because it is missing a subject or a predicate, write an *X* in the "Sink" column. If it is complete write an *X* in the "Swim" column.

	Sink	Swim
Example: The *Titanic,* the largest ship afloat.	X	
1. Sailed from Southampton, England, to New York.	____	____
2. Ruth Becker was excited about traveling on the beautiful ship.	____	____
3. Ruth peeked inside an open door to a first-class cabin.	____	____
4. The Beckers and other passengers in the lounge.	____	____
5. Forgot their life belts.	____	____
6. The *Titanic*'s twenty lifeboats.	____	____
7. She asked to get into the lifeboat.	____	____
8. Ruth Becker stood in the lifeboat.	____	____
9. Many survivors' hands.	____	____
10. Was unwilling to speak about the disaster.	____	____

Name _____

Railroad Words

Write an original story using the vocabulary words. The words may be used in any order. Be sure to give your story a title.

Vocabulary

conductor
depot
jolting
lurching
platform
satchels

Name _____

Detail Map

	Details
Waiting for the train	
Riding the train	

Name _____

The Train Ride

**Look at the summary of the Ingalls family's train ride.
Draw a line through each mistake you find and correct it
on the line to the right.**

Laura and her family are traveling by train to meet their
grandmother in a place far from Plum Creek called Golden
Lake. The family has quite a distance to go, so they have to
take a train. Travel by train is slower than traveling by
horse and buggy, so everyone knows it will be a safe ride.
Ma gets the family to the station 10 minutes early. The
train arrives at the station, and everyone climbs on board.

Because of Mary's blindness, Laura describes the car and
passengers for her. The brakeman comes by and punches
little holes in everyone's ticket. Laura watches a man go
down the aisle to get water. He turns a handle and water
flows into a paper cup. Laura goes to get some water
without Ma's permission and has a hard time walking in the
moving train. Laura brings back drinks of water for
Carrie and Mary. After a while a boy appears in the
aisle selling popcorn from a basket. Ma buys some as a
special treat on their first train ride. Suddenly it's noon
and the train ride is over.

_____
_____
_____
_____
_____
_____
_____
_____
_____

Name _____

A Hospital Chart

**Read the story. Then complete the Detail Chart
on the following page.**

"Please, Mom, Tell Me We're Not There Yet!"

When I was little and we were on a car trip, I
would ask, "Mom, are we there, yet?" every five
minutes. But just last week we went on a car trip and
I kept saying, "Please, Mom, tell me we're not there yet!"
Why? Mom was driving me to the hospital's emergency room!

It all started on the soccer field. After two minutes of play I fell,
grabbing at my stomach. Coach Toth immediately stopped the game.
Somehow I made it over to the bench on the sidelines where my
mother anxiously waited. My mother and Coach Toth carried me
to the car.

I remember looking out the car window on the way to the hospital
trying to keep my mind off the pain in my stomach. I saw that
someone had painted a house we used to live in a sickening shade of
green. I saw the tree that I once fell out of and broke my arm. Then I
started to sweat like crazy.

At the emergency room, they kept us waiting only a short time,
but it seemed like forever as the pain grew worse. Suddenly a doctor
appeared. He seemed to be about eight feet tall. He asked
me some questions and felt the sore place on my
stomach. I yelled. He asked my mom if I still
had my appendix. She told him yes. He
said, "Well, she won't for long," and
smiled at me. A nurse gave me a
shot. The next thing I knew I
was wide awake in a hospital
room—minus one appendix!

Name _____

A Hospital Chart continued

Complete these Detail Charts for the story "Please, Mom, Tell Me We're Not There Yet!"

Before the Hospital	**More Important Details**
	_____
	_____
	_____
	_____
	Less Important Details
	_____
	_____
	_____
	_____
At the Hospital	**More Important Details**
	_____
	_____
	_____
	_____
	Less Important Details
	_____
	_____
	_____
	_____

Name _____

Word Roots *tele* and *rupt*

Tele and *rupt* are word roots. They have meaning but cannot stand alone. *Tele* means "distance" or "over a distance." *Rupt* means "break."

telescope   television   interrupt   abrupt

Complete each sentence with a word from the box. Use a dictionary to check word meanings if you are not sure which word to choose.

televise	telescope	telegraph	telephone
interrupt	abrupt	disruptive	bankrupt

1. Please don't _____ the conductor when he's taking tickets.

2. One of the astronomers carried her _____ on the train.

3. Is the noise from the dining car _____?

4. Many railroads went _____ when the automobile became popular.

5. Will they _____ the first run of the new high-speed train?

6. Call me on the _____ when you reach the station.

7. The train came to an _____ stop when someone pulled the emergency brake.

8. Before the invention of the _____, Pony Express was one way to send messages quickly.

Name _____

Homophones

Homophones are words that sound alike but have different meanings and spellings. When you write a homophone, be sure to spell the word that has the meaning you want.

/stēl/   st**ee**l   a metal made from iron and carbon

/stēl/   st**ea**l   to take without having permission

Write each Spelling Word under the matching sound.

1. steel
2. steal
3. lead
4. led
5. wait
6. weight
7. wear
8. ware
9. creak
10. creek
11. beet
12. beat
13. meet
14. meat
15. peek
16. peak
17. deer
18. dear
19. ring
20. wring

TICKETS

/ē/ Sound

_____

_____

_____

_____

_____

_____

_____

_____

/ĕ/ Sound

_____

_____

/ā/ Sound

_____

Rhymes with *sing*

_____

_____

Vowel Sound + *r*

_____

_____

_____

_____

_____

Name _____

Spelling Spree

Double Trouble **Circle the correct Spelling Word.
Write the words on the lines.**

1. Please (ring/wring) the clothes dry.
2. I heard the bell (ring/wring).
3. In winter I (wear/ware) a scarf.
4. Those cabinets hold cooking (wear/ware).
5. I write with a (led/lead) pencil.
6. She (led/lead) the hikers along the trail.
7. A (beet/beat) is a red-colored vegetable.
8. She can usually (beet/beat) me at chess.
9. A pound is not a lot of (wait/weight).
10. It was a long (wait/weight) for the bus.

1. _____   6. _____
2. _____   7. _____
3. _____   8. _____
4. _____   9. _____
5. _____   10. _____

Spelling Words

1. steel
2. steal
3. lead
4. led
5. wait
6. weight
7. wear
8. ware
9. creak
10. creek
11. beet
12. beat
13. meet
14. meat
15. peek
16. peak
17. deer
18. dear
19. ring
20. wring

Hint and Hunt **Write the Spelling Word that answers
each question.**

11. What is a forest animal with four legs?   11. _____
12. What do old bones sometimes do?   12. _____
13. What is a bargain sometimes called?   13. _____
14. What do you buy from a butcher?   14. _____
15. What do you write to start a letter?   15. _____
16. What is part of a game that babies love?   16. _____

Name _____

Proofreading and Writing

Proofreading **Circle the four misspelled Spelling Words in this poster. Then write each word correctly.**

See the West the Easy Way!

All aboard! Come to the untamed West, where deer, elk, and buffalo still roam the range. Travel on to San Francisco, where the mountains meat the sea. Ride the stel rails from St. Louis all the way to the Pacific Ocean. Cross every valley, river, and creak with ease. See every canyon and snowy peek from the comfort of your passenger seat. Don't wait another minute — get your train tickets today!

---

1. _____   3. _____

2. _____   4. _____

Spelling Words

1. steel
2. steal
3. lead
4. led
5. wait
6. weight
7. wear
8. ware
9. creak
10. creek
11. beet
12. beat
13. meet
14. meat
15. peek
16. peak
17. deer
18. dear
19. ring
20. wring

✏️➤ **Write a List of Rules** Laura and her sisters were very careful to behave properly on the train. Have you ever been on a bus, a train, or in any public place where people have behaved in a rude or improper way? How did it make you feel? Think of some rules to remember when sharing a public place with other people.

On a separate sheet of paper, write five rules of good behavior to follow in public places. Use Spelling Words from the list.

Name _____

Find the Guide Words

**Match each word with the correct guide words. In the first
column, write each word under the correct guide words. Then
write each word in alphabetical order between the guide words.**

bond	boil	immediate
boggle	immense	imagine
bold	imitate	

bog/bone

1. _____

2. _____

3. _____

4. _____

bog

_____

_____

_____

bone

image/immobile

1. _____

2. _____

3. _____

4. _____

image

_____

_____

_____

immobile

Name _____

Finding Common Nouns

Read each sentence, and look for common nouns. Then write each common noun on the lines provided.

1. People waited on the platform for the train.

   _____

2. A traveler rode along at a speed of twenty miles an hour.

   _____

3. The conductor punched holes in the tickets.

   _____

4. Many weeks and months had gone by.

   _____

5. The family sat on a bench in the station.

   _____

6. The woman bought the tickets with money from her pocketbook.

   _____

7. Her dress had a collar and a cuff on each sleeve.

   _____

8. One daughter had long hair with braids and a bow.

   _____

9. Black smoke and white steam came out of the smokestack.

   _____

10. The passengers gathered up their bags and packages.

    _____

Name _____

Choosing Common Nouns

In each sentence, fill in the blank with a noun from the box. Then, on the following line, write whether the noun you chose names a person, a place, or a thing.

| weeks | holes | conductor | windows |

1. The _____ smiled.

   _____

2. The _____ on the train were clear.

   _____

3. He punched _____ in the tickets.

   _____

4. Many _____ had gone by before the trip.

   _____

Write two examples of each type of common noun.

Person	Place	Thing
5. _____	7. _____	9. _____
6. _____	8. _____	10. _____

Use one of the common nouns you wrote for each category to write your own sentence.

_____

_____

Name _____

Writing Nouns in a Series

Using Commas in a Series Good writers often combine ideas. Sometimes a sentence will have three or more words of the same kind that follow one another in a series. When three or more words are written in a series, a joining word comes before the last word, and the words are separated by commas.

Read each group of sentences. Then combine the sentences into one sentence with words in a series. Add commas where they are needed. Write your sentences on the lines below.

1. a. People carried satchels.
   b. People carried handbags.
   c. People carried packages.

   _____

   _____

2. a. Out the train window, Laura could see houses.
   b. Out the train window, Laura could see barns.
   c. Out the train window, Laura could see haystacks.

   _____

   _____

3. a. The candy was red.
   b. The candy was yellow.
   c. The candy was striped.

   _____

   _____

4. a. Ma gave the boy a nickel.
   b. Ma gave the boy three pennies.
   c. Ma gave the boy two dimes.

   _____

   _____

Name _____

Writing a Friendly Letter

The Person I Am Writing To:

My Address:

The Date:

My Greeting:

My Purpose in Writing:

The Most Important Thing I Want to Say:

Important Details I Want to Include:

My Closing:

Name _____

Using Commas in Dates and Places

In the following letter, add commas as necessary in dates and place names.

> Paducah Kentucky
> September 14 1878
>
> Dear Cousin Ethan,
>
>   I am so happy to hear that you are doing well at your new homestead. The town of Tracy South Dakota is very lucky to have someone as hardworking as you!
>
>   In your letter of April 23 1878 you described a family on the train you took to Tracy. There were several daughters. Did you ever meet them?
>
>   Now that you are settled, I would like to come visit you. I can take a train from Cincinnati Ohio all the way to Tracy If I arrive on May 4 1879 will you meet me at the station?
>
>   Your cousin,
>   Elizabeth

Name _____

Choosing the Best Answer

Use the test-taking strategies and tips you have learned to help you answer these multiple-choice questions. You may go back to *Akiak* if you need to. This practice will help you when you take this kind of test.

Read each question. Fill in the circle for the best answer in the answer row at the bottom of the page.

1 Where does the story take place?

   A Alaska   **C** Greenland

   B Canada   **D** Siberia

2 What happened when Mick caught up with Willy?

   F Willy blocked Mick from passing.

   G Mick forced Willy off the trail.

   H Willy pulled over to let Mick pass.

   J Mick took a different trail to get around Willy.

3 Why did Roscoe take Akiak's place to lead the dog team?

   A It was Roscoe's turn to lead the team.

   B Akiak was too old and tired to continue the trip.

   C Mick thought Roscoe would do a better job than Akiak.

   D Akiak had a sore pawpad.

4 What happened when the volunteer took Akiak to the airplane?

   F The dog tipped the plane over.

   G The dog ran off.

   H Mick came back for the dog.

   J The pilot had taken off because of a storm.

ANSWER ROWS   1 Ⓐ Ⓑ Ⓒ Ⓓ   3 Ⓐ Ⓑ Ⓒ Ⓓ

                2 Ⓕ Ⓖ Ⓗ Ⓙ   4 Ⓕ Ⓖ Ⓗ Ⓙ

Name _____

Choosing the Best Answer continued

5 How did Akiak survive the whiteout during the blizzard?

A She took refuge in Galena.

B She kept running along the trail.

C She stayed in a cabin with some volunteers.

D She burrowed in a snowdrift.

6 What did Akiak find when she reached Elim?

F The people had put food out for her.

G The trail volunteers were waiting to catch her.

H Mick was waiting for her.

J The mushers were ready to chase her into the community hall.

7 Why doesn't Mick put Akiak back in her usual spot at the harness?

A Mick thought Akiak was too tired to lead the dog team.

B Mick was afraid Akiak would get lost.

C Mick knew it was against the rules.

D Mick wanted Akiak to stay off her injured pawpad.

8 What was the noise that Mick heard as she approached Nome?

F It was the sound of another blizzard.

G It was a crowd of people cheering.

H It was the dog teams that were ahead of her.

J It was the roar of snowmobile engines.

ANSWER ROWS　5 Ⓐ Ⓑ Ⓒ Ⓓ　　7 Ⓐ Ⓑ Ⓒ Ⓓ

6 Ⓕ Ⓖ Ⓗ Ⓙ　　8 Ⓕ Ⓖ Ⓗ Ⓙ

Name _____

Spelling Review

Write Spelling Words from the list on this page to answer the questions.

1–15. Which fifteen words have the /ă/ or /ā/ sound or the /ĕ/ or /ē/ sound?

1. _____   9. _____

2. _____   10. _____

3. _____   11. _____

4. _____   12. _____

5. _____   13. _____

6. _____   14. _____

7. _____   15. _____

8. _____

16–24. Which nine words have the /ĭ/ or /ī/ sound or the /ŏ/ or /ō/ sound?

16. _____   21. _____

17. _____   22. _____

18. _____   23. _____

19. _____   24. _____

20. _____

25–30. Which six words have the /ŭ/,/yo͞o/,or /o͞o/ sound?

25. _____   28. _____

26. _____   29. _____

27. _____   30. _____

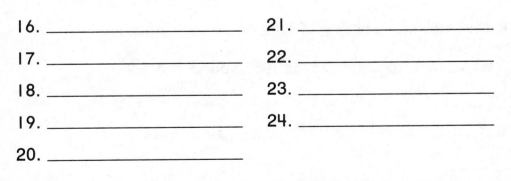

Spelling Words

1. safe
2. few
3. tube
4. steep
5. past
6. steel
7. kept
8. gain
9. suit
10. steal
11. reach
12. sigh
13. wait
14. trunk
15. gray
16. still
17. coast
18. weight
19. grown
20. gold
21. odd
22. creek
23. wrote
24. crime
25. meat
26. blind
27. true
28. crumb
29. creak
30. meet

Theme 1: **Journeys**   71

Name _____

Spelling Spree

Puzzle Play Write the Spelling Word that fits each clue.
Then use the letters in the boxes to write the secret word.
Begin the secret word with a capital letter.

Spelling Words

1. past
2. weight
3. kept
4. steel
5. creek
6. still
7. meat
8. blind
9. creak
10. steal
11. trunk
12. tube
13. crumb
14. wait
15. meet

1. did not throw out ___ ___ ___ [ ]

2. unable to see ___ ___ [ ] ___ ___

3. what toothpaste comes in [ ] ___ ___ ___

4. opposite of future ___ ___ [ ] ___

5. a large box for storage or travel ___ ___ ___ [ ] ___

6. not moving ___ ___ ___ [ ] ___

7. a tiny piece of food [ ] ___ ___ ___ ___

Secret Word: _____

Hint: This famous ship struck an iceberg and sank on its first journey.

Homophone Hunt Write two Spelling Words that sound the same
in each sentence.

8. We always _____ in the butcher shop to buy

_____.

9. I can't _____ to find out my _____!

10. In the breeze, the trees _____ near the shallow

_____.

11. The robber tried to _____ the old

_____ safe.

Name _____

Proofreading and Writing

In the News Write the Spelling Word that completes each headline. Begin each word with a capital letter.

1. Man Rescues Cat and Breathes a _____
2. Many Leave Town But _____ Return
3. Miners Look for _____ Nearby
4. Dry Cleaner Loses Man's New _____
5. Two Climbers Lost on _____ Mountain
6. Schools _____ a Lot with New Plan
7. Lost Hiker Is Found _____ but Hungry
8. _____ Behavior in Skunks Signals Rabies
9. Two Arrested During _____ Spree

Spelling Words

1. reach
2. steep
3. gain
4. gold
5. gray
6. crime
7. coast
8. grown
9. odd
10. wrote
11. few
12. true
13. safe
14. suit
15. sigh

Proofreading Circle the six misspelled Spelling Words in this travel story. Then write each word correctly.

We left early and sailed along the coste. We hoped to reech the island in a few weeks, but it took a year. Some may think it strange that I never wroat about this journey before. Now my hair is graye, and my children are grone. At last, I can tell the trewe story.

10. _____   13. _____
11. _____   14. _____
12. _____   15. _____

✏️➤ **Continue the Story** On a separate sheet of paper, write the rest of the story about the sailor's strange journey. Use the Spelling Review Words.

Name _____

The Perfect Detective

Think about the two detectives you have read about in *Focus on Mysteries*. Use the chart below to describe their characteristics. Then list which characteristics you think the perfect detective would have. How do Encyclopedia Brown and the Judge compare to your perfect detective?

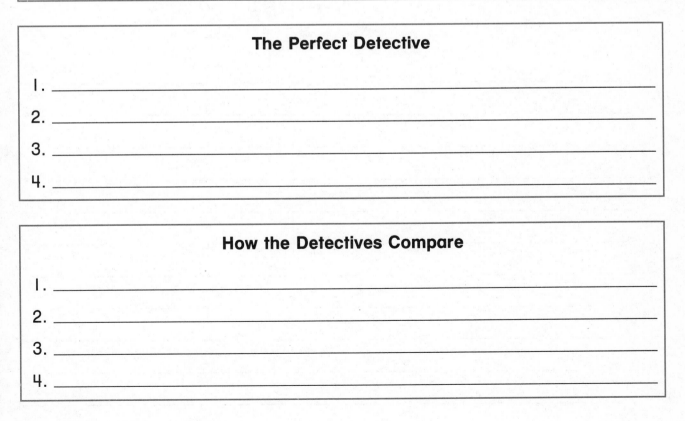

Encyclopedia Brown	**The Judge**
1. smart	1. smart
2.	2.
3.	3.
4.	4.

The Perfect Detective

1. _____
2. _____
3. _____
4. _____

How the Detectives Compare

1. _____
2. _____
3. _____
4. _____

Name _____

The Interview

Imagine that you are interviewing Encyclopedia Brown for your school newspaper. You want to show that someone Encyclopedia Brown's age can be a good detective. List the questions you would ask him. Then act out your interview with a friend.

1. _____

_____

_____

2. _____

_____

_____

3. _____

_____

_____

4. _____

_____

Name _____

Tell About America

**You are visiting another country and meet someone your age.
Your new friend wants to know about the United States,
and asks you the questions below. Help your friend learn about
the United States by answering these questions.**

1. What kind of food do people in the United States like to eat?

_____

2. What is an American school like?

_____

3. What do you and your friends like to do on weekends?

_____

**Think of another question your friend might ask. Write an
answer to it.**

_____

_____

_____

_____

Name _____

New Places

	Who is the story about? Where do they go in the story?	How are the characters' lives changed by going to the new place?
Tomás and the Library Lady		
Tanya's Reunion		
Boss of the Plains		
A Very Important Day		

Copyright © Houghton Mifflin Company. All rights reserved.

Name _____

Let's Read

Vocabulary

borrow   check out   eager   glaring   storyteller   lap

Choose the best meaning for the underlined word.
Write the letter of your answer on the line provided.

1. Many people <u>borrow</u> books and records from libraries. _____
   A. use for a short   B. lend   C. dig a hole for   D. steal
      time

2. I would like to <u>check out</u> that book for two weeks. _____
   A. pay the bill for   B. borrow   C. prove true   D. add up

3. I am very <u>eager</u> to read the book you gave me for my birthday. _____
   A. careful   B. uninterested C. demanding   D. interested

4. The old house near the bus stop, with its broken windows
   <u>glaring</u> down at us, can be scary. _____
   A. obvious   B. dark   C. sharp   D. to stare in an
                                                                angry way

5. Stories always seem better when read aloud by a good <u>storyteller</u>. _____
   A. person who   B. liar   C. actor   D. speaker
      tells stories

6. After school I will read, and my cat will quietly <u>lap</u> up her milk. _____
   A. spill   B. lick up   C. pour   D. share

Name _____

Event Map

Pages 160–161

At midnight, the family was headed by car _____
_____

↓

Pages 162–165

The boys carried water to the field, and when they got hot, they _____
_____

↓

Pages 166–167

First the library lady brought Tomás some water. Then she _____
_____

↓

Pages 168–170

All summer, whenever he could, Tomás _____
_____

↓

Pages 171–174

In the evenings, Tomás _____
_____

Name _____

Check Your Memory

Think about the selection. Then complete the sentences.

3. Tomás was able to forget about both Iowa and Texas when _____

_____

_____

_____

1. The Rivera family traveled to Iowa each summer because _____

_____

_____

_____

4. Tomás got a small sample of what it's like to be a teacher when _____

_____

_____

_____

2. Tomás wanted to learn new stories so he could _____

_____

_____

5. Tomás was sad to say the word *adiós* because _____

_____

_____

_____

A Summer Sequence

Read the story below and answer the questions on the following page.

Audrey's Dream

It was a late summer afternoon. Sitting in the shade not far from her friend Sharon, Audrey looked through the book her father had loaned her. The book was all about the world of dinosaurs. In the heat, Audrey felt sleepy.

As she read, Audrey seemed to see real dinosaurs standing by a pond and drinking cool water. Even though her eyes were closing, Audrey seemed to hear the cry of the wild snakebird. A minute later, she was on the back of a dinosaur. She felt its warm neck as she held on tight.

The dinosaur carried Audrey across fields and swamps and into forests. Together they traveled many miles toward the setting sun. At last they ended up on a grassy plain. All was still. Audrey could hear nothing, but the dinosaur was listening for something that only it could hear.

Then in the distance, Audrey saw a shadow. A moment later, she saw a huge, fierce dinosaur she recognized from the book. The dinosaur she was riding began to run.

Faster and faster it ran across the plain. Looking behind her, Audrey saw huge teeth and claws getting closer and closer. Just then she heard a loud thud.

"Audrey, wake up!" she heard Sharon say. "You fell asleep. What would your father say if he knew you let his book fall in the dirt?"

Name _____

A Summer Sequence continued

Answer the following questions.

1. What first happens to Audrey as she falls asleep?

   _____

   _____

2. What happens next, after the dinosaur carries Audrey away?

   _____

   _____

3. What causes the *loud thud*?

   _____

   _____

4. What takes place once Audrey recognizes the fierce dinosaur in the distance?

   _____

   _____

5. Which two of these questions are out of sequence?

   _____

   _____

Name _____

A Contraction Conversation

Read Marisa's conversation with her father and circle all the contractions. There are five contractions in each speech balloon.

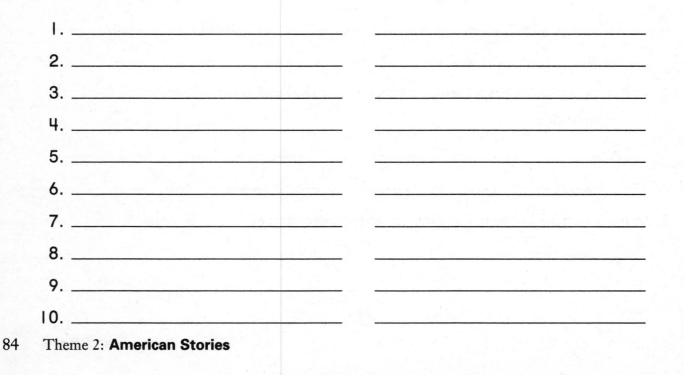

Dad, I'm ready. Let's go to the library. I've got two books to return, and I'd like to get a good mystery. Wouldn't you like to get a book too?

That's a great idea! We'll walk there. It won't take long. It's only three blocks away. Don't forget your scarf.

Write each contraction you circled on a line in the first column. Then write the two or more words that make the contraction on the matching line in the second column.

1. _____   _____
2. _____   _____
3. _____   _____
4. _____   _____
5. _____   _____
6. _____   _____
7. _____   _____
8. _____   _____
9. _____   _____
10. _____   _____

Name _____

The /ou/ and /ô/ Sounds

When you hear the /ou/ or the /ô/ sound, think of these patterns:

/ou/ *ou* or *ow*   /ô/ *aw, au,* or *a* before *l*

Remember that a consonant sound usually follows the *ou* or the *au* pattern.

/ou/ p**ou**nd, h**ow**l   /ô/ j**aw**, c**au**se, **al**ways

► In the starred word, *couple, ou* spells the /ŭ/ sound, not the /ou/ sound.

Write each Spelling Word under its vowel sound.

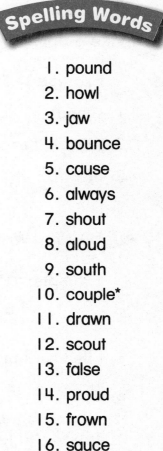

Spelling Words

1. pound
2. howl
3. jaw
4. bounce
5. cause
6. always
7. shout
8. aloud
9. south
10. couple*
11. drawn
12. scout
13. false
14. proud
15. frown
16. sauce
17. gown
18. couch
19. dawn
20. mount

/ou/ Sound	/ô/ Sound
_____	_____
_____	_____
_____	_____
_____	_____
_____	_____
_____	_____
_____	_____
_____	**Another Vowel Sound**
_____	_____
_____	_____

Name _____

Spelling Spree

Letter Swap Change the first letter of each word to make a Spelling Word. Write the word.

Example: talk   *walk*

1. sound   _____

2. down   _____

3. brown   _____

4. law   _____

Puzzle Play Write a Spelling Word to fit each clue.

Example: a joking performer who does tricks

| c | l | o | (w) | n |

5. filled with pride

6. a pair

7. a liquid topping for food

8. attracted; sketched

9. to explore for information

10. to cry out

11. to climb or get up on

12. to move with a bobbing motion

Now write the circled letters in order. They spell three words Papá Grande often said to Tomás.

Name _____

Proofreading and Writing

Proofreading Suppose Tomás sent a postcard to a friend. Circle the five misspelled Spelling Words in this postcard. Then write each word correctly.

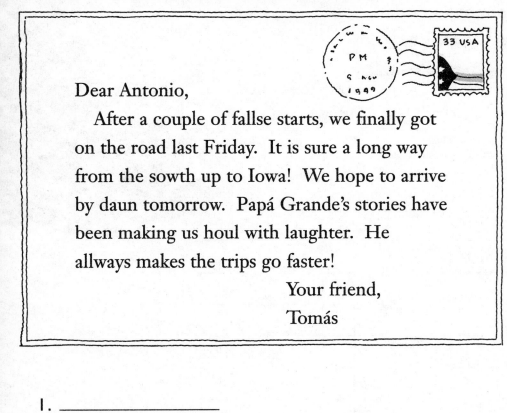

Dear Antonio,

    After a couple of fallse starts, we finally got on the road last Friday. It is sure a long way from the sowth up to Iowa! We hope to arrive by daun tomorrow. Papá Grande's stories have been making us houl with laughter. He allways makes the trips go faster!

                    Your friend,
                    Tomás

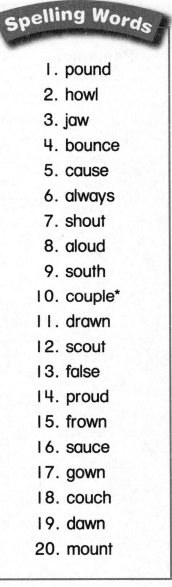

Spelling Words

1. pound
2. howl
3. jaw
4. bounce
5. cause
6. always
7. shout
8. aloud
9. south
10. couple*
11. drawn
12. scout
13. false
14. proud
15. frown
16. sauce
17. gown
18. couch
19. dawn
20. mount

1. _____

2. _____

3. _____

4. _____

5. _____

✏️ **Write a Description** Tomás and his family often made the trip between Texas and Iowa. Have you taken an interesting trip? Did you travel by car, bus, train, or plane? What did you see and do?

On a separate sheet of paper, write a description of a trip you have taken. Use Spelling Words from the list.

Name _____

Antonym Puzzle

Complete the crossword puzzle by writing the correct antonym for each clue. Choose your answers from the words in the box. Remember, an antonym is a word that means the opposite or nearly the opposite of another word.

Vocabulary

above	asleep	lost	start	true
after	least	push	sunny	winter
appear	loose	raise	top	return

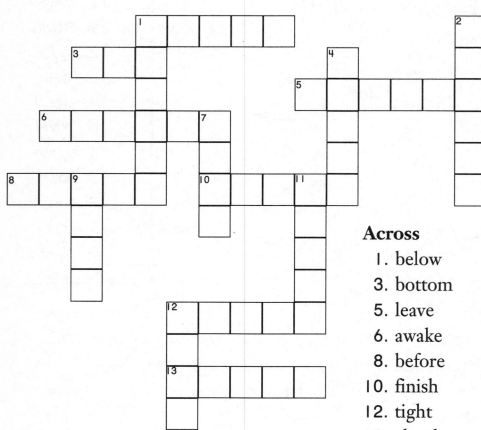

Across
1. below
3. bottom
5. leave
6. awake
8. before
10. finish
12. tight
13. cloudy

Down
1. vanish
2. summer
4. most
7. pull
9. false
11. lower
12. found

Name _____

Finding Proper Nouns

Underline the proper nouns in each sentence.

1. As a boy, Tomás Rivera traveled with his parents.
2. The Rivera family came to the United States from Mexico.
3. The family picked crops in Texas and in Iowa.
4. The young boy called his parents Mamá and Papá.
5. The boy's grandfather told stories to him and his brother, Enrique, in Spanish.
6. The boy sometimes told stories to Papá Grande in English.
7. The boy grew up to become a famous Mexican American.
8. A beautiful library in Riverside, California, is named for him.

Write each underlined proper noun in the correct space below.

Person	Place	Thing
_____	_____	_____
_____	_____	_____
_____	_____	_____
_____	_____	_____
_____	_____	_____
_____	_____	_____

Name _____

Completing with Proper Nouns

Complete each sentence with a proper noun from *Tomás and the Library Lady.*

1. Tomás's family is driving to the state of _____ .

2. Tomás calls his grandfather _____ .

3. Tomás's brother's name is _____ .

4. Their grandfather tells stories in _____ .

5. The _____ .

    is in Denton, Texas.

Write a proper noun for each person, place, or thing described.

6. the first and last name of a friend or relative _____

    _____

7. the state where you live _____

    _____

8. a language you speak _____

    _____

9. your favorite book or movie _____

    _____

10. the name of your school or library _____

    _____

Name _____

Writing Proper Nouns

Proofread the paragraph below. Find common nouns that have capital letters. Find proper nouns that need capital letters. Use the proofreading marks to show the corrections. Then write the corrected common and proper nouns in the columns below.

Proofreading Marks

Make a small letter: S̷tory

Make a capital letter: <u>m</u>exico

> The Woman who wrote the story is pat mora. She was born in El Paso, texas. The Illustrator is Raul colón. He is an Artist from puerto rico. The story is about a young Boy named tomás rivera. He learns to love Books from the kind library lady. He grew up to become a famous mexican american.

Common Nouns	**Proper Nouns**
_____	_____
_____	_____
_____	_____
_____	_____
_____	_____

Name _____

Writing an Essay

Use this page to help you plan your essay. Write your focus idea first. Then write two reasons or facts about your topic in the boxes below. Finally, think of some examples you could use to make each reason or fact clear.

My Focus Idea

_____

_____

_____

_____

_____

Reason/Fact	**Reason/Fact**

Example	**Example**

Name _____

Improving Your Writing

Read the following essay. Then add reasons to the main idea of paragraphs 2, 3 and 4 that support that idea. Write your reasons on the lines provided.

Afternoons at the Library

One afternoon a week, I usually stop by our local public library. Each time I go, I try to find at least one book that I want to read. Sometimes I find a new book of stories. Sometimes I discover an exciting mystery novel. Sometimes I find a nonfiction book about science or history.

Stories always appeal to me.
Add two or three sentences that give possible reasons why stories are appealing.

_____

_____

_____

I have to admit that mystery novels get my attention, too.
Add two or three sentences that give possible reasons why mystery novels might be interesting to read.

_____

_____

_____

Books about science and history are my favorite kinds of nonfiction.
Add two or three sentences that give reasons why science or history might be appealing choices for a reader.

_____

_____

_____

Name _____

Revising Your Description

**Reread your description. What do you need to make it better?
Use this page to help you decide. Put a checkmark in the box
for each sentence that describes what you have written.**

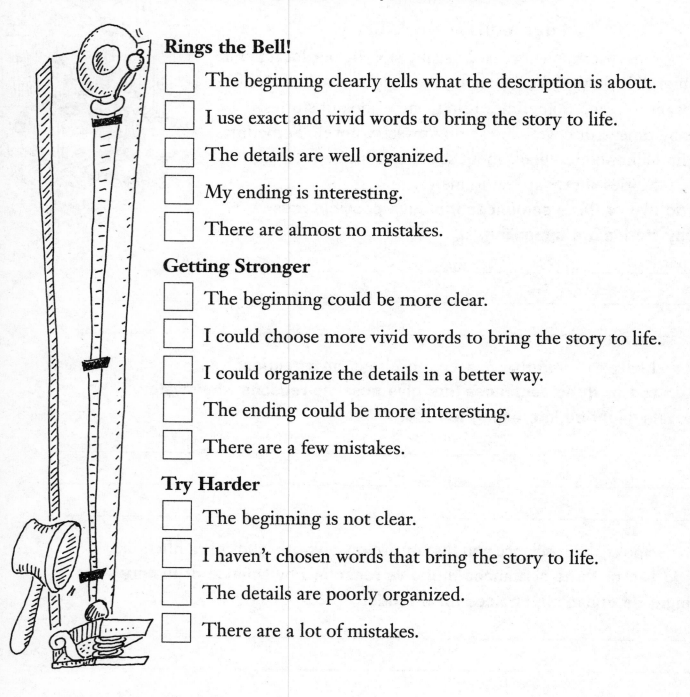

Rings the Bell!

☐ The beginning clearly tells what the description is about.

☐ I use exact and vivid words to bring the story to life.

☐ The details are well organized.

☐ My ending is interesting.

☐ There are almost no mistakes.

Getting Stronger

☐ The beginning could be more clear.

☐ I could choose more vivid words to bring the story to life.

☐ I could organize the details in a better way.

☐ The ending could be more interesting.

☐ There are a few mistakes.

Try Harder

☐ The beginning is not clear.

☐ I haven't chosen words that bring the story to life.

☐ The details are poorly organized.

☐ There are a lot of mistakes.

Name _____

Sentence Combining

Combine each pair of sentences into one sentence. Write a new sentence that has a compound subject or compound predicate, or write a compound sentence. Use the joining word in parentheses. Add commas where they are needed.

1. Mary fed the cat.
2. Ben fed the cat. (or)

_____

3. The cat sat on my favorite chair.
4. The cat took a nap. (and)

_____

5. The dog held a bone in its paws.
6. The dog chewed on it. (and)

_____

_____

7. The kitten knocked over the lamp.
8. The puppy knocked over the lamp. (or)

_____

_____

9. The kitten watched the raindrops through the window.
10. The puppy barked at the thunder. (but)

_____

_____

11. The kitten snuggled up next to the puppy.
12. Soon both animals were fast asleep. (and)

_____

_____

Name _____

Spelling Words

Words Often Misspelled Look for familiar spelling to help you remember how to spell the Spelling Words on this page. Think carefully about the parts that you find hard to spell in each word.

Write the missing letters in the Spelling Words below.

1. a _____ _____ _____
2. oth _____ _____
3. _____ _____ other
4. _____ nyone
5. ev _____ ry
6. som _____ one
7. mys _____ _____ _____
8. fam _____ ly
9. fr _____ _____ nd
10. p _____ _____ ple
11. _____ g _____ _____ n
12. _____ nything
13. _____ nyway
14. ev _____ _____ yone
15. f _____ rst

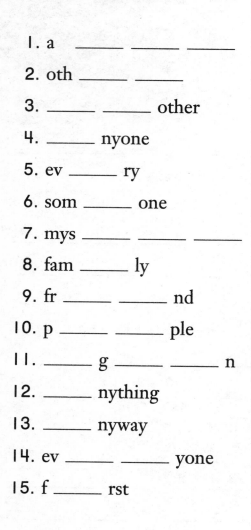

Study List **On a separate piece of paper, write each Spelling Word. Check your spelling against the words on the list.**

Name _____

Spelling Spree

Sentence Fillers **Write the Spelling Word that best completes each sentence.**

1. Did you ever find your _____ glove?

2. I'd like you to meet my best _____ , Philip.

3. My sister got _____ question on her math test right.

4. Can we get you _____ from the store?

5. It was hard to get _____ to agree on a movie.

6. Next summer, we're visiting my mom's _____ out west.

7. I'm getting _____ piece of pizza.

8. I think that _____ called our house late last night.

1. a lot
2. other
3. another
4. anyone
5. every
6. someone
7. myself
8. family
9. friend
10. people
11. again
12. anything
13. anyway
14. everyone
15. first

Word Clues **Write a Spelling Word to fit each clue.**

9. a word meaning "just the same" _____

10. one more time _____

11. a synonym for anybody _____

12. a crowd of human beings _____

13. coming before anything else _____

14. the opposite of a little _____

15. a word you use when talking about you

_____

I'll do it <u>myself</u>!

Proofreading and Writing

Proofreading Circle the five misspelled Spelling Words in this speech. Then write each word correctly.

If somone were to ask you, "What is an American?" what would you say? I think that evryone has his or her own answer. But when I ask myslef this question, my first answer is "a person who believes in democracy." It is democracy that lets each one of the American peple have a say in the direction of our country.

If there is anythin more important to being an American, I can't think of it.

Spelling Words

1. a lot
2. other
3. another
4. anyone
5. every
6. someone
7. myself
8. family
9. friend
10. people
11. again
12. anything
13. anyway
14. everyone
15. first

1. _____
2. _____
3. _____
4. _____
5. _____

✏ **Tag-Team Poetry** Pair up with a classmate. Then create a poem about America by taking turns writing lines. Use Spelling Words from the list.

Name _____

A Family Get-Together

Aunt Sally had to miss the big family party. Kara writes to tell her all about it. Complete Kara's letter by filling in the blank with the correct word from the list.

Vocabulary

arrangements
gathering
great-uncle
homestead
persisted
pitches in
reunion
satisfaction

Dear Aunt Sally,

    I am sorry that you missed the family _____. We all had great fun, and saw many relatives from both near and far away. Nearly sixty people came for the party. It was the largest family _____ in years. There were many familiar faces, and a few I didn't know at all. Two great-aunts and one _____ came all the way from Oregon. My dad made the travel _____ for them. They had not seen our house for twenty years. They called our house and the surrounding land the _____.

    One of the things that I like is that everyone _____ to prepare food. It's too much work for just a few people. I got a great deal of _____ from seeing how many of the relatives liked my potato salad. The only thing wrong with the day was that the bees _____ in buzzing around the desserts.

    I hope you can come visit soon.

Yours truly,
Your niece Sarah

Name _____

Character Development Flow Chart

Story Event or Character Detail	+	My Own Experience	=	Inference About Character
page 189 When Grandma says she's leaving for the reunion without Tanya and the family, silence falls across the dinner table.	+	I know that _____ _____ _____ _____	=	I can infer that _____ _____ _____ _____
page 196 When Tanya gets to the farm, she doesn't find what she expects.	+	I know that _____ _____ _____ _____	=	I can infer that _____ _____ _____ _____
page 196 When Aunt Kay hugs Tanya, the warm, soft hug reminds Tanya of Grandma.	+	I know that _____ _____ _____ _____	=	I can infer that _____ _____ _____ _____
page 200 Tanya stops and looks closely at the family "memories" in the sitting parlor.	+	I know that _____ _____ _____ _____	=	I can infer that _____ _____ _____ _____

Name _____

Just the Facts

Complete the following to show the setting, major events, and the ending for *Tanya's Reunion*.

Setting:

_____

_____

_____

Events:

_____

_____

_____

_____

_____

_____

_____

_____

_____

Ending:

_____

_____

_____

_____

Name _____

What Characters!

Read the story below. Then complete the chart on the following page.

Family Tree

"Let's make a family tree!" said Meghan. "We can look for family records on the Internet."

"We could never do that," said her brother Brian, shaking his head. "The Internet is too huge."

"Nonsense," said Meghan. "We know that some of our great-grandparents lived in Lowell, Massachusetts. Using the Internet, we can scan the Lowell city records for other information."

A few computer clicks later, Meghan and Brian found the city's records. "Look, there they are!" said Meghan, her hands trembling. "Bridget and James O'Toole were married in Lowell on June 11, 1896. It says her parents were Sean and Maeve Boyle. His parents were James and Rose O'Toole."

"Can we tell where they were born?" asked Brian.

"Maybe," said Meghan. "Here are passenger lists for ships arriving in Boston in the 1880s and 1890s. Let's check to see if we can find their names."

"Look!" said Brian, staring wide-eyed at the computer screen. "Here are James and Rose O'Toole listed as passengers on the *Adelaide* that sailed in 1888 from Ireland."

Meghan sighed. "That means that if we want more information, we'll have to look for records in Ireland!"

Name _____

What Characters! continued

Use the story and your own experiences to complete the following chart.

Story Event	+	My Own Experience	=	Inference About Character
Brian shakes his head when Meghan suggests searching the Internet.	+	I may shake my head _____ _____	=	I can infer that _____ _____ _____
Meghan's hands tremble when she finds the family records.	+	My hands may tremble _____ _____	=	I can infer that _____ _____ _____
Brian stares wide-eyed at the computer screen.	+	I may stare wide-eyed _____ _____	=	I can infer that _____ _____ _____
Meghan sighs when she learns that their search must extend to Ireland.	+	I may sigh _____ _____ _____	=	I can infer that _____ _____ _____

Name _____

Root It Out

The word root *sign* means "a sign or mark."
The word root *spect* means "to look at."

Example: The **spectators** cheered loudly.

The runners waited for the **signal** to start the race.

**Use the words in the box to complete the story. If you
need help, use a dictionary.**

signaled	suspected	inspect	signified	spectacular
respect	signature	spectacles	designs	expected

When Jenna woke up, she knew the raindrops hitting her

window _____ another day inside. Jenna

decided to _____ the dusty attic. A lot

of the items she found looked like junk, but Jenna knew each item

_____ an important part of her family's

history and deserved _____. Jenna loved

the colorful _____ on the old quilts.

They were _____! Next she tried

looking through _____ that she

_____ belonged to her grandmother long

ago. Then Tanya read some letters that had her great-grandfather's

_____. She hadn't

_____ to find that!

Name _____

The /o͞o/ and /o͝o/ Sounds

When you hear the /o͞o/ sound, think of the pattern *oo*.
Remember that the /o͝o/ sound is often spelled *oo* or *u*
followed by a consonant or a cluster.

/o͞o/ **too**l   /o͝o/ **woo**d, p**u**t

▶ The starred words *group*, *prove*, *soup*, and *move* use
different spelling patterns for the /o͞o/ sound.

Write each Spelling Word under its vowel sound. Include
roof **with the** /o͞o/ **sound.**

Spelling Words

1. wood
2. brook
3. tool
4. put
5. wool
6. push
7. full
8. roof
9. group*
10. prove*
11. stood
12. stool
13. hook
14. smooth
15. shoot
16. bush
17. fool
18. pull
19. soup*
20. move*

/o͞o/ Sound   **/o͝o/ Sound**

_____ _____
_____ _____
_____ _____
_____ _____
_____ _____
_____ _____
_____
_____

Theme 2: **American Stories**   105

Name _____

Spelling Spree

Hink Pinks **Write a Spelling Word that answers the question and rhymes with the given word.**

Example: What do you call a stand that sells teeth?

_____tooth_____ booth

1. What do you call a silly person on a cold day?

cool _____

2. What makes the best fires?

good _____

3. What is a large farm animal after a

meal? _____ bull

4. What would you use to "fish" at the

library? book _____

5. What do you call a mean hammer?

cruel _____

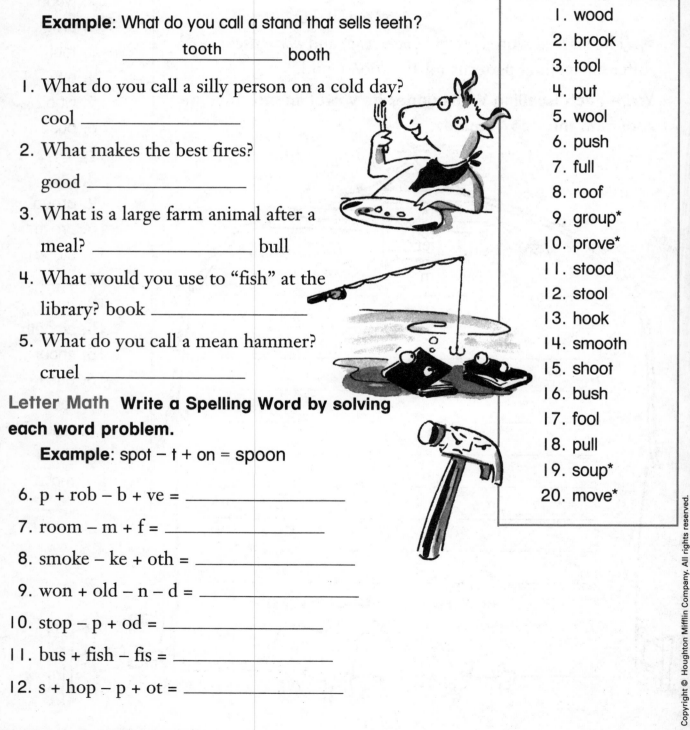

Letter Math **Write a Spelling Word by solving each word problem.**

Example: spot − t + on = spoon

6. p + rob − b + ve = _____

7. room − m + f = _____

8. smoke − ke + oth = _____

9. won + old − n − d = _____

10. stop − p + od = _____

11. bus + fish − fis = _____

12. s + hop − p + ot = _____

Name _____

Proofreading and Writing

Proofreading Circle the five misspelled Spelling Words in this diary entry. Then write each word correctly on the lines below.

> Today a groop of us made taffy for the reunion. After cooking it, we putt it on a counter. One person's job was to poush the blob of taffy down. Then two others picked it up. Their job was to pul the blob to stretch it. This helped to make the taffy smooth. We did this over and over. It was hard work! Tonight I am so sore I can hardly mouve.

Spelling Words

1. wood
2. brook
3. tool
4. put
5. wool
6. push
7. full
8. roof
9. group*
10. prove*
11. stood
12. stool
13. hook
14. smooth
15. shoot
16. bush
17. fool
18. pull
19. soup*
20. move*

_____

_____

_____

_____

_____

Write a Recipe What food dish would you like to take to a family reunion?

On a separate piece of paper, write a recipe for a dish that you might make. List what is in the dish and explain how to make it. Use Spelling Words from the list.

Name _____

Identify Parts of a Definition

Choose the correct label for each part of the definition of
family **from the list. Write the labels in the spaces provided.**

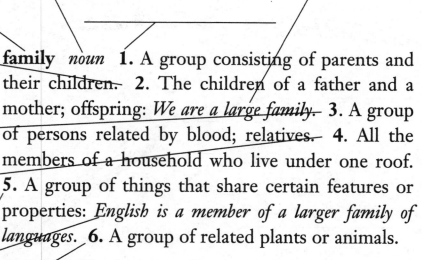

entry word	third meaning	syllable break
part of speech	fourth meaning	pronunciation
first meaning	fifth meaning	sample sentence
second meaning	sixth meaning	word form with a
part of speech	sample sentence	different ending

_____

_____

_____

_____

_____

_____

family *noun* **1.** A group consisting of parents and their children. **2.** The children of a father and a mother; offspring: *We are a large family.* **3.** A group of persons related by blood; relatives. **4.** All the members of a household who live under one roof. **5.** A group of things that share certain features or properties: *English is a member of a larger family of languages.* **6.** A group of related plants or animals.

fam•i•ly (făm′ ə lē) noun, plural, **families**

_____

_____

Name _____

Finding Singular and Plural Nouns

In each sentence, circle each singular common noun. Underline each plural common noun.

1. Tanya didn't like traveling on buses.

2. In the barnyard, Tanya couldn't see any horses.

3. From inside the house, Tanya saw raindrops on the window.

4. The girl and her cousins played games.

5. Lights far away seemed like torches through the sheets of rain.

6. Patches of ground were soaked.

7. In the kitchen, boxes were scattered all over.

8. The trees in the orchard were full of ripe apples.

Write each plural noun in the correct column below.

Adds *s* to form the plural	Adds *es* to form the plural

Name _____

Puzzle with Plurals

Complete the crossword puzzle about things that Tanya saw on her trip to the family reunion in Virginia. Use the general clues to write the plural forms of these exact nouns from the story.

ACROSS

3. fields for growing fruit trees
5. rooms for cooking
7. soft, gentle winds
9. daytimes before noon
10. farm buildings

DOWN

1. containers made of cardboard or wood
2. farm birds that lay eggs
4. fees paid to governments
6. body parts for seeing
8. tools for sweeping

Create a Puzzle Use the plural forms of these nouns to create your own crossword on a separate sheet of paper. Trade puzzles with a classmate and complete one another's puzzles.

| porch | horse | pocket |
| glass | bus | farm |

Name _____

Using Exact Nouns

Read each sentence below. Then rewrite the sentence on the lines below it, substituting an exact noun for the general noun or words in parentheses.

1. Everyone was going to a family (get-together).

   _____

   _____

2. Tanya had been on the bus for nine (periods of 60 minutes).

   _____

   _____

3. Tanya grew hungry when she smelled delicious (smells).

   _____

   _____

4. From the porch, Tanya could see the (place where fruit trees grow).

   _____

   _____

5. Before she went to the barn, Tanya put on a pair of (heavy shoes).

   _____

   _____

Name _____

A Character Sketch

Use this page to help you plan a character sketch. Write at least two specific details about what the person looks like, what the person says and does, and how you feel about the person.

Introduction

Whom is my character sketch about?

_____

What the Person Looks Like

Details: 1. _____

2. _____

3. _____

What the Person Says

Details: 1. _____

2. _____

3. _____

What the Person Does

Details: 1. _____

2. _____

3. _____

Conclusion: How I Feel About the Person

_____

_____

On a separate sheet of paper, write your character sketch.

Name _____

Improving Your Writing

▶ Two or more sentences that run together make a **run-on sentence**.
▶ Correct run-on sentences by making separate sentences. Add
sentence end marks and capital letters where they are needed.

**Read the character sketch. Find all the run-on sentences. Then
rewrite the character sketch, including corrections you made.**

My Grandmother

I think my grandmother is my favorite relative, she
knows more than anyone I know. I sometimes wonder if I'll
ever know all that she knows.

She can cook anything you can name, and it always tastes delicious.
You should see her spice cabinet, it's full of all kinds of herbs and spices
for cooking. She says she learned how to use them from her mother and
grandmother.

Sometimes I wonder how she remembers all the things she does.
Maybe I can learn a part of what she knows. Then I'll know a lot about
many things, that's why my grandmother is my favorite relative.

_____

_____

_____

_____

_____

_____

_____

_____

_____

Name _____

Go West!

Like John Stetson, many people traveled west in the 1800s to seek their fortunes. Complete the story by filling in each blank with the correct word from the list. Then answer the question.

adventurers
determined
frontier
gear
opportunity
pioneers
settlers
tanned
wranglers

Many _____ came from the East to live out West. They were seeking an _____ to make their fortunes. A great number of them were _____ to find gold.

New people were arriving at the _____ almost daily. These people were true _____ who had traveled across the prairie to the Colorado territory. They stayed to become _____ of the new area. Those who drove cattle were called _____. The hide of the cattle was often _____ to make useful items like hats, boots, and belts. In addition, cowboys needed other special _____ for their outdoor work. What piece of equipment might a cowboy need for outdoor work?

_____

Name _____

Generalization Chart

Question: What was St. Joseph, Missouri, like in 1859? (page 224)

Details: _____

_____

Generalization: _____

Question: What was the reaction to the hat samples John sent out west? (pages 233–234)

Details: _____

_____

_____

Generalization: _____

Question: What does the story show about the process of inventing something?

Details: _____

_____

Generalization: _____

Question: Look at the reasons why the Boss of the Plains became successful. What things are needed for an invention to be a success?

Details: _____

_____

_____

Generalization: _____

Name _____

What's It About?

Complete the description for each part of a three-part documentary about the life of John Stetson.

Television — What's On TV This Week

Monday, 8:00 P.M., Part 1

Twelve-year-old John Batterson Stetson is hard at work in the family's hat-making shop in New Jersey. Young John first hears about the West _____.

In 1859, John B. Stetson, now a young man, decides to head west

_____.

Wednesday, 8:00 P.M., Part 2

John mines for gold and realizes the hat he is wearing offers very little protection from the weather. John decides to make _____

_____.

One day a horseman rides into camp and _____

_____.

Thursday, 8:00 P.M., Part 3

John decides to move to Philadelphia and _____

_____.

The shop is not successful until one day John remembers the horseman who bought his hat. John spends all his money making samples of the hat and sends them _____.

For weeks, John hears nothing. Then suddenly the orders roll in. In no time, John Stetson's Boss of the Plains _____

_____.

General Statements

**Read the article below and complete the chart on the
following page.**

Settling Colorado

Before Colorado became a state in 1876, some Native Americans
lived in the mountain valleys and on the plains. A few people
wandered through the mountains looking for gold and other valuable
minerals. Only a few farming families lived anywhere in the region.

In 1858, people found gold near what is now Denver. Soon,
thousands of people had settled in the region. Tiny settlements
became large towns. Farmers and ranchers settled in the mountain
valleys.

Today, residents of Colorado no longer live in the wide-open
spaces of the Old West. Instead, four out of every five people in the
region live in one of six large cities. Many people move to these cities
every year. Also, many of the mountain areas still have no residents.

Name _____

General Statements continued

In the chart below write the details that answer
the questions. Then form the generalizations.

What was the population like in Colorado before the 1850s?

Details: _____

_____

_____

Generalization: _____

_____

How did Colorado change after the 1850s?

Details: _____

_____

_____

Generalization: _____

_____

What is the population of Colorado like today?

Details: _____

_____

_____

Generalization: _____

_____

Name _____

Super Suffixes

Write the word from the box that matches each clue. Write only one letter on each line. Remember, the endings *-er, -or,* and *-ist* each mean "someone who." If you need help, use a dictionary. To solve the riddle, write the numbered letter from each answer on the line with the matching number.

composer	sailor	teacher
conductor	traveler	settler

1. Someone who sails   __ __ __ __ __ __
                                      6

2. Someone who takes a trip   __ __ __ __ __ __ __ __
                                         1

3. Someone who settles
a new place   __ __ __ __ __ __ __
                     5

4. Someone who is in
charge of a train   __ __ __ __ __ __ __ __ __
                4

5. Someone who teaches   __ __ __ __ __ __ __
                       3

6. Someone who writes music   __ __ __ __ __ __ __ __
                                    2

Riddle: What did the alien say to the book?

Take me to your __ __ __ __ __ __ !
               1   2   3   4   5   6

Name _____

The /îr/, /är/, and /âr/ Sounds

When you hear the /îr/, /är/, and /âr/ sounds, think of these patterns and examples:

Patterns	Examples
/îr/ *ear, eer*	g**ear**, ch**eer**
/är/ *ar*	sh**ar**p
/âr/ *are, air*	st**are**, h**air**y

► The spelling patterns for the vowel + *r* sounds in the starred words are different. In *heart*, the /är/ sound is spelled *ear*. In *weird*, the /îr/ sound is spelled *eir*. In *scarce*, the /âr/ sound is spelled *ar*.

Write each Spelling Word under its vowel + *r* sound.

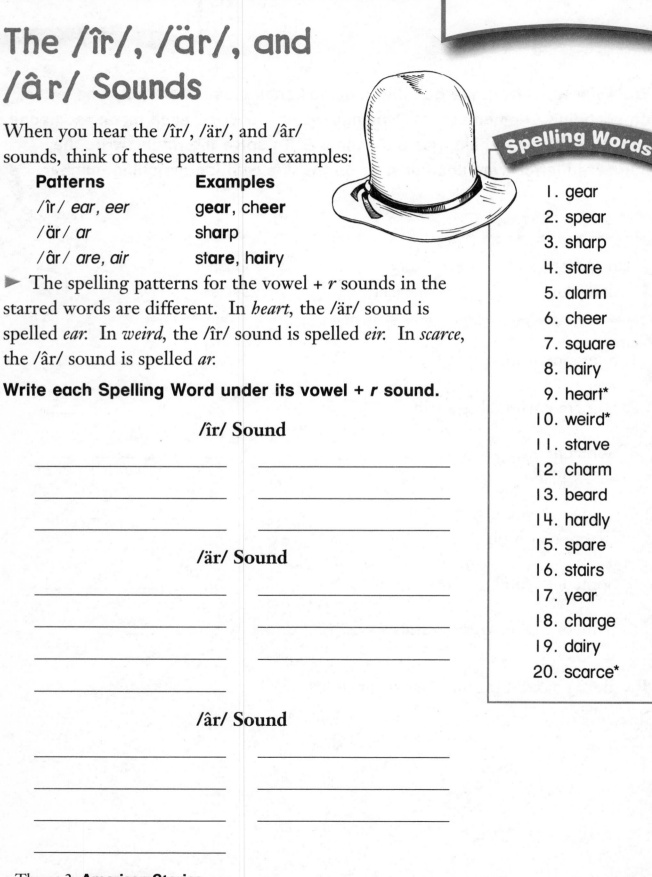

/îr/ Sound

_____   _____

_____   _____

_____   _____

/är/ Sound

_____   _____

_____   _____

_____   _____

_____

/âr/ Sound

_____   _____

_____   _____

_____   _____

_____

Spelling Words

1. gear
2. spear
3. sharp
4. stare
5. alarm
6. cheer
7. square
8. hairy
9. heart*
10. weird*
11. starve
12. charm
13. beard
14. hardly
15. spare
16. stairs
17. year
18. charge
19. dairy
20. scarce*

Name _____

Spelling Spree

Word Search **Write the Spelling Word that is hidden in each sentence.**

Example: Ea<u>ch air</u>plane was on time. *chair*

1. Does the diver need air yet? _____

2. This harp has a broken string. _____

3. How often does the spa replace the mud? _____

4. The royal armada sailed the seas. _____

5. Children of that age are cute. _____

6. The show will star very famous people. _____

7. How much armor did knights wear? _____

8. His pea rolled off his fork. _____

Book Titles **Write the Spelling Word that best completes each funny book title. Remember to use capital letters.**

Example: *Something's in the* ___Air___
by Lotta Smoke

9. *Getting by When Money Is* _____ by B. A. Tightwad

10. *Ways to* _____ *Up a Gloomy Pal* by May Kem Laff

11. *Climb the* _____ *to Success* by Rich N. Famous

12. *Taking* _____ *of Your Life* by U. Ken Dewitt

9. _____ 11. _____

10. _____ 12. _____

Spelling Words

1. gear
2. spear
3. sharp
4. stare
5. alarm
6. cheer
7. square
8. hairy
9. heart*
10. weird*
11. starve
12. charm
13. beard
14. hardly
15. spare
16. stairs
17. year
18. charge
19. dairy
20. scarce*

Name _____

Proofreading and Writing

Proofreading **Circle the five misspelled Spelling Words in this paragraph from a story. Then write each word correctly.**

Suddenly, a hush came over the room. I could hardely hear a sound. I turned, and there in the doorway stood a huge cowpoke with a long beerd. I couldn't help but stayre at him because he looked so odd. A Stetson hat sat on his head. His weard hands were as hairy as bear paws. He was covered with dust too. Then he grinned and said shyly, "Howdy, folks!" Someone yelled, "It's Big John, home from a yier on the trail!" The crowd broke into a cheer, and everyone ran up to shake John's hand.

1. gear	
2. spear	
3. sharp	
4. stare	
5. alarm	
6. cheer	
7. square	
8. hairy	
9. heart*	
10. weird*	
11. starve	
12. charm	
13. beard	
14. hardly	
15. spare	
16. stairs	
17. year	
18. charge	
19. dairy	
20. scarce*	

1. _____   4. _____

2. _____   5. _____

3. _____

✏ **Write an Ad** **If you were to create a new style of hat, what would it look like? Why would people want to buy one of your hats?**

On a separate piece of paper, write an ad that tells about your hat. Make the hat seem so great that everyone will want to buy one. Use Spelling Words from the list.

Name _____

It's All in the Context

Choose the correct definition from the list below for
each underlined word in the paragraph. Write the letter
after the number matching the word. Use context clues
to help choose the right definition.

a. to protect or cover

b. small in amount

c. explore for valuable metals

d. one-of-a-kind

e. the flat, broad lower edge of a hat

f. beautiful; scenic

g. setting a person or thing apart
from others

h. a rock containing gold or silver

i. strike out; make a new path

j. a remote area with few people

John Stetson and the Pikes Peakers headed away from

the cities and into the <u>frontier</u>. Along the way, they passed
₁

<u>picturesque</u> landscapes that seemed to be painted in red
₂

and gold. John's <u>distinctive</u> hat made him stand out from
₃

the rest. It was <u>unique</u>; no one else had anything like it.
₄

John liked the way the hat's wide <u>brim</u> managed to <u>shield</u>
₅   ₆

his face from the sun. When they reached Colorado, John

saw men <u>prospect</u> for gold. In some rocks they found <u>ore</u>
₇   ₈

containing silver. Mostly, though, results were so <u>meager</u>
₉

that many miners left Colorado to <u>blaze</u> a new trail to the
₁₀

California goldfields.

1. _____

2. _____

3. _____

4. _____

5. _____

6. _____

7. _____

8. _____

9. _____

10. _____

Name _____

Finding More Plural Nouns

Underline each plural noun in the sentences below.

1. The West offered many opportunities for making money.

2. In Eastern cities, a Stetson hat wouldn't sell.

3. In the territories of the West, many men wore one.

4. Behind many a herd of sheep rode a cowboy with a Stetson.

5. A horse might carry a settler's supplies, but the settler wore his Stetson.

6. Ladies were impressed by a stylish broad-brimmed hat.

7. If you picked berries, you could always put them in your Stetson.

8. Did anyone ever see sheep or deer wearing headgear like that?

On the line at the right of each singular noun given, write the correct plural form. Use a dictionary to help you.

9. duty _____

10. woman _____

11. bison _____

12. sky _____

13. moose _____

14. child _____

15. ditty _____

Name _____

Rewriting Plural Nouns

**Rewrite each sentence on the lines provided, using the
plural of the noun in parentheses.**

1. Many (family) went west to seek wealth.

_____

2. Some came from (city) in the East.

_____

3. Hats like (derby) were not useful in bad weather.

_____

4. In this new land, people needed special kinds of (supply).

_____

5. (Man) who worked in the open needed a hat to protect them.

_____

6. Against (sky) full of rain or snow, a Stetson offered protection.

_____

7. Herders of (sheep) wanted to keep the sun out of their eyes.

_____

8. John Stetson's new hat pleased cowboys and (woman) alike.

_____

9. In all the (territory) you could see Stetsons everywhere.

_____

10. Everyone, including (child), sported a Stetson.

_____

Name _____

Proofreading for Noun Endings

Proofread the paragraph below. Find plurals of nouns that are incorrectly spelled. Circle each misspelled plural. Then correctly write each misspelled plural on the lines provided. Use a dictionary to help you.

Proofreading Marks   ⬭ spell correctly

Would you like a hat to protect you from rainy skyes? How about one to keep the sun out of your eyies? You can use these hats to hold grainies for your horsers or to carry freshly picked strawberris. You can make two earholes in these hats and put them on your sheeps or oxes. What kind of hat can entire familys wear — men, woman, and childs? Are they derbys? No, these hats are Stetsones.

Regular	Changes *y* to *i* and adds *es*	Special plural	Same as singular
_____	_____	_____	_____
_____	_____	_____	_____
_____	_____	_____	_____
_____	_____	_____	_____

Name _____

Writing a Business Letter

Use this page to help you plan a business letter.

My Purpose for Writing _____

    Writer's Address _____

    _____

    _____

_____ Inside Address

_____

_____

_____ Greeting

Introductory Paragraph

_____

_____

Middle Paragraph

_____

_____

Concluding Paragraph

_____

_____

Closing

_____

Signature

_____

Name _____

Improving Your Writing

Read the business letter. Find details that do not keep to the point. Mark them to be deleted. Then recopy the letter, with these details omitted, on another sheet of paper.

1407 Green Street
Urbana, Illinois 61801
January 19, 2001

Ms. Angela O'Byrne
Public Relations Director
Kitchenwares Incorporated
920 Main Street
Mineola, New York 11502

Dear Ms. O'Byrne:

I am writing to request information about the new Whiz food processor. I am in the cooking class at school. We are learning to bake now. Our class needs a new processor. We saw an advertisement in the newspaper. The processor in your ad seems to be a good one.

Our teacher asked me to write to you for information about what the processor costs and what it will do. I like to write. I always get good grades on my compositions. I will take the information you send and present it to our class. The class will decide if the Whiz is the one for us.

Thank you for your help. I hope the Whiz will be the food processor that we get for our class. I am sure the information you send will help us make our decision.

Sincerely,
Maria Lopez

Name _____

Becoming a Citizen

Miguel's grandparents want to become citizens, but they don't know what to do. Miguel tells them what to expect. Complete Miguel's story by filling in each blank with the correct word from the list.

Vocabulary

allegiance
chamber
citizen
citizenship
enrich
examiner
oath
petitioners

When someone wants to become a _____ of the United States, that person must go through a special ceremony. The ceremony takes place in a United States government courthouse. The people all gather in a room called a _____. When everyone is seated, a person called an _____ calls out each person's name. Then each of the _____ walks up to the desk, is given a certificate, and signs his or her name. After this is done, a judge comes into the room to administer the _____ of _____. All the people stand up and pledge their _____ to the United States. After the ceremony, friends and relatives offer their congratulations to the new citizens. Hopefully, the new citizens will _____ their lives and the lives of others as citizens of their new country.

Name _____

Who/What Chart

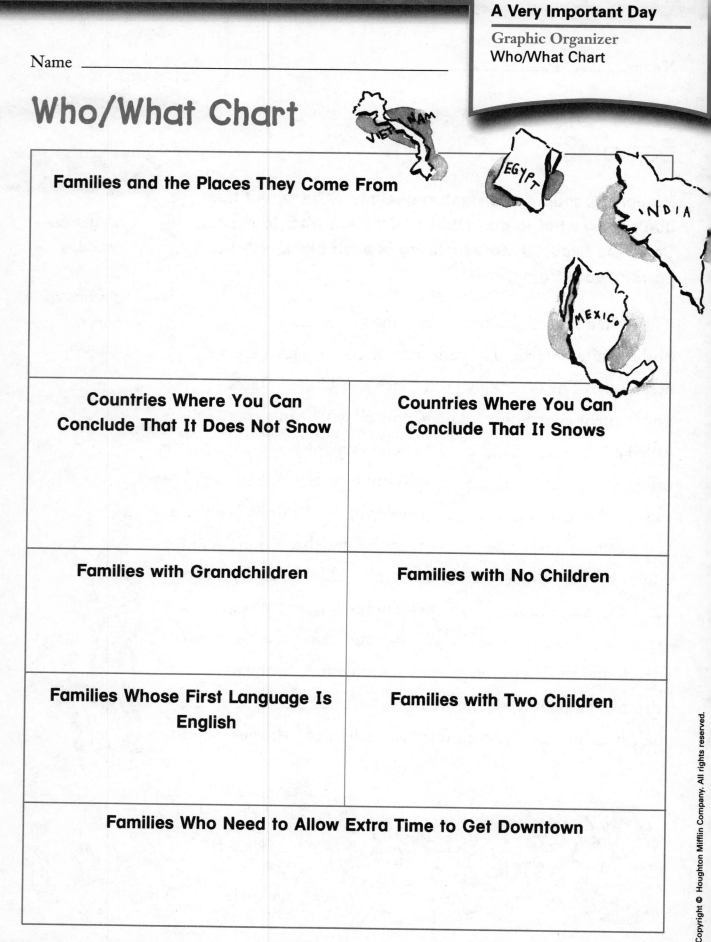

Families and the Places They Come From	
Countries Where You Can Conclude That It Does Not Snow	**Countries Where You Can Conclude That It Snows**
Families with Grandchildren	**Families with No Children**
Families Whose First Language Is English	**Families with Two Children**
Families Who Need to Allow Extra Time to Get Downtown	

Name _____

Jacket Information

Complete the summary for the book jacket for *A Very Important Day*.

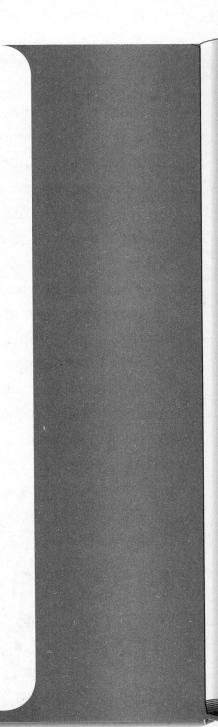

Snow is falling on New York City as different families awaken early one winter day. The members of each family worry because

_____

_____

Each family member is an immigrant who has come to America from a foreign country. Today is special because

_____

At the courthouse, the examiner _____

_____

When the certificates are handed out, the judge leads everyone

_____

_____

When the oath is finished, the judge welcomes all the new citizens and wishes them good luck. Then everyone in the courtroom stands

_____

_____

All the new citizens congratulate each other and then head for home to celebrate a very special day.

Name _____

Classified Information

Read the article below and complete the chart on the following page.

Arriving at Ellis Island

Ellis Island, in New York harbor, was the first stop in the United States for millions of immigrants in the early twentieth century. When they arrived on ships, immigrants were taken there to be checked by doctors and most were then allowed to enter the United States. Among them were my grandparents, who arrived in 1913.

In Europe, my grandparents had traveled through Austria, Hungary, Germany, and France to reach the ship that brought them to New York. With them were their friends Mr. and Mrs. Radowsky, Mr. and Mrs. Graff, and Mr. Stead.

When they reached Ellis Island, they were taken to a huge hall. Around them were immigrants from Russia, China, Jamaica, Brazil, and South Africa. People were dressed in different types of clothes and spoke many different languages.

My grandparents and their friends were examined by doctors. Mr. Stead was found to be ill, and he was not allowed into the United States. Yet my grandparents and their other friends were allowed to enter. My grandparents and the Radowskys settled in Brooklyn. The Graffs settled in Chicago.

Name _____

Classified Information continued

Answer the following questions based on the article.

1. Which countries are in Europe?

_____

_____

2. Who can be classified as friends of the grandparents?

_____

_____

3. Who can be classified as new residents of the United States?

_____

_____

4. What would you name the category that has the grandparents and the Radowskys as its only members?

_____

_____

Name _____

Picturing Possessives

Write a sentence to tell about each picture. Make the noun beside each picture possessive, and use it in your sentence.

A possessive noun is a noun that shows ownership.
▶ Add an apostrophe (') and *s* to a singular noun.
▶ Add just an apostrophe (') to plural nouns ending in *s*.
▶ Add an apostrophe (') and *s* to plural nouns that do not end in *s*.

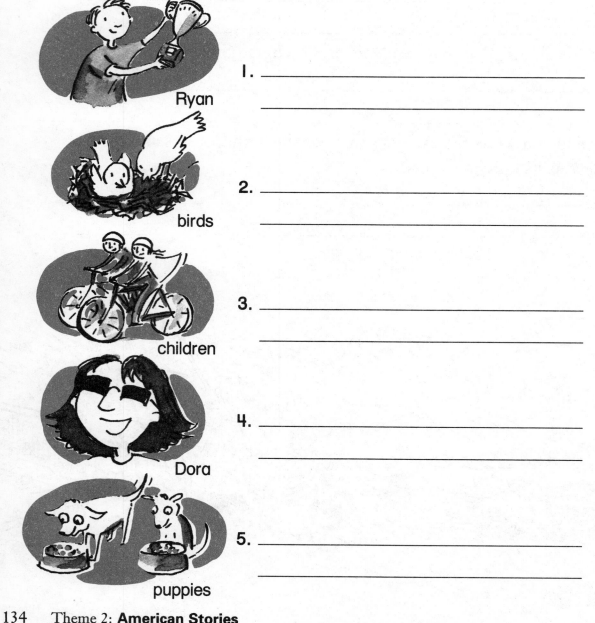

Ryan

1. _____

   _____

birds

2. _____

   _____

children

3. _____

   _____

Dora

4. _____

   _____

puppies

5. _____

   _____

134   Theme 2: **American Stories**

Name _____

The /ôr/, /ûr/, and /yŏŏr/ Sounds

When you hear the /ôr/, /ûr/, or /yŏŏr/ sounds, think of these patterns and examples:

Patterns	Examples
/ôr/ *or, ore*	h**or**se, ch**ore**
/ûr/ *ur, ir, ear, or*	f**ir**m, c**ur**ve, l**ear**n, w**or**m
/yŏŏr/ *ure*	p**ure**

► The /ôr/ sound is usually spelled *or* or *ore*.

► They /ûr/ sound is usually spelled *ir*, *ur*, *ear*, or *or*.

► The /yŏŏr/ sound is usually spelled *ure*.

► The spelling patterns for the /ôr/ sounds in the starred words *board* and *course* are different.

Write each Spelling Word under its vowel + *r* sounds.

/ôr/ Sounds

_____   _____

_____   _____

_____   _____

/ûr/ Sounds

_____   _____

_____   _____

_____   _____

_____   _____

/yŏŏr/ Sounds

_____   _____

Spelling Words

1. horse
2. chore
3. firm
4. learn
5. dirty
6. curve
7. world
8. pure
9. board*
10. course*
11. heard
12. return
13. cure
14. score
15. worm
16. thirteen
17. worn
18. curl
19. shirt
20. search

Name _____

Spelling Spree

Word Addition **Write a Spelling Word by adding the beginning of the first word to the end of the second word.**

   Example: hum + part *hurt*

1. curb + dive _____
2. chop + store _____
3. wool + corn _____
4. seat + march _____
5. cut + girl _____
6. fix + term _____
7. boat + hard _____
8. cut + tore _____
9. ship + dart _____
10. put + care _____

Questions **Write a Spelling Word to answer each question.**

11. What number is one more than twelve?
12. What is the name for a large animal that has a long mane?
13. What word describes a room that has not been cleaned?
14. What small, soft-bodied animal crawls through the soil?
15. What do you do when you hit a home run in baseball?

11. _____   14. _____
12. _____   15. _____
13. _____

Spelling Words

1. horse
2. chore
3. firm
4. learn
5. dirty
6. curve
7. world
8. pure
9. board*
10. course*
11. heard
12. return
13. cure
14. score
15. worm
16. thirteen
17. worn
18. curl
19. shirt
20. search

Name _____

Proofreading and Writing

Proofreading Circle the five misspelled Spelling Words in this friendly letter. Then write each word correctly.

Dear Genya,

    I have the best news in the wurld. I am going to become an American! Thirteen of us are taking a special corse. We all have to lern facts about our new country. Then we take a test. If I get a high score, I will become a citizen. Isn't this the greatest news you have ever heared?

    Next year, we hope to retern to Russia for a visit. I can teach you a lot about America then!

Love,
Olga

Spelling Words

1. horse
2. chore
3. firm
4. learn
5. dirty
6. curve
7. world
8. pure
9. board*
10. course*
11. heard
12. return
13. cure
14. score
15. worm
16. thirteen
17. worn
18. curl
19. shirt
20. search

1. _____ 4. _____

2. _____ 5. _____

3. _____

✏️→ **Write a Description** What could you tell a friend in another country about your city or town? Does it snow where you live? Are there palm trees on your street?

On a separate sheet of paper, write a paragraph telling about the place where you live. Use Spelling Words from the list.

Name _____

One Word, Many Meanings

In each of the following sentences, the underlined word has at least two possible meanings. Choose the meaning that fits the sentence. Mark your choice with an X.

1. "We came early so we wouldn't <u>miss</u> you," said the Pitambers.

   A. _____ fail to meet   B. _____ avoid or escape

2. "Trinh," said her mother, "come and let's <u>board</u> the bus."

   A. _____ plank of wood   B. _____ get onto

3. Jorge was grateful for his father's <u>company</u> on the ferry.

   A. _____ companionship   B. _____ business

4. The subway ride was <u>over</u>, and it was time for breakfast.

   A. _____ finished   B. _____ above

5. The table had just been <u>set</u> by Veena when the doorbell rang.

   A. _____ decided on   B. _____ made ready

6. Nelia's son was <u>fast</u> asleep until she woke him up.

   A. _____ completely   B. _____ quickly

7. "She'll get <u>used</u> to snow, living here," said Kostas.

   A. _____ not new; secondhand   B. _____ accustomed

8. The race between Kwame and Efua ended in a <u>tie</u>.

   A. _____ an equal score   B. _____ make a knot

Name _____

In Search of Possessive Nouns

In each sentence, underline each possessive noun form.

1. Nelia's family in the Philippines had never seen snow.

2. Miguel's family was going to the courthouse.

3. The Patels' neighbors and children were invited to breakfast.

4. Eugenia's whole family took the subway downtown.

5. Grandfather's hands were full of wet snow.

6. Mrs. Soutsos laughed at little Kiki's reaction to snowflakes.

7. The family's restaurant was closed for the day.

8. Passengers' bundles fell to the floor when the driver
   had to stop.

9. The judge's voice was loud and clear in the courtroom.

10. The citizens' voices could be heard saying the Pledge
    of Allegiance.

On the line at the right of each noun, write the correct possessive form.

11. relative _____

12. woman _____

13. children _____

14. Eugenia _____

15. friends _____

16. sister _____

17. mouse _____

18. babies _____

19. crowd _____

20. city _____

Name _____

Replacing with Possessive Nouns

Rewrite each sentence, replacing the underlined words with a singular or plural possessive noun.

1. Nelia heard <u>the voice of the announcer</u> telling about the snow.

   _____

2. <u>The sister of Miguel</u> woke him up.

   _____

3. Niko, <u>the brother of Kiko</u>, helped her sweep snow off
   the sidewalk.

   _____

4. Everyone in <u>the family of the Leonovs</u> had waited for the big day.

   _____

5. Down from the window came a gift from <u>a friend of Yujin</u>.

   _____

6. Becoming a citizen was <u>the goal of an immigrant</u>.

   _____

7. Everyone heard the examiner call out each of <u>the names of</u>
   <u>the Castros</u>.

   _____

8. All the people in the room could hear <u>the words of the judge</u>.

   _____

Name _____

Proofreading for Apostrophes

Proofread each sentence. Find any possessive nouns that lack apostrophes or have apostrophes in the wrong place. Circle each incorrect possessive noun. Then write the corrected sentence on the line below it.

1. The days main event for many families was becoming United States citizens.

   _____

   _____

   _____

2. To one womans surprise, the DJ predicted six inches of snow.

   _____

   _____

3. The Huerta familys goal was to be at the courthouse early.

   _____

   _____

4. Kwames wife, Efua, had her picture taken.

   _____

   _____

   _____

5. All the Castros signatures were on the court papers.

   _____

   _____

Name _____

Writing Journal Entries

Answer these questions. Then use your answers to help write your own journal entry.

1. What new word, fact, or idea did you learn today? Now, write it down, along with a few words telling why you found it interesting.

   _____

   _____

2. If you could ask anybody in the world a question, who would that person be and what question would you ask?

   _____

   _____

3. As you look around, what object catches your eye? Name the object, and write a few words to describe it.

   _____

   _____

4. What is a recent movie or television show that you've seen? Now, give your opinion of it.

   _____

   _____

5. What is one thing that makes you smile? Write what it is and why it makes you smile.

   _____

   _____

Name _____

Improving Your Writing

**Suppose Kostas kept a journal. Read the journal entry below.
Then write a journal entry as if you were one of the other
characters in *A Very Important Day*. Write your observations and
feelings in words that give your writing your own personal voice.**

From Kostas's Journal

January 18

*Today will be very special. Mother and Father are
becoming United States citizens. I don't have to do that,
because I'm already a citizen. I was born in this country. I
feel very proud that they will become citizens, too. Tonight,
we'll have a wonderful party to celebrate.*

*It is snowing. I like snow. The city becomes quieter when it
snows. The street sounds are muffled, and the city seems
peaceful. I hope there will be enough snow to make a
snowman. Maybe there will be enough snow to make two!*

_____

_____

_____

_____

_____

_____

_____

_____

Name _____

Filling in the Blank

Use the test-taking strategies and tips you have learned to help you answer fill-in-the-blank items. This practice will help you when you take this kind of test.

Read each item. At the bottom of the page, fill in the circle for the answer that best completes the sentence.

1. Tomás and his family picked fruit and vegetables for Texas farmers in the —

   A summer   **C** spring

   B winter   **D** fall

2. Right after Tomás and Enrique carried water to their parents, they —

   F visited the library

   G went to the town dump

   H picked corn in the fields

   J played with a ball

3. When Tomás got to the library, he saw —

   A that the building was closed

   B Papá Grande telling a story

   C children leaving with books

   D his brother Enrique reading a book

4. Just after Tomás went inside the library and got a drink of water, —

   F the librarian brought him some books

   G he read a book about dinosaurs

   H he listened to Papá Grande tell a story

   J the librarian told him that the library was closing

ANSWER ROWS   1 Ⓐ Ⓑ Ⓒ Ⓓ   3 Ⓐ Ⓑ Ⓒ Ⓓ

                   2 Ⓕ Ⓖ Ⓗ Ⓙ   4 Ⓕ Ⓖ Ⓗ Ⓙ

Name _____

Filling in the Blank continued

5. Tomás imagined he was riding one, when he read a book about —

    A horses

    B camels

    C dinosaurs

    D tigers

6. Before Tomás could leave with any of the library books, the librarian had to —

    F get him a library card

    G talk to his parents

    H check them out in her name

    J write down his address

7. When Tomás went to the town dump with his family, he looked for —

    A toys

    B iron

    C pencils

    D books

8. Before Tomás left to go back to Texas, the librarian gave him a —

    F ride on a horse

    G new book

    H package of sweet bread

    J library card

ANSWER ROWS   5 Ⓐ Ⓑ Ⓒ Ⓓ   7 Ⓐ Ⓑ Ⓒ Ⓓ
               6 Ⓕ Ⓖ Ⓗ Ⓙ   8 Ⓕ Ⓖ Ⓗ Ⓙ

Name _____

Spelling Review

Write Spelling Words from the list on this page to answer the questions.

1–14. Which fourteen words have the /ou/, /ô/, /o͝o/, or /o͞o/ sounds?

1. _____   8. _____
2. _____   9. _____
3. _____   10. _____
4. _____   11. _____
5. _____   12. _____
6. _____   13. _____
7. _____   14. _____

15–22. Which eight words have the /îr/, /är/, or /âr/ sounds?

15. _____   19. _____
16. _____   20. _____
17. _____   21. _____
18. _____   22. _____

23–30. Which eight words have the /ôr/ or /ûr/ sounds?

23. _____   27. _____
24. _____   28. _____
25. _____   29. _____
26. _____   30. _____

Spelling Words

1. gear
2. howl
3. wood
4. bounce
5. jaw
6. put
7. year
8. false
9. couch
10. dawn
11. push
12. sauce
13. spare
14. tool
15. full
16. search
17. roof
18. pull
19. hardly
20. world
21. dairy
22. chore
23. curl
24. dirty
25. alarm
26. cheer
27. charge
28. horse
29. heard
30. return

Name _____

Spelling Spree

Context Clues **Write the Spelling Word that completes each sentence.**

1. You rode a black _____ at the farm.

2. When I come back, I _____.

3. I _____ my coat in the closet.

4. We _____ noises in the kitchen.

5. Mom likes to _____ her hair.

Rhyme Time **Write the Spelling Word that makes sense and rhymes with the word in dark print.**

6. **Thirty** _____ rabbits hopped.

7. We always **yawn** at _____.

8. **Ouch**! I fell off of the _____.

9. Choose **good** _____ for the fire.

10. Wolves sometimes **growl** or _____.

American Places **Use the Spelling Words to complete these sentences about American cities.**

11. New York is one of the biggest cities in the _____.

12. There are many _____ farms in Wisconsin.

13. Many people visit Austin, Texas, each _____.

14. Sometimes you can _____ see in the fog of San Francisco.

15. Boston chefs make delicious spaghetti _____.

Spelling Words

1. howl
2. couch
3. dawn
4. sauce
5. wood
6. put
7. hardly
8. year
9. dairy
10. horse
11. dirty
12. curl
13. heard
14. world
15. return

Proofreading and Writing

Proofreading **Circle the six misspelled Spelling Words in this advertisement. Then write each word correctly.**

Come visit a real log cabin. You will bownce along an old lane for about one mile. Then you will see smoke from the chimney on the ruf. The charg is three dollars.

In the 1700s, people had little spair time. Each child had at least one chor to do. Every day was ful of work.

1. _____   4. _____

2. _____   5. _____

3. _____   6. _____

What's the Message? **After his visit, Harry e-mailed his cousin. Use Spelling Words to complete the message.**

Is it true or 7. _____ that you are sick? I hope this note will 8. _____ you up. My 9. _____ dropped when we visited a log cabin. No 10. _____ in the cabin was electric! You would need muscles to 11. _____ and 12. _____ logs into place! Except for a fire 13. _____ in the roof, it is the same as it was long ago. We can 14. _____ for a place like this where we can bring our camping 15. _____.

✏️ **Write a Diary Entry** **On a separate sheet of paper, write a diary entry about life in a log cabin. Use the Spelling Review Words.**

Name _____

Adapting a Book to a Play

Choose a book (or one of the selections from the previous themes) to adapt into a play. Explain why you have chosen it. Make a list of all the elements of a play that must be included.

_____

_____

_____

_____

_____

Next write the cast of characters, the setting, and the time of the play.

_____

_____

_____

_____

_____

_____

_____

_____

_____

_____

Name _____

Write a Character Analysis

Write a character analysis, or description, for the following characters from *Tales of a Fourth Grade Nothing*. Describe what kind of person the character is. Be sure to use descriptive adjectives that tell about the character's personality. Refer to the play for examples to support your descriptions.

1. Peter: _____

_____

_____

_____

_____

_____

_____

_____

_____

_____

2. Mrs. Yarby: _____

_____

_____

_____

_____

_____

_____

_____

_____

_____

Name _____

Make It Amazing!

Change the underlined words in the paragraph below to make it amazing. The first one is done for you.

When I <u>walked</u> into my <u>house</u> yesterday, I saw <u>my</u> <u>mother</u> on the <u>sofa</u>. She was <u>reading the newspaper</u>. When she <u>looked up</u>, I told her about my day at <u>school</u>.

When I _____ *flew* _____ into my _____

yesterday, I saw _____ on the

_____. She was

_____. When she

_____, I told

her about my day _____.

Continue the story to tell about your amazing day!

_____

_____

_____

_____

_____

_____

_____

★ **Bonus To make your story even more amazing, rewrite the paragraph, adding adjectives to describe the important nouns. Here are two examples: "my <u>upside down</u> house" and "the <u>floating</u> sofa."**

Name _____

That's Amazing!

	What in the story was realistic?	What amazing things happened in the story?
The Stranger		
Cendrillon		
Heat Wave!		

Which of these stories was most amazing to you? Put a mark on the line for each story, labeled with the story's title, to show how realistic you think each one was!

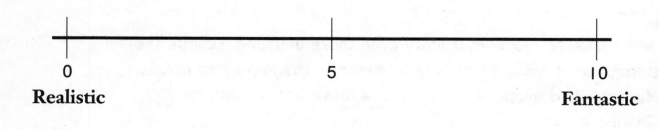

0   5   l0

Realistic   **Fantastic**

Name _____

Chilly Crossword

Complete the puzzle using words from the vocabulary list. Write the word that fits each clue.

Across

2. season of year between summer and winter
4. very thin covering of ice
6. an instrument that measures temperature
8. a flow of air

Down

1. strange, odd
3. silvery metal used in thermometers
5. made a design by cutting lines
7. shy; easily frightened

Vocabulary

autumn
draft
etched
frost
mercury
peculiar
thermometer
timid

Name _____

Detail Map

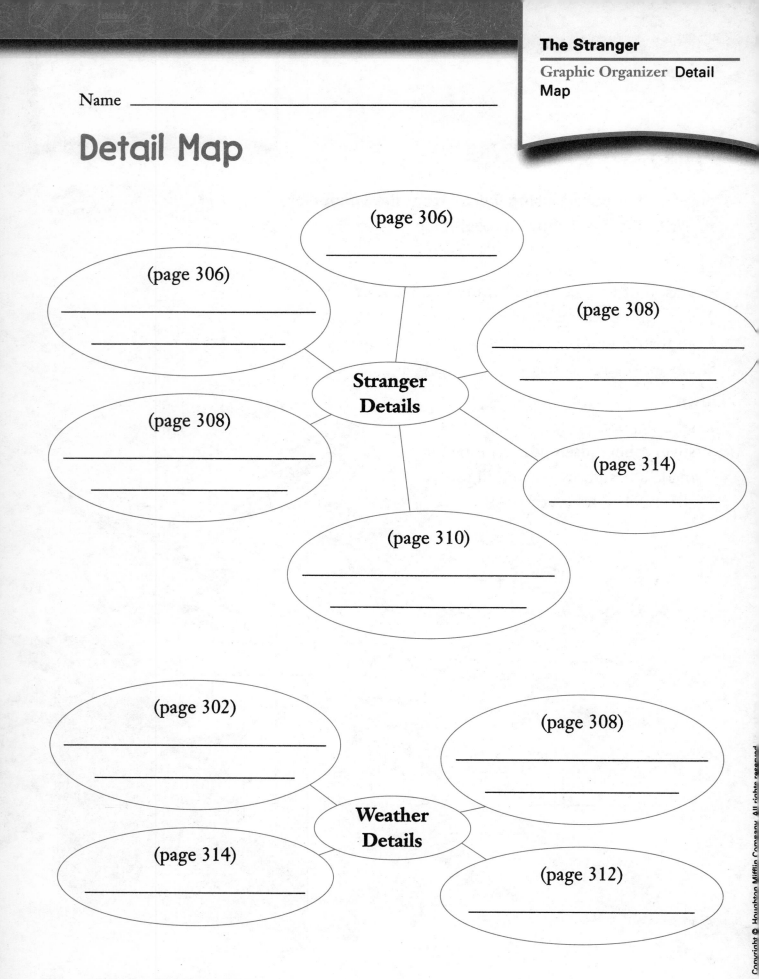

(page 306)

_____

(page 306)

_____

_____

(page 308)

_____

_____

**Stranger
Details**

(page 308)

_____

_____

(page 314)

_____

(page 310)

_____

_____

(page 302)

_____

_____

(page 308)

_____

_____

**Weather
Details**

(page 314)

_____

(page 312)

_____

Name _____

A Nose for Details

Think about the selection. Then answer these questions.

1. What time of year does the story take place?

   _____

2. What happens when Mr. Bailey is driving his truck?

   _____

3. What was the stranger wearing?

   _____

4. What does the stranger **not** do?

   _____

5. The stranger pulls a leaf off a tree and does what?

   _____

6. What happens to the weather and the leaves after the stranger leaves?

   _____

7. What words are etched in frost on the farmhouse windows every year?

   _____

Name _____

Think About It

Read the story. Then complete the detail map on the next page.

What's Your Name?

Mr. Downing's first attempt at a garden since his retirement was a huge disappointment. He had tried everything—plant food, pruning, bug control, and water. It still looked like even the smallest field mouse couldn't get a meal from it.

One day an elderly lady wearing a large hat covered with flowers passed by the fence in front of Mr. Downing's house. She called over to him, "Looks like you could use a little help there." The lady walked over to the garden, tucked her long, curly, gray hair up into her hat, bent down, and immediately began tending the plants.

As Mr. Downing watched her in stunned silence he noticed that the flowers in her hat were real. "How odd," he thought. Then he heard the lady softly talking. He was about to ask her to speak up when he realized she wasn't talking to him but the plants instead.

Mr. Downing focused his eyes on the lady for quite some time. Finally she stood up and spoke to him. "Remember, a little conversation never hurts." She began to walk away.

A little confused, Mr. Downing looked from her to his garden. He was amazed at the sight before his eyes. The flowers were blooming and there were vegetables on the vines. He turned back, thanked the lady and asked her name.

"Everybody just calls me Mother," she said, with a smile full of sunshine.

Name _____

Think About It

Complete this Detail Map for the story "What's Your Name?"

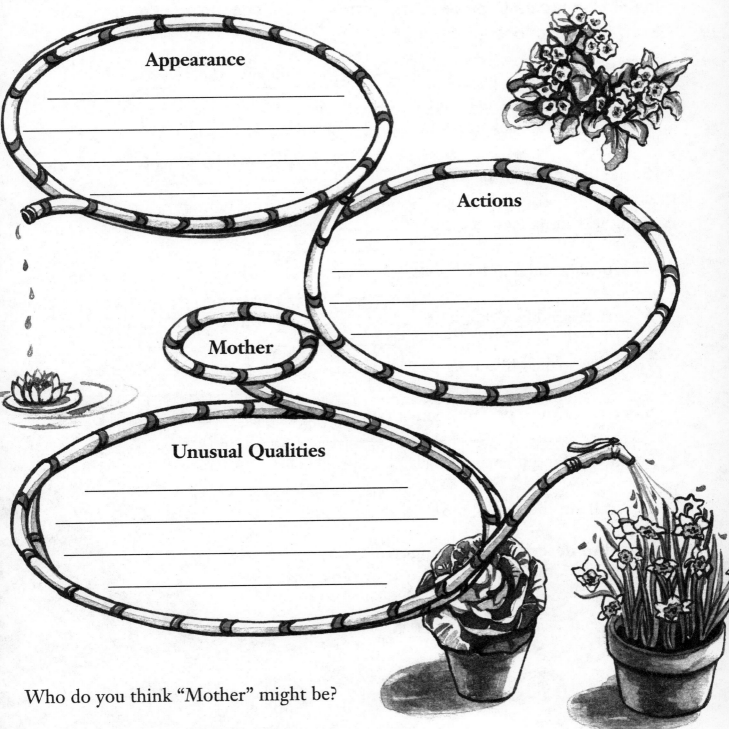

Appearance

_____
_____
_____
_____

Actions

_____
_____
_____

Mother

Unusual Qualities

_____
_____
_____
_____

Who do you think "Mother" might be?

_____

Name _____

Compound Challenge

**Write the compound word that matches each clue. Then write
the circled letters in order at the bottom of the page to spell a
word that describes the Stranger.**

1. carousel ⬡□□□□-□□-□□□□□

2. a yard at the back of a house □□□□Ⓞ□□□

3. the first meal of the day □□□□□□□□Ⓞ□

4. light coming from stars □Ⓞ□□□□□□□

5. Saturday and Sunday □□□□Ⓞ□□

6. a truck used by firefighters □□Ⓞ□ □□□□□□

7. a bank shaped like a pig □Ⓞ□□ □□□□

8. a coat worn to protect against rain □□□□□Ⓞ□□

9. a house for a dog □□□□□Ⓞ□□

10. a walk on the side of a road Ⓞ□□□□□□□

A word to describe the Stranger:

◯◯◯◯◯◯◯◯◯◯

Name _____

Compound Words

A **compound word** is made up of two or more smaller words. To spell a compound word correctly, you must know if it is written as one word, as two words joined by a hyphen, or as two separate words.

rail + road = railroad   **ninety + nine** = ninety-nine

seat + belt = seat belt

▶ In the starred word *already*, an *l* was dropped in *all* to make one word.

Write each Spelling Word under the heading that tells how the word is written.

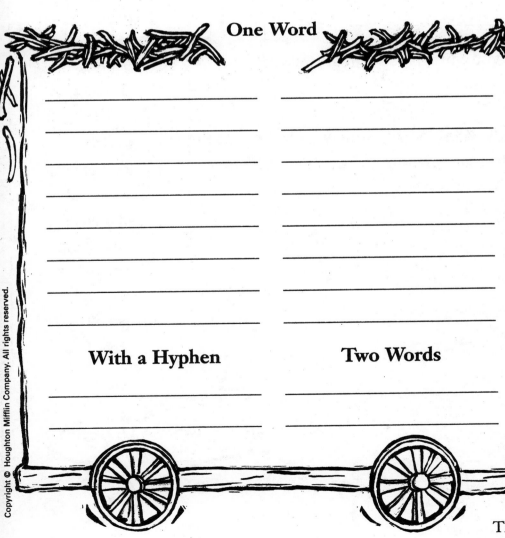

One Word

With a Hyphen   **Two Words**

Spelling Words

1. railroad
2. airport
3. seat belt
4. everywhere
5. homesick
6. understand
7. background
8. anything
9. ninety-nine
10. already*
11. fireplace
12. ourselves
13. all right
14. forever
15. breakfast
16. whenever
17. everything
18. meanwhile
19. afternoon
20. make-believe

Name _____

Spelling Spree

What Am I? **Write the Spelling Word that answers each riddle.**

1. I'm cereal and juice, and I happen before lunch.

   What am I? _____

2. I'm really quite old, but less than one hundred.

   What am I? _____

3. I'm the part of the day between morning and night.

   What am I? _____

4. Fasten me and I'll save you from crashes.

   What am I? _____

5. If going by plane, you must pass through me.

   What am I? _____

Finish the word **Each of the words below forms part of a Spelling Word. Write the Spelling Words on the lines.**

6. any _____

7. home _____

8. under _____

9. back _____

10. where _____

11. our _____

12. all _____

13. when _____

14. while _____

15. believe _____

Spelling Words

1. railroad
2. airport
3. seat belt
4. everywhere
5. homesick
6. understand
7. background
8. anything
9. ninety-nine
10. already*
11. fireplace
12. ourselves
13. all right
14. forever
15. breakfast
16. whenever
17. everything
18. meanwhile
19. afternoon
20. make-believe

162   Theme 3: **That's Amazing!**

Name _____

Proofreading and Writing

Proofreading Circle the five misspelled Spelling Words in the newspaper article. Then write each word correctly.

Weird Weather Grips Town

Up until two days ago, everyone was enjoying the warm fall weather. Local farmers reported that everthing was still growing at an amazing rate. Enormous pumpkins had allready been harvested. Then winter arrived without notice. Experts are predicting snow that may cause railrode and airport delays. Weather reporter Storm Sky says the cold snap won't last foreever. Stay indoors today, though. This is the perfect time to curl up by the firplace with a good book.

Spelling Words
1. railroad
2. airport
3. seat belt
4. everywhere
5. homesick
6. understand
7. background
8. anything
9. ninety-nine
10. already*
11. fireplace
12. ourselves
13. all right
14. forever
15. breakfast
16. whenever
17. everything
18. meanwhile
19. afternoon
20. make-believe

1. _____   4. _____

2. _____   5. _____

3. _____

✏️ **Write Helpful Hints** The stranger in the story was unfamiliar with many things in the Bailey house. Have you ever helped a person in an unfamiliar situation? What information would be helpful to that person?

On a separate sheet of paper, write a list of helpful tips for newcomers to your town or neighborhood. You might include information such as where to get the best pizza. Use Spelling Words from the list.

Name _____

Strange Synonyms

Suppose that the Baileys have a neighbor, and the neighbor wrote this letter to a cousin. She uses the word *strange* in almost every sentence. From the word list, choose synonyms to add variety to the letter. Some of the words are exact synonyms for *strange,* while others give a better sense of the sentence. Some words will fit in more than one sentence, but use each word only once. Use the sentence context to help decide which words fit best.

Dear Cousin Joe,

Our town had a very 1. __strange__ autumn. Every leaf stayed green for weeks, which is 2. __strange__ for these parts. A 3. __strange__ wind blew in the trees, making it feel just like summer. Everyone noticed the 4. __strange__ weather, even the new person in town. He was a little 5. __strange__ — he didn't talk much, but he sure could play the fiddle! He had a 6. __strange__ gift with animals. But the weather must have been too 7. __strange__ for him, because he left suddenly. The town felt 8. __strange__ without him. We missed him a lot. Shortly after he left, the 9. __strange__ summer weather turned to fall. It's too bad that the 10. __strange__ stranger left so soon. I think he would have liked autumn.

Your cousin,
Freda

Vocabulary

unusual
shy
unique
warm
unknown
rare
unfamiliar
new
odd
special
cool
weird
sad
uncommon
timid
quiet
different
lonely

1. _____   6. _____

2. _____   7. _____

3. _____   8. _____

4. _____   9. _____

5. _____   10. _____

Name _____

Letter with Action Verbs

What if Katy Bailey had a cousin and she wrote a letter to him? Read the letter. Circle each action verb and write it on the lines below.

Dear Cousin,

We have a new guest at our house. I think he lives in the forest near us. He wears a leather shirt and pants. His breath makes things cold. I call him "Jack Frost." He likes my mother's cooking, though. He especially enjoys her homemade vegetable soup. I hope you meet him soon.

Love,

Katy

_____   _____

_____   _____

_____   _____

_____   _____

Name _____

Take Action!

**Suppose Katy tells her class about the stranger who
came to stay with her family. Complete Katy's story by
filling each blank with an action verb. Choose verbs
from the box or use action verbs of your own.**

change
disappears
drives
grows
hears
jams
helps
jumps
listens
works

One fall day as my father _____ his

truck along the road, he _____ a loud

thump. He _____ on the brakes and

_____ out of the truck. Father

_____ the stranger into his truck.

The doctor _____ to the stranger's

heart. The stranger _____ stronger and

_____ with Father on the farm. When

the stranger _____, the leaves

_____ color and the weather turns cold.

Name _____

Using Action Verbs

Using Exact Verbs   Good writers use verbs that name specific actions to produce a vivid image in the reader's mind. Read each sentence below. Then rewrite the sentence. Substitute an exact verb for the general word or phrase in parentheses.

1. The doctor (looks at) the man's body.

_____

2. The doctor (finds) a lump on the man's head.

_____

3. The stranger (does the same thing as) Katy as she cools her soup.

_____

4. The cold breath (makes) a chill up Mrs. Bailey's spine.

_____

5. The rabbits do not (act frightened by) the stranger.

_____

6. The stranger (goes) along when Mr. Bailey works in the fields.

_____

7. Two weeks (go by) and the stranger can't remember his name.

_____

8. The stranger (wondered about) the colors of the leaves on the trees.

_____

Name _____

Writing an Explanation

Use this page to plan your explanation. You can explain why something happens or how something happens. Then number your reasons or facts in the order you will use them.

Topic:
Title:

Topic Sentence:

Reason / Fact:	**Reason / Fact:**

Reason / Fact:	**Reason / Fact:**

Name _____

Audience

Writers are always aware of their audience. A good writer will adapt the style of writing to fit the reader.

► Formal writing is used for reports, presentations, many school assignments, and business letters.

Formal: Deer can be found in almost all regions of the United States. Although they are wild animals, they can become quite used to the presence of human beings.

► Informal writing is for friendly letters, postcards, or e-mails between friends.

Informal: We saw the most incredible deer today. I was careful to walk up to it really slowly. I stretched out my hand, and it sniffed my palm. It felt really funny!

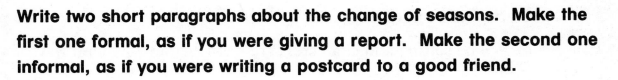

Write two short paragraphs about the change of seasons. Make the first one formal, as if you were giving a report. Make the second one informal, as if you were writing a postcard to a good friend.

The Change of Seasons

Formal:

_____

_____

_____

_____

Informal:

_____

_____

_____

_____

Name _____

Revising Your Story

Reread your story. What do you need to make it better? Use this page to help you decide. Put a checkmark in the box for each sentence that describes your story.

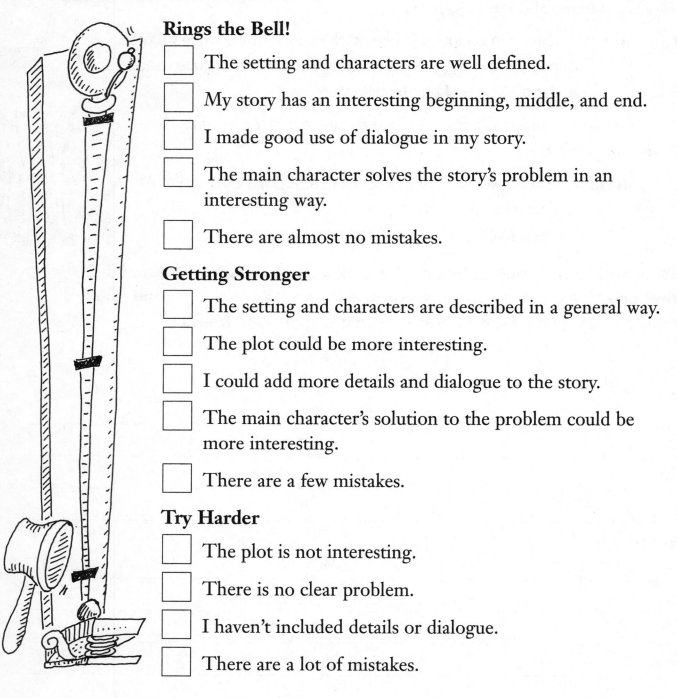

Rings the Bell!

☐ The setting and characters are well defined.

☐ My story has an interesting beginning, middle, and end.

☐ I made good use of dialogue in my story.

☐ The main character solves the story's problem in an interesting way.

☐ There are almost no mistakes.

Getting Stronger

☐ The setting and characters are described in a general way.

☐ The plot could be more interesting.

☐ I could add more details and dialogue to the story.

☐ The main character's solution to the problem could be more interesting.

☐ There are a few mistakes.

Try Harder

☐ The plot is not interesting.

☐ There is no clear problem.

☐ I haven't included details or dialogue.

☐ There are a lot of mistakes.

Name _____

Using Possessives

A **possessive** shows ownership.
► Add *'s* to make nouns possessive.
► For plurals that end in *s*, add an apostrophe.

**Rewrite each phrase, using a possessive noun. Then
use the new phrase in a sentence of your own.**

1. the pouch of the kangaroo _____
   _____
   _____

2. the roar of the lion _____
   _____
   _____

3. the buzz of the flies _____
   _____
   _____

4. the cleverness of the foxes _____
   _____
   _____

5. the prey belonging to the tiger _____
   _____
   _____

6. the symphony of the frogs _____
   _____
   _____

Name _____

Spelling Words

Words Often Misspelled Look for familiar spelling patterns to help you remember how to spell the Spelling Words on this page. Think carefully about the parts that you find hard to spell in each word.

Write the missing letters in the Spelling Words below.

1. ton _____ _____ _____ t
2. _____ _____ ole
3. _____ _____ ile
4. c _____ _____ _____ d
5. w _____ _____ ld
6. _____ _____ iting
7. b _____ _____ ld
8. s _____ _____ ool
9. fini _____ ed
10. mo _____ _____ ing
11. c _____ _____ ing
12. sto _____ _____ ed
13. ge _____ _____ ing
14. g _____ _____ s
15. g _____ ing

Spelling Words

1. tonight
2. whole
3. while
4. could
5. world
6. writing
7. build
8. school
9. finished
10. morning
11. coming
12. stopped
13. getting
14. goes
15. going

Study List **On a separate piece of paper, write each Spelling Word. Check your spelling against the words on the list.**

Name _____

Spelling Spree

Write a Spelling Word to fit each clue.

Spelling Words

1. a word meaning "at the same time as" _____

2. a two-syllable synonym for *done* _____

3. the opposite of *going* _____

4. a pencil helps you with this _____

5. what the car did at the red light _____

6. the whole wide _____

7. a synonym for *leaving* _____

8. what carpenters do _____

9. a place for learning _____

10. not broken into smaller pieces _____

Spelling Words

1. tonight
2. whole
3. while
4. could
5. world
6. writing
7. build
8. school
9. finished
10. morning
11. coming
12. stopped
13. getting
14. goes
15. going

Word Addition **Combine the first part of the first word with the second part of the second word to write a Spelling Word.**

11. goat + sees _____

12. couch + mold _____

13. tons + light _____

14. more + inning _____

15. germ + sitting _____

Theme 3: **That's Amazing!**   173

Name _____

Proofreading and Writing

Proofreading Circle the five misspelled Spelling Words in this newspaper item. Then write each word correctly.

The latest episode of *Amazing and Incredible* will be on tonigt at eight o'clock. It coud be an interesting program. Most of the show is about a woman who tried to build a house out of old soft drink bottles. Apparently, she finnished most of two stories. However, she stoped when she realized that the bottles wouldn't be able to support a roof. There will also be an interview with a person who's trying to row a boat around the werld. This show can be seen on Channel 9.

1. tonight
2. whole
3. while
4. could
5. world
6. writing
7. build
8. school
9. finished
10. morning
11. coming
12. stopped
13. getting
14. goes
15. going

1. _____

2. _____

3. _____

4. _____

5. _____

 **Rhyming Sentences** Pick five Spelling Words from the list. Then write a sentence for each word. In each sentence, include a word that rhymes with the Spelling Word. Underline the rhyming words.

174   Theme 3: **That's Amazing!**

Name _____

A Perfect Match

Write the letter to match each word with its definition.

_____ **crossly**   a. a woman who acts as a child's parent

_____ **elegant**   b. relating to a poor farm worker

_____ **god-mother**   c. thinking highly of oneself

_____ **orphan**   d. in a grumpy or grouchy way

_____ **peasant**   e. a child whose parents are dead

_____ **proud**   f. marked by good taste

Write your own sentence for each vocabulary word.

1. orphan: _____

_____

2. god-mother: _____

_____

3. elegant: _____

_____

4. proud: _____

_____

5. crossly: _____

_____

6. peasant: _____

_____

Name _____

Venn Diagram

Vitaline and Cendrillon

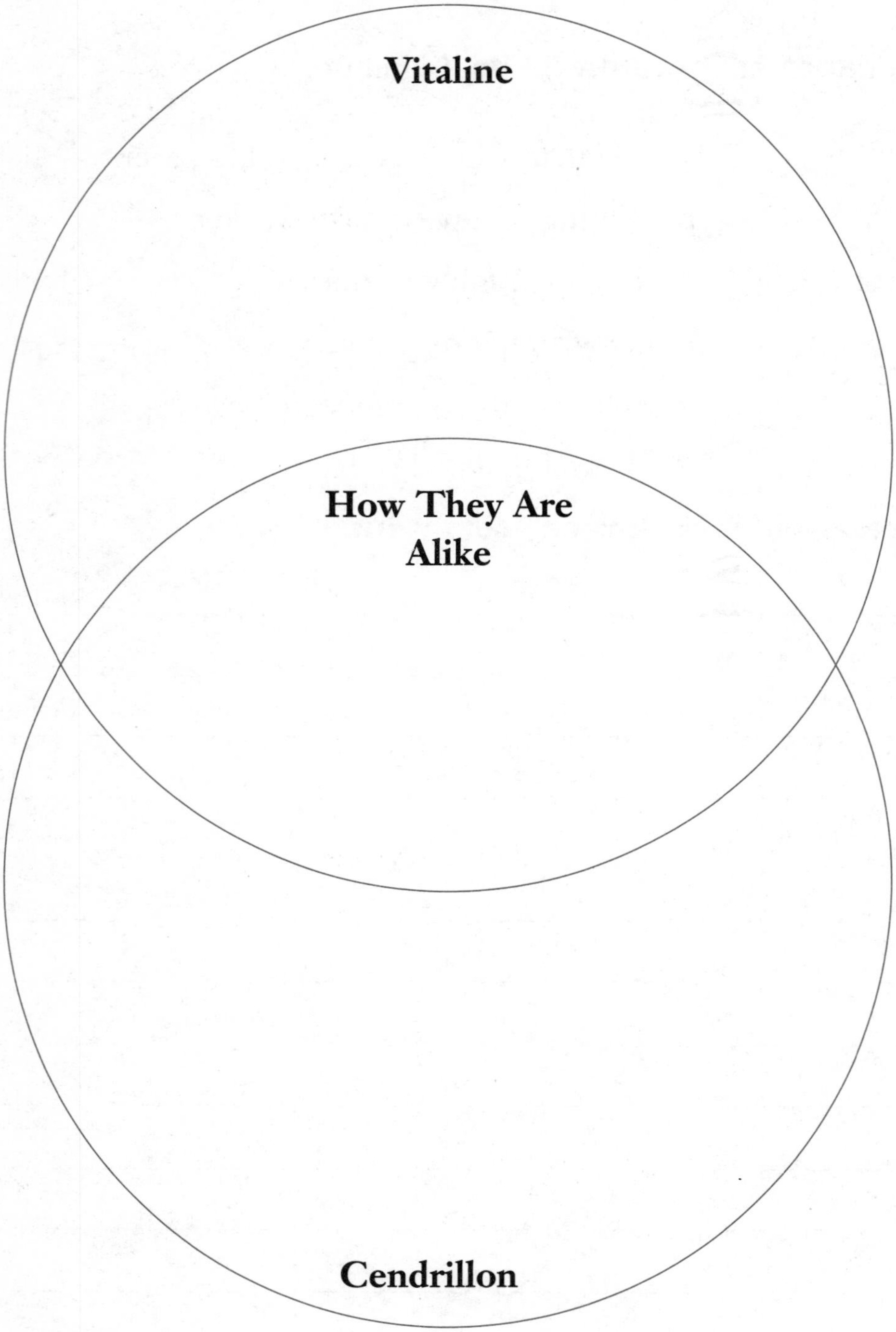

Vitaline

**How They Are
Alike**

Cendrillon

Name _____

Memory Check

Think about the selection. Then complete the sentences.

1. The wand given to the narrator had the power to

_____

_____

2. One day, Cendrillon came sad-faced to the river because

_____

_____

3. Cendrillon's godmother turned breadfruit and six agoutis into

_____

_____

4. While running from the ball, Cendrillon stumbled and left behind

_____

_____

5. Cendrillon told her godmother "No more spells" because

_____

_____

Name _____

A Resourceful Parent

**Read the story. Then complete the Venn diagram on the
following page.**

A Costume for the Carnival

It was carnival time and everyone was hurrying to make or
find the most original costume to win the grand prize.
Pantaloon, a rich boy, and Harlequin, a poor boy, both wanted
to win.

Pantaloon's rich father ordered a costume from a famous
tailor. When completed, the costume was spectacular. It was
made of gold cloth, trimmed with yellow diamonds, complete
with purple gloves and a hat with feathers.

Since Harlequin was poor, he didn't know what to do.
His mother suggested, "Why don't you ask if you can borrow
an extra costume from one of your friends?"

Harlequin ran to the house of every one of his friends, but
at every house it was the same. "I'm sorry, Harlequin, I don't
have an extra costume. But I have these scraps of cloth left
over. You may have them—if they will help."

Sadly, Harlequin brought the scraps to his mother. His
mother had an idea and sent him off to bed. Harlequin did as he
was told. The next morning there, at the foot of his bed, lay the
most beautiful costume he had ever seen! His mother had used
the scraps and cut them into diamond shapes. Then she had sewn
all the shapes together to create a costume with every color of the
rainbow! She had sewn on sequins so the costume caught the light
and shined and sparkled. He even had a matching hat with feathers!

Harlequin pulled on his costume and hurried to the Square.
Did his costume win the prize for the most original?
Well, what do you think?

Name _____

A Resourceful Parent continued

Complete the Venn Diagram for the story "A Costume for the Carnival."

Harlequin's Costume

1. _____
2. _____
3. _____

How the Costumes are Alike

1. _____
2. _____

Pantaloon's Costume

1. _____
2. _____
3. _____

If you were one of the costume judges, would you award the prize to Harlequin or Pantaloon? Why? Use complete sentences.

_____

_____

_____

Name _____

A Suffix Story

**Fill in each blank with a word from the box and the suffix
-able. Then finish the fairy tale by writing what happens
next. Try to use at least one word with the suffix *-able* in
your story ending.**

Word Bank

play
comfort
find
solve
read
imagine
value
wear
accept

Once upon a time, Angelina was given a magic wand
by her fairy godmother. This magic wand was the most
marvelous thing _____. It could
make a hard wooden chair _____.
It could make the most difficult book
_____. One wave of the wand, and
an old game became _____ or a
shirt that was too small became _____
again. Even a lost jewel or a tiny charm became
_____.

But one day, the _____ wand
disappeared! Angelina looked everywhere. Finally she cried,
"This is not _____! Where is my
wand?" Was the problem _____?

_____
_____
_____
_____
_____

Name _____

Final /ər/ and Final /l/ or /əl/

A syllable is a word or word part that has one vowel sound. The final syllable of some words ends with a weak vowel sound + *r* or *l*. This weak vowel sound is called **schwa** and is shown as /ə/. When you hear the final /ər/ sounds in a two-syllable word, think of the patterns *er*, *or*, and *ar*. When you hear the final /l/ or /əl/ sounds in a two-syllable word, think of the patterns *el*, *al*, and *le*.

final /ər/   *er, or, ar* (weath**er**, harb**or**, sug**ar**)
final /l/ or /əl/   *el, al, le* (mod**el**, fin**al**, midd**le**)

Write each Spelling Word under its spelling of the final /ər/, /l/, or /əl/ sounds.

er

_____

_____

_____

_____

or

_____

_____

ar

_____

_____

_____

el

_____

_____

al

_____

_____

le

_____

_____

_____

_____

Name _____

Spelling Spree

Crossword Use the Spelling Words from the box to complete the crossword puzzle.

Across

2. a brother of your mother or father
4. cloth used to dry things
7. unusual or exceptional
8. polite
9. home for a boat
11. a small copy
13. a brief rain
14. work

Down

1. container for liquids
3. part of a shirt
5. a section of a book
6. rain, sun, or snow
10. someone who begs
12. someone who pratices medicine
13. a substance used to sweeten food

Spelling Words

1. harbor
2. final
3. middle
4. weather
5. labor
6. model
7. chapter
8. special
9. sugar
10. bottle
11. medal
12. collar
13. proper
14. towel
15. beggar
16. battle
17. trouble
18. shower
19. uncle
20. doctor

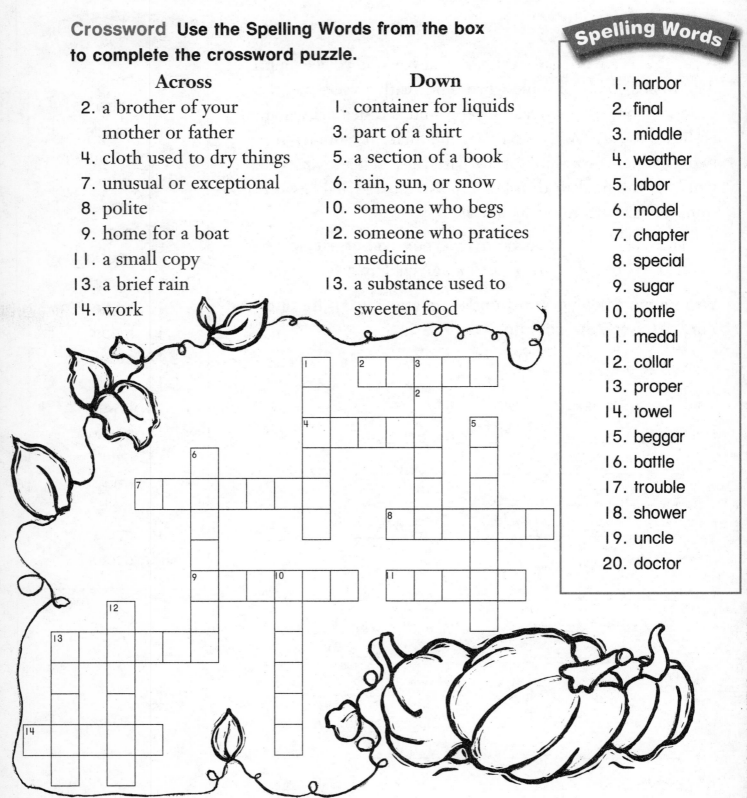

Name _____

Proofreading and Writing

Proofreading Circle the five misspelled Spelling Words in this diary entry. Then write each word correctly.

Dear Diary,

It was a battel against all odds, but I got to the ball after all! Nannin' helped me with her special wand. She deserves a medle for her efforts. I looked so fine in my blue velvet gown and pink slippers. Alas, right in the middel of the ball, everything went wrong. Nannin' said we would be in truble if we didn't leave right away. Then I stumbled and lost one of my slippers. By the finel stroke of midnight my gown had turned to rags. All I have left is one slipper. I am determined to find the other one, even if I have to knock on every door in town!

Spelling Words

1. harbor
2. final
3. middle
4. weather
5. labor
6. model
7. chapter
8. special
9. sugar
10. bottle
11. medal
12. collar
13. proper
14. towel
15. beggar
16. battle
17. trouble
18. shower
19. uncle
20. doctor

1. _____   4. _____

2. _____   5. _____

3. _____

✏ **Write an Explanation** Think about *Cendrillon* and other fairy tales you have read. What do you like about these stories? Are there things about fairy tales that you don't like?

On a separate sheet of paper, write a paragraph giving reasons why you like or dislike fairy tales. Use some of the Spelling Words from the list.

Name _____

Make a Spelling Table Pronunciation Key

Write the words in the correct blanks to complete the spelling table/pronunciation key below. Then underline the letters in those words that match the sound.

wand	fruit	chime
coach	round	guests
lost	spoil	gasp
blaze	scarf	stood

Spelling Table / Pronunciation Key

Sound	Sample Words
/ă/	hand, _____
/ā/	face, _____
/ä/	march, _____
/ĕ/	bread, _____
/ī/	my, _____
/ŏ/	hot, _____
/ō/	most, _____
/ô/	fall, _____
oi	boy, _____
/o͝o/	cook, _____
/o͞o/	move, _____
ou	crowd, _____

Name _____

Identifying Verbs

Underline the whole verb in each sentence. Then write the main verb and the helping verb on the lines below.

1. Cendrillon's stepmother has made the girl a servant.

   Main verb: _____

   Helping verb: _____

2. Cendrillon and her godmother have washed clothes at the river.

   Main verb: _____

   Helping verb: _____

3. Cendrillon has suffered without complaint.

   Main verb: _____

   Helping verb: _____

4. Who has arrived at the ball?

   Main verb: _____

   Helping verb: _____

5. Her godmother has accompanied her to the ball.

   Main verb: _____

   Helping verb: _____

Name _____

Writing Helping Verbs

Change each verb in the sentences below by adding *has* or *have*. Write the new sentence on the lines.

1. Cendrillon's stepmother scolded her.

   _____

   _____

2. Cendrillon and her godmother washed clothes for the family.

   _____

   _____

3. The godmother changed the agoutis into horses.

   _____

   _____

4. The carriage traveled over the bridge.

   _____

   _____

5. Cendrillon and the handsome young man danced all evening.

   _____

   _____

Name _____

Using Helping Verbs

Good writers often combine two sentences that have the same subject and helping verb but different main verbs. Read each pair of sentences below. Then rewrite the two sentences as one sentence by combining the main verbs and helping verbs. Write your new sentence on the lines provided.

1. Cendrillon's godmother has tapped the breadfruit with her wand. She has turned it into a gilded coach.

   _____

   _____

2. The godmother has turned the agoutis into carriage horses. She has changed the lizards into tall footmen.

   _____

   _____

3. The carriage has crossed the bridge. The carriage has arrived at the mansion.

   _____

   _____

4. All the guests have looked at Cendrillon. They have talked about her.

   _____

   _____

5. Cendrillon has heard the bells. She has run from the ball.

   _____

   _____

Name _____

Writing an Announcement

Use the chart to organize your ideas for an announcement. Then write an announcement about a birth, wedding, concert, fair, parade, or other special event.

Who?	What?	Where?
When?	Why?	How?

_____
_____
_____
_____
_____
_____
_____
_____

Name _____

Ordering Important Information

► When writing an announcement, first decide what information is most important. Put that information first.
► Put other information in order of importance from most important to least important.
► Be sure your announcement includes all the necessary information that answers some or all of these questions: who, what, where, when, why, how.

Use the following outline to write a wedding announcement for Cendrillon and Paul. Fill in the information in the outline. Then put the information in the order that makes the most sense.

Where will it take place?
_____

What is the occasion?
_____

What time?
_____

When will it take place?
_____

Who is the announcement about?

_____
_____
_____
_____
_____

Name _____

What Do You Mean?

Write the word from the box that fits each definition.

Vocabulary

affected
horizon
miscalculated
singe
temperature
weather vane

1. to burn slightly

   _____

2. moveable pointer that shows wind direction

   _____

3. figured incorrectly

   _____

4. measure of heat or coldness

   _____

5. the line along which the sky and the earth seem to meet

   _____

6. caused a change in

   _____

Write the word from the vocabulary list that belongs in each group.

7. Words about fire

   burn   char   scorch   _____

8. Words that tell about making mistakes

   misspelled   misjudged   mistaken   _____

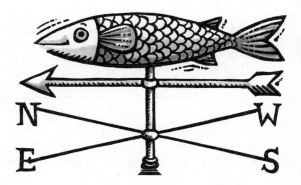

Name _____

Fantasy/Realism Chart

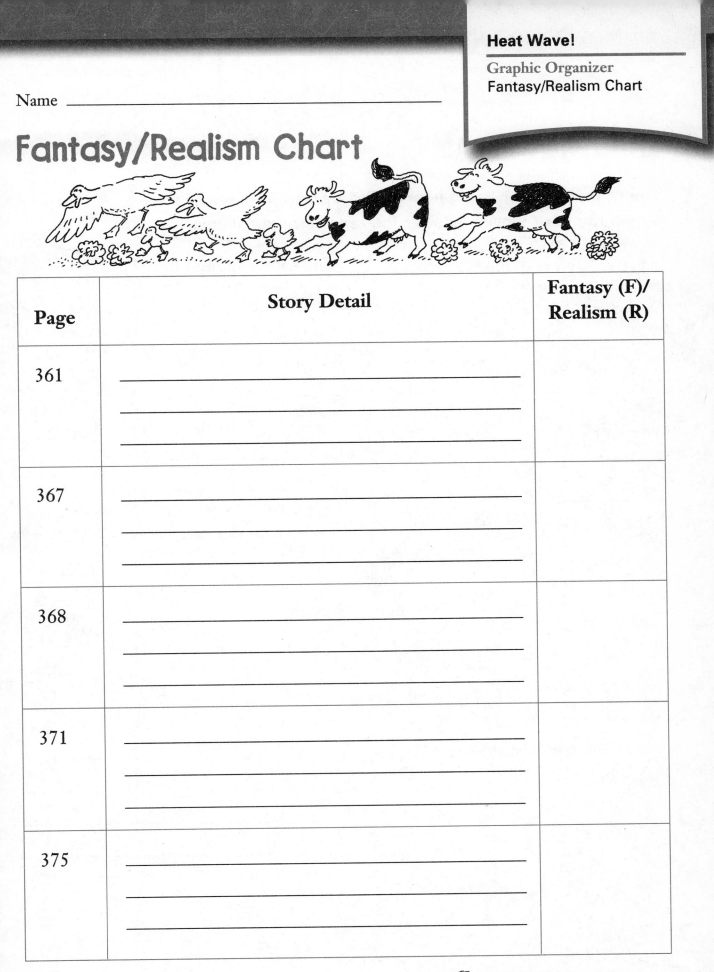

Page	Story Detail	Fantasy (F)/ Realism (R)
361	_____ _____ _____	
367	_____ _____ _____	
368	_____ _____ _____	
371	_____ _____ _____	
375	_____ _____ _____	

Name _____

Interview Time

You're the narrator being interviewed by reporters after you defeat the Heat Wave. Answer the reporters' questions.

Name _____

That's Fantastic!

Read the story and complete the chart on the next page.

The Big Little Machine

My name is Julius G. Malone. My middle initial stands for *genius*. Why? I have invented a machine that makes big things little. You simply place an object inside the machine, turn the dial, and *presto!* Big to little, large to small.

I made sure it worked by turning my dad's golf clubs into toothpicks. I also made my sister's new school clothes just the right size for her doll. I even made two ceiling lights into glow-in-the-dark earrings for my mother.

I was really excited about my new invention. Just as I was bragging about it to my sister, my mother called, "Everybody to the kitchen! We need to have a family meeting to solve a big problem!"

My dad began the meeting by saying, "Julius, perhaps you should limit your experiments to your own belongings." My sister, Lily, stuck her tongue out at me. When I promised to no longer shrink any of their things, Dad said, "Good. Thank you. This family meeting is officially over."

Just then our dog, Gruffly, ran into the room, chasing our cat. Before anyone could stop him, Gruffly ran right into the Big Little Machine as my hand slipped on the dial. In a second, he went from the size of a giant sheepdog down to the size of a pencil eraser.

Lily began crying. My mother frowned. And my dad said, "Attention, please. This family meeting is NOT officially over!"

That's Fantastic! continued

Complete this chart for the story "The Big Little Machine." Label the details with an F if it's *fantasy* or R if it is *realism*. Write in other details when the letter F or R is provided for you.

Story Detail	Fantasy (F) or Realism (R)?
golf clubs becoming toothpicks	
sister's clothes fitting her doll	
_____ _____	R
having a family meeting to solve a problem	
_____ _____	R
Gruffly, the dog, chasing the cat	
_____ _____	F
_____ _____	F

194   Theme 3: **That's Amazing!**

Name _____

Add the Ending

► When a base word ends with *e*, the *e* is dropped before adding *-ed* or *-ing*. *move/moved/moving*

► When a base word ends with one vowel followed by a single consonant, the consonant is doubled before adding *-ed* or *-ing*. *pop/popped/popping*

Read each sentence. Choose a word from the box similar in meaning to the word or words in dark type. Complete the puzzle by adding *-ed* or *-ing* to your word.

| turn |
| rise |
| bake |
| stir |
| race |
| drive |
| switch |
| grab |
| hop |
| scrub |

Across

1. My brother **changed** his tune when the Heat Wave hit.
4. Pa started **washing** the cows as hard as he could.
6. The cows were **jumping** around like rabbits.
7. The dough was **going up** so fast we ran for our lives.
8. We **hurried** into the barn, but it was too late.
9. I **snatched** a shovel and ran to the cornfield.

Down

2. Ma was **steering** the truck out to the cornfield.
3. We watched the Heat Wave **twisting** in the sky.
4. I **mixed** the water and the flour in a trough.
5. The dough **cooked** in the heat.

Theme 3: **That's Amazing!**   195

Name _____

Words with *-ed* or *-ing*

Each of these words has a base word and an ending. A **base word** is a word to which a beginning or an ending can be added. If a word ends with *e*, drop the *e* before adding *-ed* or *-ing*. If a one-syllable word ends with one vowel followed by a single consonant, double the consonant before adding *-ed* or *-ing*.

race + **ed** = rac**ed**   land + **ed** = land**ed**

snap + **ing** = sna**pping**

Write each Spelling Word under the heading that tells what happens to its spelling when *-ed* or *-ing* is added.

No Spelling Change

_____

_____

_____

_____

Final Consonant Doubled

_____

_____

_____

_____

_____

_____

Final *e* Dropped

_____

_____

_____

_____

_____

_____

_____

Spelling Words

1. dancing
2. skipped
3. hiking
4. flipped
5. snapping
6. raced
7. landed
8. pleasing
9. checking
10. dared
11. dimmed
12. rubbing
13. striped
14. wasting
15. traced
16. stripped
17. tanning
18. smelling
19. phoning
20. fainted

Name _____

Spelling Spree

joke
top

care wrap

joking topping

wrapped cared

Word Factory **Write Spelling Words by adding -ed or -ing to each word below.**

1. flip _____

2. please _____

3. land _____

4. stripe _____

5. check _____

6. trace _____

7. rub _____

8. tan _____

9. strip _____

1. dancing	
2. skipped	
3. hiking	
4. flipped	
5. snapping	
6. raced	
7. landed	
8. pleasing	
9. checking	
10. dared	
11. dimmed	
12. rubbing	
13. striped	
14. wasting	
15. traced	
16. stripped	
17. tanning	
18. smelling	
19. phoning	
20. fainted	

Meaning Match **Write a Spelling Word that has each meaning and ending below.**

Example: repair + ing *fixing*

10. pass out + ed _____

11. detect an odor + ing _____

12. run at top speed + ed _____

13. go on a long walk + ing _____

14. challenge someone + ed _____

15. make a cracking sound + ing _____

Name _____

Proofreading and Writing

Proofreading Circle the five misspelled Spelling Words in the following memo. Then write each word correctly.

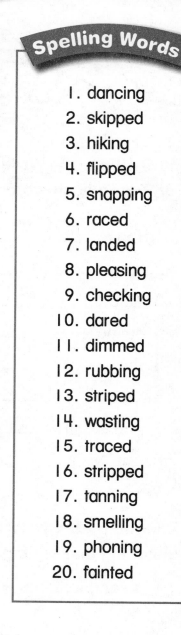

To: All city workers
From: Mayor Cole Breeze

Summer's first heat wave is here, and I ask all city workers to follow these guidelines:

- Carry on with all normal work. The heat is no excuse for skiped tasks.
- Shut fire hydrants to avoid wasteing water.
- Save energy by keeping office lights dimed.
- Keep checking on anyone doing heavy outdoor work.
- Avoid foning my office for the latest bulletins.

Finally, don't miss the official heat wave party on Saturday. Bring your danceing shoes!

Spelling Words

1. dancing
2. skipped
3. hiking
4. flipped
5. snapping
6. raced
7. landed
8. pleasing
9. checking
10. dared
11. dimmed
12. rubbing
13. striped
14. wasting
15. traced
16. stripped
17. tanning
18. smelling
19. phoning
20. fainted

1. _____ 4. _____

2. _____ 5. _____

3. _____

✏️ **Write a Funny Weather Report** Have you ever experienced a long period of hot or cold weather, snow, or heavy rain? Try to remember what it was like. Then imagine what might happen if the weather's effects were greatly exaggerated.

On a separate sheet of paper, write a funny weather report predicting severe weather. Use Spelling Words from the list.

Name _____

Divide and Conquer

Here are sixteen words from *Heat Wave!* Divide each word into syllables. Then write each word in the correct column on the chart below.

disappeared	everyone	brother	girls
feeding	lettuce	miserable	horizon
Hank	altogether	commotion	tease
farmers	everybody	thermometer	fight

Words with One Syllable

_____

_____

_____

_____

Words with Two Syllables

_____

_____

_____

_____

Words with Three Syllables

_____

_____

_____

_____

Words with Four Syllables

_____

_____

_____

_____

Name _____

Getting the Tense

**Underline the verb in each sentence. Then write each
verb in the correct column, under *Present Tense*,
Past Tense, or *Future Tense*.**

1. Hank will tease me again.
2. I feed the chickens every day.
3. The clump of yellow air rolled across the sky.
4. The heat roasted the geese in midair.
5. The flowers will wilt soon in this heat.
6. I wrap a blanket around the hound dog.
7. The cows hopped around like rabbits.
8. The cows' milk will turn to butter.
9. We pour butter over the popcorn.
10. The oats dried in the field.

Present Tense	**Past Tense**	**Future Tense**
_____	_____	_____
_____	_____	_____
_____	_____	_____
	_____	

Reporting in the Past Tense

Help the reporter complete the news story by writing the correct past-tense forms of the verbs in parentheses.

Last week an unusual thing _____.
(happen) We _____ a very sudden heat
wave. (suffer) No one quite _____ the
temperature. (believe) The mercury just
_____ out of the thermometer at one
farm here. (blast) The ground was so hot, cows
_____ up and down. (jump) Their
movements _____ their milk to butter.
(turn) The farmer's daughter _____ the
hot cows down and _____ them. (hose)
(cool) She _____ wetting down the oats
but she only _____ a huge, lumpy field
of oatmeal. (try) (create) If you have any other stories about
the heat wave, call the newspaper immediately.

Write three sentences of your own about the heat wave, using past tense verbs.

_____

_____

_____

_____

Name _____

Using the Correct Tense

Good writers make sure to choose the verb tense that correctly shows the time of the action described. Read the diary entry that the girl in the story might have written. Rewrite it so that all of the verbs show that the events have already happened.

Dear Diary,

Yesterday begins like a normal day. It turns out to be a strange day. It will start with a hot wind blowing in. The wind sounds like the roar of a lion. The wind quickly heats up everything.

This wind created lots of trouble. It nearly burns all the crops. We save the popcorn, though. At one point, I almost will drown in oatmeal. Finally, some crows flap their wings and cool us off.

_____

_____

_____

_____

_____

_____

_____

_____

_____

Name _____

Writing a Summary

Use this page to plan a summary of the first few pages of *Heat Wave!* Write the main idea for the story in the top box. Then write an important detail for each page of the story.

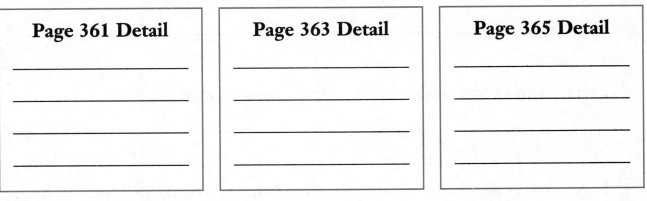

Main Idea

_____

_____

_____

Page 361 Detail	**Page 363 Detail**	**Page 365 Detail**
_____	_____	_____
_____	_____	_____
_____	_____	_____
_____	_____	_____

Name _____

Paraphrasing

► Writers use paraphrasing when they write a summary or notes for a report.
► Paraphrasing is restating an idea in your own words, without changing the author's meaning.

"Then we heard a commotion in the pasture."

Which paraphrasing does not change the author's meaning?

☑ Then we heard noise coming from the pasture.

☐ Then we saw something in the pasture.

Paraphrase each sentence.

1. The ground had gotten too hot, so we herded the cows inside the barn.

_____

_____

2. As it turned out, the cows had jumped so much, they'd churned their milk to butter.

_____

_____

3. We scrubbed a couple of shovels and the beds of the pickup trucks.

_____

_____

4. I sent Pa and Hank to the field to fill the pickups with popcorn.

_____

_____

5. In no time at all, they sold every last bit of that popcorn, then hurried home.

_____

_____

Name _____

Writing a Personal Response

Use the test-taking strategies and tips you have learned to help you answer this kind of question. Then read your answer and see how you may make it better. This practice will help you when you take this kind of test.

Write one or two paragraphs about one of the following topics.

a. You have just read *Heat Wave!* What do you think would happen if it could really get hot enough for corn to start popping while it is growing in the field? What other crops might be affected by this kind of heat? What would happen to those crops?

b. In the story, the narrator came up with unbelievable solutions for cooling the Heat Wave. Use your imagination to think of another way to cool the Heat Wave. What would you do? How would it work?

_____

_____

_____

_____

_____

_____

_____

_____

_____

_____

_____

_____

Name _____

Writing a Personal Response continued

Read your answer. Check to be sure that it

- focuses on the topic
- is well organized
- has details that support your answer
- includes vivid and exact words
- has few mistakes in capitalization, punctuation, grammar, or spelling

Now pick one way to improve your response. Make your changes below.

_____

_____

_____

_____

_____

_____

_____

_____

_____

_____

_____

_____

_____

_____

Name _____

Spelling Review

Write Spelling Words from the list on this page to answer the questions.

Spelling Words

1–10. Which ten words are compound words? They can be written as one word, as hyphenated words, or as two words.

1. _____   6. _____

2. _____   7. _____

3. _____   8. _____

4. _____   9. _____

5. _____   10. _____

11–20. Which ten words end with the /ər/, /l/, or /əl/ sounds? Bonus: Put a check mark beside the compound word above that ends with the /ər/ sound.

11. _____   16. _____

12. _____   17. _____

13. _____   18. _____

14. _____   19. _____

15. _____   20. _____

21–30. Which ten words end with *-ed* or *-ing*?

21. _____   26. _____

22. _____   27. _____

23. _____   28. _____

24. _____   29. _____

25. _____   30. _____

Spelling Words

1. weather
2. doctor
3. airport
4. understand
5. raced
6. smelling
7. anything
8. uncle
9. pleasing
10. ninety-nine
11. fainted
12. beggar
13. seat belt
14. final
15. all right
16. proper
17. battle
18. make-believe
19. towel
20. snapping
21. whenever
22. skipped
23. hiking
24. trouble
25. medal
26. striped
27. homesick
28. railroad
29. dimmed
30. checking

Theme 3: **That's Amazing!**   207

Name _____

Spelling Spree

Book Titles Write the Spelling Word that best completes
each book title. Remember to use capital letters.

1. *Aunt Angela and* _____ *Ed*
   by Watt A. Life

2. *Fasten Your* _____*! Blast Off!*
   by Rock Ottship

3. *Our* _____ *Day in the Jungle*
   by I. M. Lost

4. *Now I* _____*: Science Made*
   Simple by Sy N. Smaster

5. *The Mystery of the* _____
   Without Planes by A. D. Tektiv

6. *The* _____ *Station at the End*
   of the Tracks by Steem N. Jin

7. *Eat Vegetables* _____ *You Like:*
   A Guide to Healthy Eating by Dr. Eetmore Greenes

Spelling Words

1. battle
2. airport
3. all right
4. homesick
5. railroad
6. understand
7. anything
8. make-believe
9. whenever
10. trouble
11. ninety-nine
12. seat belt
13. final
14. proper
15. uncle

The Next Word Write the Spelling Word that belongs
with each group of words.

8. seventy-seven, eighty-eight, _____

9. correct, right, fitting, _____

10. nothing, something, _____

11. fight, struggle, war, _____

12. good, okay, _____

13. lonesome, sad, _____

14. fantasy, pretend, _____

15. problem, worry, _____

Name _____

Proofreading and Writing

Proofreading **Circle the six misspelled Spelling Words in Professor Mick Stupp's diary of backward adventures. Then write each word correctly.**

August 32nd At ten this morning it was just getting dark. The wether was fine, but it was raining hard. Now I've seen anything! I met a begger sitting on a towle. I gave him a million-dollar bill, and he faynted. I went hikeing down the street to find him a docter. What a day!

1. _____   4. _____
2. _____   5. _____
3. _____   6. _____

Mixed-up News **Use Spelling Words to complete the following paragraph of a TV news report.**

Our reporter has been 7. _____ on Professor

Stupp's latest adventure. She has not 8. _____ any

details. The professor ended up 9. _____ like fish, after he fell

into a fish barrel. The mayor awarded him a 10. _____ on a

blue-and-white 11. _____ ribbon. The ribbon was

12. _____ to most, but Professor Stupp's smile 13. _____

when he saw it wasn't red! Still, he 14. _____ quickly offstage,

15. _____ his fingers and saying, "Time for adventure!"

➤ **Create an Adventure** **On a separate sheet of paper, write about another adventure of Professor Mick Stupp. Use the Spelling Review Words.**

Spelling Words

1. fainted
2. checking
3. beggar
4. towel
5. hiking
6. dimmed
7. weather
8. snapping
9. pleasing
10. doctor
11. medal
12. raced
13. smelling
14. striped
15. skipped

Name _____

Be a Problem Solver!

Many problems have more than one solution. For each of the following problems, write down at least two different ways to solve it!

Problem #1: One of the wheels on your bicycle breaks.

_____

_____

Problem #2: You're having a hard time understanding your math homework.

_____

_____

Problem #3: Your parents won't give you money to buy the game you want.

_____

_____

Name _____

Problem Solvers

	Who is the main character? What problem does he or she have?	What are some benefits that result from solving the problem?
My Name Is María Isabel		
Marven of the Great North Woods		
The Last Dragon		
Sing to the Stars		

Name _____

Vocabulary Scramble

Unscramble the vocabulary words and write them on the lines.

ddppiisantoe __ __ __ __ __ __ __ __ __ __ __ __

Hint: means "having unsatisfied hopes or wishes"

youvernsl __ __ __ __ __ __ __ __ __ __

Hint: means "with worry or concern"

aeeiytttnvl __ __ __ __ __ __ __ __ __ __ __

Hint: means "alertly or with great attention"

lbreetoosum __ __ __ __ __ __ __ __ __ __ __

Hint: means "causing trouble or difficulty"

uddsstmiinnnerag

__ __ __ __ __ __ __ __ __ __ __ __ __ __ __ __

Hint: means "a failure to understand"

Unscramble the circled letters to answer the question.

What does the chorus do before a winter concert?

__ __ **w** __ __ __ __ __ __ __

Name _____

Prediction Chart

Details about María Isabel	
María Isabel at School _____ _____ _____ _____ _____	**What María Isabel Likes** _____ _____ _____ _____ _____
María Isabel's Life at Home _____ _____ _____ _____ _____ _____ _____ _____	**What María Isabel Wishes** _____ _____ _____ _____ _____ _____ _____ _____

What will happen in next year's school pageant?

_____

_____

_____

Name _____

A Diary Entry

What if María Isabel kept a diary? Help her finish this page in her diary by completing the sentences.

Because there are two other girls named María in my class, my teacher

doesn't call me _____.

_____ are the only three

kids who don't have parts in the play.

The others don't mind, but I feel _____.

My only comfort is _____.

My problems don't seem so bad compared with _____.

When I rode the bus home today, I sang _____

_____ and I felt a little better.

I cannot tell _____ that I am not in
the pageant, because they will be so disappointed.

I'm so glad I wrote an essay on _____
because it led me to get a part in the pageant.

Name _____

What Might Happen?

Read this story and then answer the questions on the following page.

My Mean Brother

It was the first day of the new school year, and my first day of fifth grade. This meant going to a new school, the same one as my older brother, Kevin. He was in seventh grade.

Kevin had been trying to scare me all summer about Mrs. D., my new teacher. He'd say things such as, "Look out, Bryan, Mean Mrs. D. doesn't like kids. She once sent me to the principal's office for sneezing! She doesn't let you erase your mistakes. And she even does surprise fingernail checks to make sure they are neat and clean!" I laughed at Kevin, wondering if he was telling the truth.

Being really nervous about the first day of school, I couldn't believe my luck when I missed the bus. Kevin made me go back in the house to get his lunch, but when I did, the bus drove by and Dad told me Kevin already took his lunch!

My dad took me to school that day, telling me not to let Kevin bother me. But I was bothered by the fact that we were late! All I could think about was what Mean Mrs. D. was going to do to me!

When we arrived, I ran up and down the hallway, searching for Mrs. D.'s classroom. I guess I was making a lot of noise because Mrs. D. opened her door as I skidded to a stop in front of her.

"Oh, you must be Bryan," she said. "I was worried about you. Glad you made it. Why don't you get a drink of water, and then come to class."

Name _____

What Might Happen? continued

Answer each of the following questions with a prediction about what will happen and the details from the story that support that prediction.

1. What do you think Bryan will do when he and Kevin return home from school?

   Prediction: _____

   _____

   _____

   Supporting Details: _____

   _____

   _____

2. What kind of student do you think Bryan will be in Mrs. D.'s class?

   Prediction: _____

   _____

   _____

   Supporting Details: _____

   _____

   _____

3. What do you think Bryan would be like as an older brother?

   Prediction: _____

   _____

   Supporting Details: _____

   _____

   _____

Name _____

Is It Poss*ible?*

Write T if the statement is true. Write F if the statement is false.
If you are unsure of a word's meaning, use a dictionary.

_____ 1. Chocolate cake is <u>edible</u>.

_____ 2. It is <u>sensible</u> to play with matches.

_____ 3. It is easy to see things that are <u>invisible</u>.

_____ 4. A <u>collapsible</u> tent is one that you can fold up when you are not using it.

_____ 5. A <u>convertible</u> car can be changed so that it has no top.

_____ 6. If something is <u>permissible</u>, you are allowed to do it.

_____ 7. If something is <u>audible</u>, you can smell it.

_____ 8. Rubber is a <u>flexible</u> material.

_____ 9. A <u>reversible</u> jacket always looks the same.

_____ 10. It is <u>responsible</u> to forget your homework at home.

Name _____

The /k/, /ng/, and /kw/ Sounds

Remember these spelling patterns for the /k/, /ng/, and /kw/ sounds:

/k/	*k, ck, c*	(shar**k**, atta**ck**, publi**c**)
/ng/	(before *k*) *n*	(si**n**k)
/kw/	*qu*	(**qu**estion)

► In the starred words *ache* and *stomach*, /k/ is spelled *ch*.

Write each Spelling Word under the correct heading.
Circle the words with the /ng/ sound.

/k/ Spelled *ck*

_____   _____
_____   _____

/k/ Spelled *k* or *c*

_____   _____
_____   _____
_____   _____
_____   _____
_____   _____

Other Spellings for /k/

_____   _____

/kw/

_____   _____

Spelling Words

1. shark
2. attack
3. risk
4. public
5. sink
6. question
7. electric
8. jacket
9. blank
10. ache*
11. crooked
12. drink
13. topic
14. track
15. blanket
16. struck
17. mistake
18. junk
19. squirrel
20. stomach*

Name _____

Spelling Spree

Daily News **Write the Spelling Word that best completes each sentence.**

Swimmer Bumped by Unidentified Object

Vacationers were upset by a report that a

(1) _____ had been spotted in the water.

Fred Finn was (2) _____ in the leg by "a huge

white fish." A family that had just spread out their

(3) _____ on the sand nearby claimed the fish

was indeed a "great white." Police Chief Ann Summer

wasn't convinced this was an actual (4) _____.

"Unless there's a real (5) _____ of someone

getting bitten, the beach will remain open," she declared.

Mr. Finn escaped with an (6) _____ in his leg.

He said, "I'm just glad I didn't end up as a meal in that

monster's (7) _____!"

Write a Spelling Word by adding the beginning of the first word to the end of the second word.

8. topcoat + music

9. size + think

10. jackpot + bonnet

11. crooning + wicked

12. job + trunk

13. election + metric

14. squirm + barrel

15. blue + tank

8. _____

9. _____

10. _____

11. _____

12. _____

13. _____

14. _____

15. _____

Spelling Words

1. shark
2. attack
3. risk
4. public
5. sink
6. question
7. electric
8. jacket
9. blank
10. ache*
11. crooked
12. drink
13. topic
14. track
15. blanket
16. struck
17. mistake
18. junk
19. squirrel
20. stomach*

Name _____

Proofreading and Writing

Proofreading Circle the five misspelled Spelling Words in this billboard advertisement. Then write each word correctly.

There's no kwestion about it!

Potato latkes are great! They're crispy and tasty and easy to make. It doesn't matter whether you're celebrating Hanukkah or just want to enjoy a fantastic treat. Serve them with a tall drinck and a mound of applesauce. Make no misstake! An admiring publick will sing your praises. Be careful cooking, though. There's always a risk of getting splattered with hot oil, and remember to keep trak of hot cookware at all times.

1. _____

2. _____

3. _____

4. _____

5. _____

Spelling Words

1. shark
2. attack
3. risk
4. public
5. sink
6. question
7. electric
8. jacket
9. blank
10. ache*
11. crooked
12. drink
13. topic
14. track
15. blanket
16. struck
17. mistake
18. junk
19. squirrel
20. stomach*

Write a Letter How does your family celebrate a special day? Do you exchange presents? Do you cook special food or sing special songs? Do friends and relatives come to visit?

On a separate sheet of paper, write a letter to tell a friend what happens at your house on the special day. Use Spelling Words from the list.

Name _____

Will You Find the Word in the Entry?

Read each sentence. In the space write *yes* if you think the underlined word would be part of a dictionary entry for the base word. Write *no* if you think it would not be part of the base word entry. Then circle the base words for *yes* answers in the word find box.

1. Everything at school <u>revolved</u> around plans for the Winter Pageant. _____

2. The class <u>talked</u> about Hanukkah and other holidays. _____

3. María Isabel's problems were <u>smaller</u> than Wilbur's. _____

4. Wilbur was in danger of <u>becoming</u> the holiday dinner. _____

5. She felt herself getting <u>sadder</u> each day. _____

6. What was <u>waiting</u> for her in the next few days? _____

7. The teacher asked, "What is your <u>greatest</u> wish? _____

8. The boy <u>dropped</u> his crutch only once during rehearsal. _____

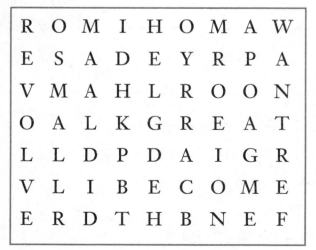

R	O	M	I	H	O	M	A	W
E	S	A	D	E	Y	R	P	A
V	M	A	H	L	R	O	O	N
O	A	L	K	G	R	E	A	T
L	L	D	P	D	A	I	G	R
V	L	I	B	E	C	O	M	E
E	R	D	T	H	B	N	E	F

Name _____

Completing with *be*

Complete each sentence by filling in the blank with the form of
***be* that goes with the subject. Use the correct form for the**
tense named in parentheses.

1. This photo _____ a picture of my mother and father.
   (present)

2. We _____ in Santo Domingo for the holidays. (past)

3. My family _____ there two years ago. (past)

4. Those two melodies _____ very familiar to me. (present)

5. Many of the songs _____ from other countries. (present)

6. Three students _____ not in the play. (past)

7. What _____ your favorite story about animals? (present)

8. Wilbur _____ the main character in María Isabel's
   favorite story. (present)

9. What _____ your wish for the new year? (past)

10. What _____ María Isabel's full name?
    (present)

Name _____

To be in the Past or the Present

Complete the sentences by writing a form of the verb
***be*. In the first four sentences, use the past. In the last**
four sentences, use the present.

1. María Isabel _____ troubled about Wilbur.

2. María Isabel _____ unhappy about not being in the

   pageant.

3. Her parents _____ there two years ago.

4. _____ María Isabel nervous in front of

   the class?

5. María Isabel _____ happy about leading the song.

6. The butterfly barrettes _____ a present from

   María Isabel's father.

7. The Hanukkah song _____ María Isabel's favorite.

8. María Isabel wrote, "Most of all, I _____ proud

   of my name."

Now make up two sentences of your own, telling
something about María Isabel and her experiences at school.
Use a different tense of *be* in each sentence.

_____

_____

_____

_____

Name _____

Writing with the Verb *be*

Using Forms of the Verb *be* Good writers are careful to use tense forms of *be* that match the subjects. Read the paragraph below. Rewrite the paragraph, correcting tense forms of *be* so that they match the subject of the sentence.

I think that holiday songs is my favorite kind of music. These songs be very tuneful. Our school program will have a lot of them. The first song on the program are for guitar and voice. It were once a lullaby. You and I know the music by heart. We is in the chorus.

Name _____

Writing an Opinion

Use this page to plan how you will write a paragraph expressing your *opinion* in a convincing way. Use facts or reasons to support your opinion. Number your facts or reasons in the order you will present them. Finally, restate your opinion.

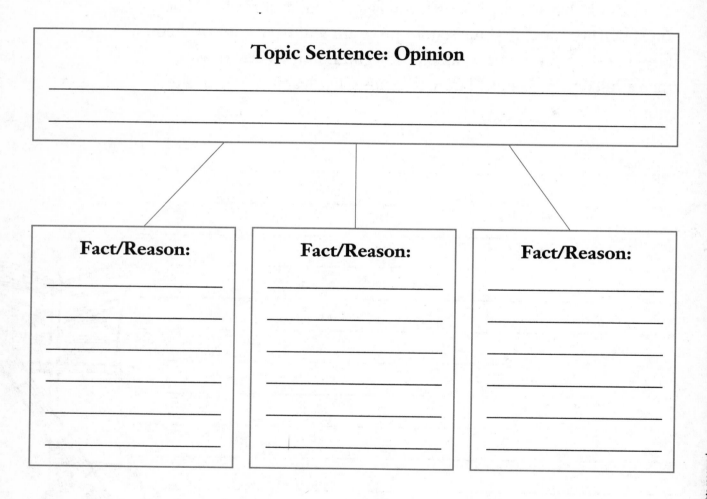

Topic Sentence: Opinion

_____

_____

Fact/Reason:

_____

_____

_____

_____

_____

_____

Fact/Reason:

_____

_____

_____

_____

_____

_____

Fact/Reason:

_____

_____

_____

_____

_____

_____

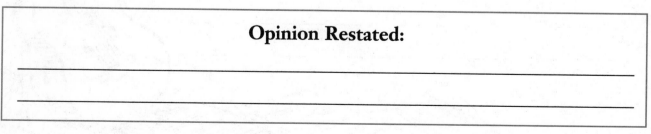

Opinion Restated:

_____

_____

Name _____

Using Commas with Introductory Phrases

A phrase is a small group of words that acts as a part of speech. A phrase at the beginning of a sentence is called an **introductory phrase**. Good writers use introductory phrases to vary sentence length and make sentences interesting. Introductory phrases should be set off with a comma.

At first, María Isabel Salazar López did not know she was being addressed.

Read the following sentences. If the sentence has an introductory phrase, write the sentence on the lines below and add a comma to set off the introductory phrase.

1. After helping with the dishes she finished her homework.

   _____

   _____

2. In time María Isabel told her parents about her problem.

   _____

   _____

3. The teacher agreed to the request made by María Isabel's parents.

   _____

   _____

4. Pleased to be called by her full name María Isabel agreed to sing her favorite song.

   _____

   _____

5. María Isabel's mother and father were there to hear her sing.

   _____

Revising Your Persuasive Essay

Reread your persuasive essay. What do you need to do to make it better? Use this page to help you decide. Put a checkmark in the box for each sentence that describes your persuasive essay.

Rings the Bell!

☐ My essay has a beginning that will get my readers' attention.

☐ I stated my goal clearly and gave reasons to support the goal.

☐ I used facts and examples to support my opinion.

☐ The essay is interesting to read and convincing.

☐ There are almost no mistakes.

Getting Stronger

☐ I could make the beginning more attention grabbing.

☐ I stated my goal, but I could add some reasons to support it.

☐ I need to add more facts and examples to make this convincing.

☐ There are a few mistakes.

Try Harder

☐ I need a better beginning.

☐ I didn't state my goals or reasons for my opinion.

☐ I need to add facts and examples.

☐ This isn't very convincing.

☐ There are a lot of mistakes.

Name _____

Subject-Verb Agreement

► Add *-s* or *-es* to most verbs to show the present tense if the subject is singular.

That frog jump**s** high.   He watch**es** frogs all day.

► Do not add *-s* or *-es* to most verbs to show the present tense if the subject is plural or the word *I*.

Frogs swim in our pond.   I watch frogs all day.

Complete each sentence. Circle the correct form of each verb.

1. Frogs (is/are) amphibians.

2. An amphibian (has/have) wet skin.

3. Amphibians (live/lives) both on land and in the water.

4. Toads (is/are) actually a type of frog.

5. Toads (has/have) dry skin and a stumpy body.

6. Both frogs and toads (breathe/breathes) through their skin.

7. Scientists (worry/worries) about frogs.

8. One scientist (blame/blames) ozone loss for the problem.

9. Gaps in the ozone layer (let/lets) dangerous UV rays through.

10. The UV rays (damage/damages) frogs.

Name _____

Spelling Words

Words Often Misspelled Look for familiar spelling patterns to help you remember how to spell the Spelling Words on this page. Think carefully about the parts that you find hard to spell in each word.

Write the missing letters in the Spelling Words below.

1. ___ ure

2. h ___ ___ ___

3. ___ ___ ew

4. m ___ ___ ___ t

5. pre ___ ___ y

6. rea ___ ___ y

7. v ___ ___ y

8. ___ ___ ere

9. lit ___ ___ ___

10. unt ___ ___

11. int ___

12. o ___ ___

13. s ___ ___ d

14. ___ ___ r

15. let ___ ___ r

Study List On a separate piece of paper, write each Spelling Word. Check your spelling against the words on the list.

Name _____

Spelling Spree

Contrast Clues The second part of each clue contrasts with the first part. Write a Spelling Word for each clue.

1. not there, but _____

2. not ugly, but _____

3. not on, but _____

4. not a phone call, but a _____

5. not big, but _____

6. not your, but _____

7. not out of, but _____

Word Magic Replace or add one letter in each word below to make a Spelling Word. Write it on the line.

8. untie _____

9. rally (add one letter) _____

10. knee _____

11. right _____

12. sand _____

13. vary _____

14. pure _____

15. here _____

Spelling Words

1. sure
2. here
3. knew
4. might
5. pretty
6. really
7. very
8. where
9. little
10. until
11. into
12. off
13. said
14. our
15. letter

Name _____

Proofreading and Writing

Proofreading Circle the five misspelled Spelling Words in this dialogue. Then write each word correctly.

Spelling Words

Pam: Well, they said that was the last bus untill 6:15.

Zack: So I guess we're stuck hear for another three hours.

Pam: I guess you mite say that.

Zack: I'm sorry—I was shur I'd have time to run and get a snack. Who new that the bus would leave on time?

Pam: There's *got* to be some other way of getting home.

Spelling Words
1. sure
2. here
3. knew
4. might
5. pretty
6. really
7. very
8. where
9. little
10. until
11. into
12. off
13. said
14. our
15. letter

1. _____
2. _____
3. _____
4. _____
5. _____

Stating the Problem What are some problems you would like to see someone try to solve? On a separate piece of paper, write four sentences that describe problems you think need solving. Use Spelling Words from the list.

Bus stop schedule

Name _____

Words in the Woods

Vocabulary

bunkhouse	cords (of wood)	immense	landscape
lumberjacks	snowshoes	timber	woodsman

The woods are full of words from the vocabulary list. Write each word above the tree trunk that shows its meaning.

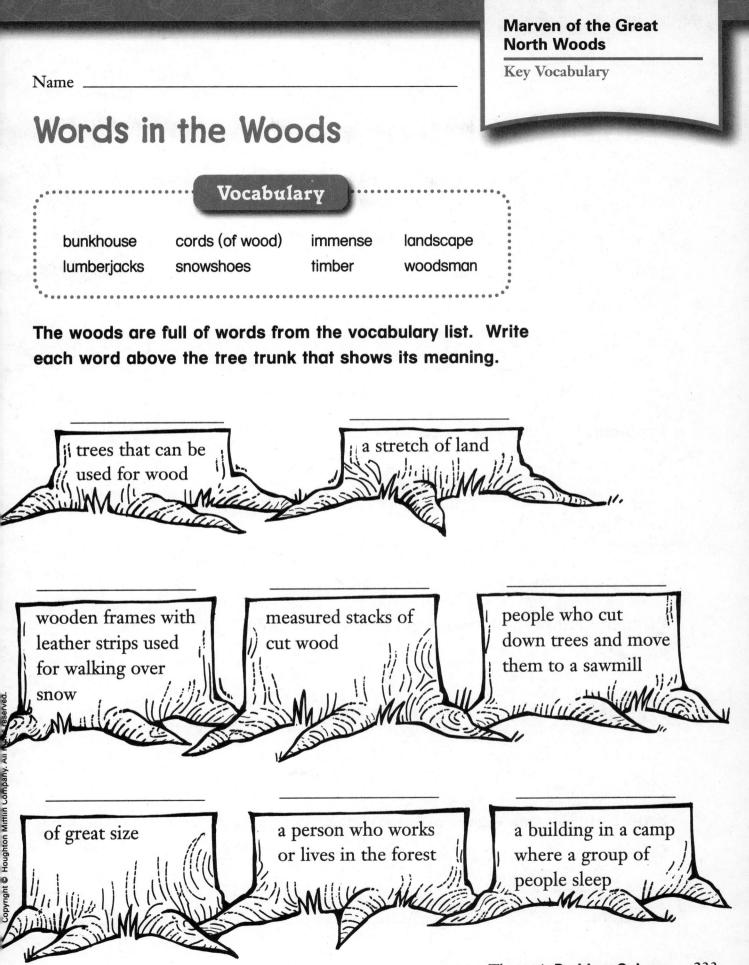

trees that can be used for wood

a stretch of land

wooden frames with leather strips used for walking over snow

measured stacks of cut wood

people who cut down trees and move them to a sawmill

of great size

a person who works or lives in the forest

a building in a camp where a group of people sleep

Name _____

Problem-Solution Frame

Page 419

Problem: How can Marven learn French?

Steps: _____

_____

Solution: _____

Page 430

Problem: How can Marven eat food that isn't kosher?

Steps: _____

_____

Solution: _____

Page 433

Problem: How can Marven organize the bookkeeping system?

Steps: _____

_____

Solution: _____

Pages 436–437

Problem: How can Marven avoid worrying about his family?

Steps: _____

_____

Solution: _____

Name _____

Write a Letter

Suppose Marven wrote a letter to his aunt and uncle. Help him complete the letter.

Dear Aunt Ghisa and Uncle Moishe,

    I know it was a good idea for me to leave the city to make sure I didn't get _____, but I miss all of you.

    Here at the logging camp, Mr. Murray asked me to

_____ since I have a good head

for numbers.

    One of the scariest things I had to do my first morning at

camp was to _____.

    Now I have lots of fun with _____,

a huge lumberjack, because we are friends.

    No matter how much fun I have in the great north woods, I will

be happy in spring when I can _____,

_____.

           Your nephew,
           Marven

Name _____

A Cold Adventure

Read the story. Then complete the chart on the following page.

Race to the Pole

In the far north, a group of men struggled against
icy wind. It was 60 degrees below zero. It was so cold that
frostbite could occur in minutes. The explorers wore thick fur
parkas, gloves, and boots to protect themselves against the cold.
Robert Peary and Matthew Henson would not give up. They
wanted to be the first explorers to reach the North Pole.

In 1909, no one had ever been to the North Pole. People
believed it was somewhere in the Arctic Ocean at the very top of the
world. That far north it is light for six months and dark for six
months. The explorers could not cross the ice in the dark. But if
they waited too long to leave, the summer sun would melt the ice
before they could cross it coming back.

The Arctic Ocean this far north also contains great chunks of ice.
The men had to cut through the ice to move on. They carried their
supplies on sledges, long sleds pulled by teams of dogs. The dogs had
to be fed, too, which meant the men had to carry a lot of food.

The pull of the moon's gravity and the movement of Earth often
crack the ice in the Arctic. This creates lanes of water called leads,
which can split open at any time, plunging the explorers into the
freezing water. So the team must always be prepared to get out of the
water and change clothes quickly. If they did not get into dry clothes,
they could freeze to death in minutes.

Peary and Henson had tried to reach the North Pole twice before.
Both times they had been beaten by the freezing winds, huge blocks of
ice, and starvation. Could they make it this time? They would not have
another chance.

Name _____

A Cold Adventure continued

Problem	Solution
The extreme cold could cause frostbite.	
In the Arctic, it is light for six months and dark for six months.	
The men need help carrying their supplies.	
The moon's gravity and Earth's movement cause lanes of water in the ice to open up.	

If you were exploring a cold and icy place like the North Pole, what do you think would be the greatest problem you would face? Why? How would you solve it?

_____

_____

_____

_____

Name _____

Prefix Precision

Answer the questions.

1. Why might a **misprinted** book need to be **reprinted**?

   _____

   _____

2. Why is it an **excellent** idea to recycle?

   _____

   _____

3. Why should you try to **respell** a word that you have

   misspelled?

   _____

   _____

4. Why is it important to **reread** the directions during an **exam**?

   _____

   _____

5. Why should you **retrace** your steps when you **misplace**

   something?

   _____

   _____

Write the word in dark type above next to its meaning.

put in the wrong place   _____

outstanding   _____

printed again   _____

read again   _____

Name _____

Final /ē/

When you hear the final /ē/ sound in a two-syllable word, think of the spelling patterns *y* and *ey*.

beauty   honey

► In the starred word *movie*, the final /ē/ sound is spelled *ie*.

Write each Spelling Word under its spelling of final /ē/.

<table>
<tr><td align="center">*y*</td><td align="center">*ey*</td></tr>
<tr><td>_____</td><td>_____</td></tr>
<tr><td>_____</td><td>_____</td></tr>
<tr><td>_____</td><td>_____</td></tr>
<tr><td>_____</td><td>_____</td></tr>
<tr><td>_____</td><td>_____</td></tr>
<tr><td>_____</td><td>**Another Spelling**</td></tr>
<tr><td>_____</td><td>_____</td></tr>
<tr><td>_____</td><td></td></tr>
<tr><td>_____</td><td></td></tr>
</table>

Spelling Words

1. beauty
2. ugly
3. lazy
4. marry
5. ready
6. sorry
7. empty
8. honey
9. valley
10. movie*
11. duty
12. hungry
13. lonely
14. alley
15. body
16. twenty
17. turkey
18. hockey
19. fifty
20. monkey

Name _____

Spelling Spree

Word Search Circle the 15 Spelling Words in the puzzle. Then write them on the lines below.

```
L  R  E  E  A  S  H  O  C  K  E  Y  T  H  E
A  C  L  A  S  P  W  S  T  T  R  I  P  T  M
Z  F  I  S  H  H  U  T  H  U  L  E  E  H  P
Y  O  V  E  U  K  T  U  E  S  S  M  A  R  T
E  A  E  Y  N  A  F  R  Y  L  H  O  N  E  Y
T  H  S  U  G  H  H  K  I  M  O  V  E  E  S
S  H  Y  R  R  O  S  E  E  A  P  I  X  E  L
F  I  F  T  Y  L  E  Y  A  Y  B  E  T  A  N
U  P  V  S  H  Y  U  L  H  M  S  W  E  E  T
M  A  T  I  E  U  G  L  Y  O  U  E  N  Y  W
A  L  I  M  Y  S  L  O  A  N  B  N  O  S  E
R  R  A  L  A  K  E  T  W  K  I  T  T  E  N
R  B  O  D  Y  Y  L  O  N  E  L  Y  I  V  T
Y  N  Q  U  E  E  S  T  A  Y  A  L  L  E  Y
```

1. beauty
2. ugly
3. lazy
4. marry
5. ready
6. sorry
7. empty
8. honey
9. valley
10. movie*
11. duty
12. hungry
13. lonely
14. alley
15. body
16. twenty
17. turkey
18. hockey
19. fifty
20. monkey

1. _____   9. _____

2. _____   10. _____

3. _____   11. _____

4. _____   12. _____

5. _____   13. _____

6. _____   14. _____

7. _____   15. _____

8. _____

Name _____

Proofreading and Writing

Proofreading Circle the five misspelled Spelling Words in this poem. Then write each word correctly.

Marven's Adventure

His father said, "My son, go forth."

So ten-year-old Marven headed north.

Met in a vally by a stranger

Far from the city, out of danger.

He took a break from his daily dutie,

Skied in search of woodland beuty.

Though the lumberjack life was steady,

He missed his family and he was readey

To ski home over the springtime snow.

And his friends were sory to see him go.

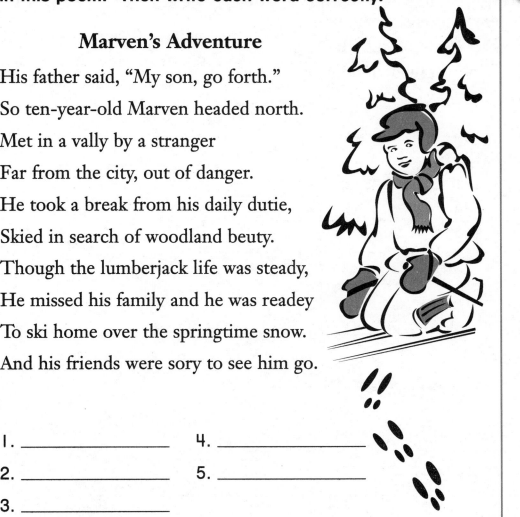

1. _____   4. _____

2. _____   5. _____

3. _____

Spelling Words
1. beauty
2. ugly
3. lazy
4. marry
5. ready
6. sorry
7. empty
8. honey
9. valley
10. movie*
11. duty
12. hungry
13. lonely
14. alley
15. body
16. twenty
17. turkey
18. hockey
19. fifty
20. monkey

✏️ **Write a Journal Entry** Pick your favorite incident or picture from *Marven of the Great North Woods*.

On a separate sheet of paper, write a journal entry that describes what happened in the scene from Marven's point of view. Use Spelling Words from the list.

Name _____

All in the Word Family

In each box, read the clues and add endings to the underlined word to make words that fit the word family. Remember, an ending sometimes changes the spelling of the base word. The first word family is written for you.

<u>t o w e r</u>
two or more: <u>t</u> <u>o</u> <u>w</u> <u>e</u> <u>r</u> <u>s</u>
very tall: <u>t</u> <u>o</u> <u>w</u> <u>e</u> <u>r</u> <u>i</u> <u>n</u> g
in the past: <u>t</u> <u>o</u> <u>w</u> <u>e</u> <u>r</u> <u>e</u> <u>d</u>

<u>f i d d l e</u>

two or more: ___ ___ ___ ___ ___ ___

person who plays a fiddle: ___ ___ ___ ___ ___ ___ ___

playing a fiddle: ___ ___ ___ ___ ___ ___ ___

played in the past: ___ ___ ___ ___ ___ ___ ___

<u>t h i c k</u>

more thick: ___ ___ ___ ___ ___ ___ ___

most thick: ___ ___ ___ ___ ___ ___ ___

in a thick way: ___ ___ ___ ___ ___ ___ ___ ___

<u>f r e e z e</u>

turning to ice: ___ ___ ___ ___ ___ ___ ___

a very cold place for food: ___ ___ ___ ___ ___ ___ ___

becomes ice: ___ ___ ___ ___ ___ ___ ___ ___

Challenge Use the base word "camp" or "wild" and write clues for other words in the same family. Swap puzzles with a classmate.

Name _____

Irregular Completion

Complete each sentence by writing the correct past tense form of the verb named in parentheses.

1. All the jacks have _____ snowshoes every day this winter. (wear)

2. The jack _____ the axe directly at the tree. (throw)

3. Marven's family _____ him to the train station. (take)

4. The train _____ to a full stop at Bemidji. (come)

5. Marven had _____ a new part of his life now. (begin)

6. Marven's father had _____ him skis for his sixth birthday. (give)

7. Marven's skis never _____ on his way from the station. (break)

8. Marven _____ latkes and knishes with him. (bring)

9. The days have _____ much shorter now. (grow)

10. Marven never _____ snow could stay white so long. (know)

Verbs in a Letter

Write a letter to the author, Kathryn Lasky, to tell her why you enjoyed *Marven in the Great North Woods*. Use as least five of the verbs on the verb tree in your letter. Vary the verb tenses. A sample has been done for you.

Dear Ms. Lasky,

When I began to read your story about Marven at the lumber camp, I couldn't stop. I knew Marven would come to enjoy life in the north woods. I even brought the story home to show my parents. Thanks for writing such a good story. You have given me lots of interesting information about what it was like to grow up in the early 1900s.

give
wear
know
take
begin
come
break
throw
bring
grow

Name _____

Using Irregular Verbs

Using the Correct Verb Form Read the first draft of the report
on one day in Marven's life at the logging camp. On the lines
below, rewrite the report, replacing any incorrect forms of
irregular verbs with correct forms.

Marven had bring his skis along. One Friday, Marven put the skis
on and taked off on the sled paths into the woods. He wear his heavy
coat. Everything growed still and white. When he come to a frozen
lake, he stopped. He know the scenery would be beautiful. He heard
a growl. He begun to tremble. Was it a bear? Had a branch broke
off? It give him quite a scare. Luckily, the noise had came from his
friend Jean Louis.

_____

_____

_____

_____

_____

_____

_____

Name _____

How to Take Notes

Use this page to *take notes* on a winter activity. Research a sport or hobby that interests you, or take notes on the article about snowshoeing on pages 446–449 of your anthology.

Research Question:

_____

_____

Main idea 1: _____

supporting detail: _____

supporting detail: _____

supporting detail: _____

Main idea 2: _____

supporting detail: _____

supporting detail: _____

supporting detail: _____

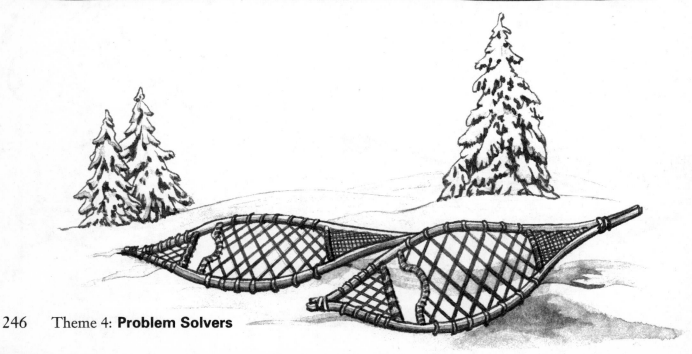

Name _____

Choosing What's Important

When writers take notes, they list main ideas and the important details that support the main ideas. To check whether a detail supports the main idea, reread the main idea. Ask: *Is this detail about the main idea?*

Main idea: use safety when snowshoeing
supporting detail: go with a partner
supporting detail: tell an adult where you are going
supporting detail: ~~snowshoes are 6,000 years old~~   *This detail is not about snowshoe safety.*

Read the following sets of notes. Use this proofreading mark ⟲
to delete the details that do not support the main idea.

1. **Main idea:** some mammals are well-adapted to life in the arctic
          regions
   detail: musk oxen and reindeer have large feet that allow them
          to walk on snow
   detail: lemmings, arctic fox, and gray wolves grow white
          winter coats
   detail: some kinds of whales are endangered worldwide

2. **Main idea:** some animals hibernate during the winter
   detail: bears and bats hibernate in caves
   detail: certain fish are found only in tropical waters
   detail: animals fatten up to hibernate

Name _____

Scrambled Dragons

Unscramble the letters to make a word from the vocabulary list. Then solve the riddle.

gheoma __ __ __ __ __ __
            1
Hint: means "honor or respect"

lessac __ __ __ __ __ __
              2
Hint: means "small, thin, flat parts that cover a reptile"

densak __ __ __ __ __ __
                  3
Hint: means "moved like a snake"

ecefir __ __ __ __ __ __
        4
Hint: means "wild and mean"

crachearts __ __ __ __ __ __ __ __ __ __
                5   6
Hint: means "marks or signs used in writing"

gniemet __ __ __ __ __ __ __
          7   8
Hint: means "to be full or crowded"

sterc __ __ __ __ __
          9
Hint: means "something that grows out of an animal's head"

Write each numbered letter in the space with the same number to solve the riddle.

What does a dragon's breath feel like?

__ __ __ __ __ __ __ __ __
5 1 7   2 6   4 8 9 3

Name _____

Conclusions Chart

	Details	Conclusions
page 455 The dragon		
page 459 Peter's reaction		
pages 467–468 The dragon's eyes		

Name _____

Peter's Adventure

Complete the story map to tell about *The Last Dragon*.

Setting

Where does the story take place?

_____

Events

What does Peter find?

_____

What is the problem with what he finds?

_____

Who helps Peter? List at least four people.

_____

_____

Ending

What happens on the last night of Peter's visit with Great Aunt?

_____

_____

Name _____

A Snapshot of America

Read the article. Then read the statements on the next page. Decide if the statement is *true, false,* or if *not enough information* is given to draw a conclusion.

United States Population to Double

Washington, DC — By the year 2100, there will be twice as many Americans as there are today. Imagine twice as many cars on the highways. Imagine twice as many people in line at the supermarket. Can our nation handle the change?

Today about 275 million people live in the United States. According to the Census Bureau, by 2100 that number will be about 571 million. That would make our population density (people per area) a bit over 160 people per square mile. In comparison, the density of Germany today is over 400 people per square mile. It's a good thing that our country is large and vast.

Today there are around 65,000 people age 100 or older. In 2100, there may be 5 million. The elderly will make up one-fifth of our population. The median age (the age at which half the population is older and half younger) will rise by 2100 to over 40, compared to around 36 today.

The Hispanic population of the United States is expected to triple in the next 50 years. The Asian and Pacific Islander population will more than triple. Today, non-Hispanic white people make up about three-quarters of the population. Although that group will grow, too, by 2050, they will make up only about one-half of the total.

Name _____

A Snapshot of America continued

1. The Hispanic population in the United States is expected to double in the next 50 years.

   true   false   not enough information

2. The population density of Germany is greater than the population density of the United States.

   true   false   not enough information

3. Germany has a larger population than the United States has.

   true   false   not enough information

4. There are more Asian Americans than Hispanic Americans in the United States today.

   true   false   not enough information

5. In the year 2100, there will be more people in the United States over 100 years old than today.

   true   false   not enough information

6. Doubling the amount of cars will cause terrible gridlock.

   true   false   not enough information

7. By the year 2050, our population will be around 571 million.

   true   false   not enough information

8. The United States is vaster than Germany.

   true   false   not enough information

Name _____

Complete Prefix Control

**Write two words from the box that together match each
description. Use each word only once. Use a dictionary if
you need help.**

Example:

No one "exactly expected" how the dragon would look when finished.
In other words, no one **precisely predicted** how it would look.

commercial	concert	congratulations	preowned
committee	concise	constant	prerecorded
companion	concrete	construction	preserved
completely	condition	consumer	preteen
computer	confused	prehistoric	preventable

1. steady friend: _____

2. mixed-up group: _____

3. advertisement taped earlier: _____

4. buyer between the ages of 9 and 12:

_____

5. totally saved from an earlier time:

_____

6. used machine that runs programs:

_____

7. very old musical performance:

_____

8. brief words to express joy for someone's good luck:

_____

Name _____

Final /j/ and /s/

Remember these spelling patterns for the final /j/, /ĭj/, and /s/ sounds:

/j/ in a one-syllable word	*dge, ge*	(bri**dge**, stran**ge**)
/ĭj/ in a word of more than one syllable	*age*	(vill**age**)
/s/	*ce*	(en**ce**)

Remember that in words with a short vowel sound, final /j/ is spelled *dge*. In words with a long vowel sound, final /j/ is spelled *ge*.

Write each Spelling Word under the correct heading.

/j/ in One-Syllable Words

_____

_____

_____

_____

_____

_____

_____

/ĭj/ in Two-Syllable Words

_____

_____

_____

_____

_____

_____

_____

Final /s/ Spelled *ce*

_____

_____

_____

_____

1. village
2. cottage
3. bridge
4. fence
5. strange
6. chance
7. twice
8. cage
9. change
10. carriage
11. glance
12. ridge
13. manage
14. damage
15. since
16. marriage
17. edge
18. lodge
19. cabbage
20. dodge

254   Theme 4: **Problem Solvers**

Name _____

Spelling Spree

Rhyming Pairs Complete each sentence by writing a pair of rhyming Spelling Words.

1–2. I had to duck and _____ snowboarders on my way to the ski _____.

3–4. The bride and groom rode off in a horse-drawn _____ to begin their _____.

5–6. I know this outfit looks a little _____, so I think I'll go back home and _____.

7–8. We must cross the _____ to get to the _____ on the other side of the river.

1. _____   5. _____

2. _____   6. _____

3. _____   7. _____

4. _____   8. _____

Quick Pick Write the Spelling Word that best matches the meaning of each word or group of words below.

Example: courtroom official _judge_

9. animal carrier _____

10. vegetable _____

11. barrier around a garden _____

12. small town _____

13. small house _____

14. quick look _____

15. rim or border _____

Spelling Words

1. village
2. cottage
3. bridge
4. fence
5. strange
6. chance
7. twice
8. cage
9. change
10. carriage
11. glance
12. ridge
13. manage
14. damage
15. since
16. marriage
17. edge
18. lodge
19. cabbage
20. dodge

Name _____

Proofreading and Writing

Proofreading Circle the five misspelled Spelling Words in this ad. Then write each word correctly.

HELP WANTED

Experts Needed to Repair Dragon

At first glanse, he might not look like much. All this Chinese dragon needs, though, is tender loving care to repair a little damidge. If you can manige to spare some time to help, please ask for Peter at the noodle factory. In return for sewing, painting, frame repair, and blessings, I promise to run errands and do small jobs (sins I don't have any money for payment). Don't think twice. All the dragon needs is a chanse!

1. _____   4. _____

2. _____   5. _____

3. _____

Spelling Words

1. village
2. cottage
3. bridge
4. fence
5. strange
6. chance
7. twice
8. cage
9. change
10. carriage
11. glance
12. ridge
13. manage
14. damage
15. since
16. marriage
17. edge
18. lodge
19. cabbage
20. dodge

✏ **Write a Thank-You Note** Peter had help from a tailor, his great-aunt and her friends, a kite maker, a painter, and others. Choose one of the people who worked on the dragon and write that person a thank-you note that Peter might have written.

On a separate sheet of paper, write your note. Be sure to include the task the person performed and why the person's help was important. Use Spelling Words from the list.

Name _____

Add the Correct Suffix

Rewrite each sentence below, replacing the words in italics with one word. Make the new word by adding the suffix *-ful*, *-less*, or *-ly* to the underlined word. Use a dictionary if you need help remembering the meanings of the suffixes.

1. Great Aunt thought the old dragon was *without <u>hope</u>*.

   Great Aunt thought the old dragon was _____.

2. Great Aunt's *full of <u>cheer</u>* friends repaired the dragon's crest.

   Great Aunt's _____ friends repaired the dragon's crest.

3. Peter waited *in a <u>patient</u> way* for Mr. Pang to repair the dragon's body.

   Peter waited _____ for Mr. Pang to repair the dragon's body.

4. *With respect to <u>luck</u>*, Dr. Fong located eyes for the dragon.

   _____, Dr. Fong located eyes for the dragon.

Add *two* suffixes to the underlined word in each sentence below.

5. The dragon moved *in a manner without <u>effort</u>* on silken legs.

   The dragon moved _____ on silken legs.

6. Peter and his friends restored the dragon *in a way full of <u>beauty</u>*.

   Peter and his friends restored the dragon _____.

Name _____

Being Specific with Adjectives

Complete each sentence with the adjective from the box that fits best. Use each adjective only once. Underline the noun each adjective modifies. Write whether the adjective tells *what kind* or *how many*.

two	tasty	loud	big	new

1. Its mouth opened with a _____ sound.

   _____

2. Fixing the dragon will be a _____ job.

   _____

3. Miss Tam made _____ dumplings.

   _____

4. Peter did _____ things for Miss Rose.

   _____

5. The kite shop was not far from the _____

   restaurant. _____

Complete each sentence by choosing the correct article in parentheses. Then write your choice in the blank.

6. Peter noticed _____ severed tail. (an, the)

7. Miss Rose had _____ idea. (a, an)

Name _____

Dragon Menu

The pictures below show what foods might have been served at Peter's farewell dinner at the Golden Palace Restaurant. Write a caption for each picture, describing the food shown and how it tastes. Use adjectives to tell what kind and how many. Color the pictures to show what the foods look like and to help you describe them.

Won-ton Soup

_____
_____
_____
_____

Noodles

_____
_____
_____
_____

Peppery Shrimp

_____
_____
_____
_____

Vegetables

_____
_____
_____
_____

On a separate sheet of paper, write a description of something else you would like to see on the menu.

Name _____

Expanding with Adjectives

Good writers add interest and detail to their sentences by including adjectives that tell what kind and how many. Read the sentences below. Rewrite each sentence using specific adjectives that tell what kind or how many.

1. The crest on the dragon's head was _____ and _____.

   _____

2. Peter didn't like Great Aunt's _____, _____ apartment.

   _____

3. Peter was carrying a sack of _____, _____ crabs.

   _____

4. The _____ jaw could move easily now.

   _____

5. Miss Rose sewed _____, _____ scales on the tail.

   _____

6. The _____ streets of Chinatown were filled with people.

   _____

Name _____

Writing a Comparison/ Contrast Composition

Use this page to plan your *comparison/contrast composition.*
Fill in the graphic organizer with details about how two places,
activities, or books are alike and different. Then, on a separate
sheet of paper, write a comparison/contrast composition.
When you have finished your composition, exchange papers
with a partner.

Comparison/Contrast of

1. _____ and 2. _____

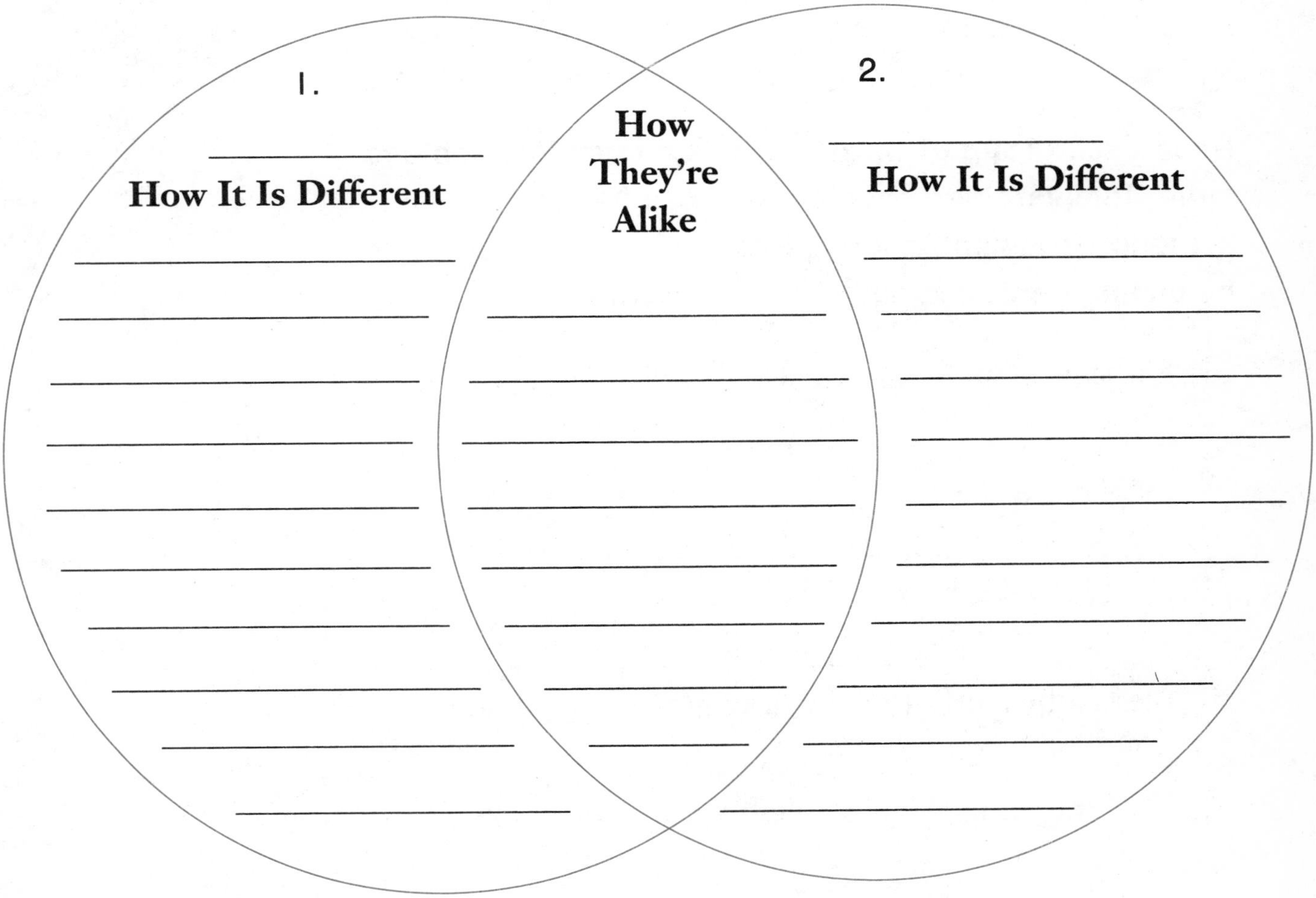

1.
_____

How It Is Different

_____
_____
_____
_____
_____
_____
_____

How They're Alike

_____
_____
_____
_____
_____
_____

2.
_____

How It Is Different

_____
_____
_____
_____
_____
_____

Name _____

Correcting Sentence Fragments

Writers know that **sentence fragments** can be
used for any note-taking graphic organizer. Good
writers also know to use complete sentences when writing paragraphs,
essays, or reports. Complete sentences have subjects and predicates.

        subject   predicate
The English teacher / suggested showing the dragon to a kite maker.

Sentence fragments that only have a subject need a predicate.
    subject: Great Aunt's apartment
    needs predicate: is in Chinatown.

Sentence fragments that only have a predicate need a subject.
    predicate: made a new crest for the dragon.
    needs subject: Great Aunt's downstairs neighbor, Mrs. Li

**Read each group of words. If it is a complete sentence,
write Complete Sentence on the lines below. If it is a
sentence fragment, change it into a complete sentence
by adding a missing subject or predicate.**

1. Did chores and ran errands.

_____

2. Something special about that dragon.

_____

3. Dr. Fong's herb shop.

_____

4. Blessed by a priest or the dragon will stay blind.

_____

5. The dragon paraded through the restaurant.

_____

Name _____

Musical Meanings

Fill in the blanks with words from the vocabulary list to complete the news article.

⇒The News⇐

Student Band Gives First Concert

The student band is warming up for its _____. The leader checks the _____ to make sure the music can be heard at the back of the hall. Then the concert begins. The drummer sets the _____ with his flying drumsticks. The trumpets are _____ out a _____ tune. The final song they played is an updated version of an old _____ melody. There was not a _____ from the audience as the band played. Everyone agreed the band has made great _____ since they first began playing together.

Vocabulary

amplifiers
blaring
classical
debut
murmur
rhythm
strides
jazz

On the lines below write a sentence that uses two of the vocabulary words.

_____

_____

_____

Name _____

Story Structure Map

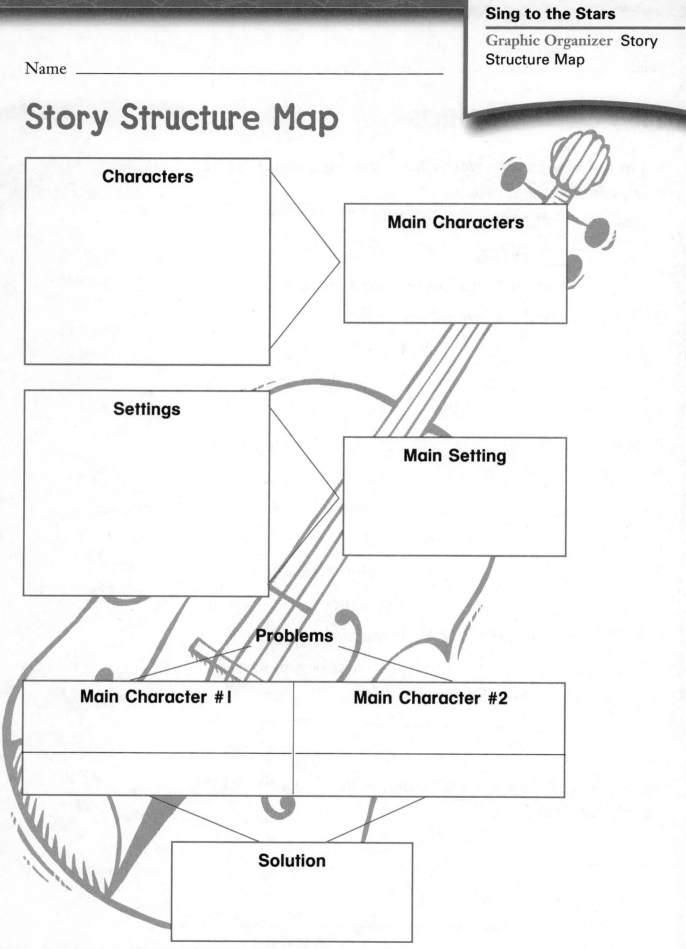

Characters

Main Characters

Settings

Main Setting

Problems

Main Character #1

Main Character #2

Solution

Name _____

Hear the Music

Complete each sentence to tell about *Sing to the Stars*.

1. Mr. Washington always knew that Ephram was coming because

_____

_____

2. When a rapper on the corner yelled to Ephram to get himself an electric guitar, Ephram

_____

_____

3. Mr. Washington stopped playing the piano when

_____

_____

4. Ephram said that he did not think he would play at the benefit concert because

_____

_____

5. The title of this story, *Sing to the Stars*, refers to

_____

_____

_____

Theme 4: **Problem Solvers**   265

Name _____

What Did You Say?

Read the story. Then complete the following page.

The Talking Yam

Once upon a time, a long time ago, not far from the city of Accra, a farmer went to dig some yams from his garden. While he was digging, one of the yams said to him, "Go away and leave me alone!" The farmer turned and looked at the cow in amazement. "Did you say something?"

The cow didn't answer, but the dog said, "The yam spoke to you. The yam says leave him alone."

The man became angry, so he kicked a stone. The stone yelled, "Hey, cut that out!" Frightened, the man ran to the village. On the way, he met a fisherman carrying a large fish. "What's your hurry?" the fisherman asked.

"My yam is talking to me! My dog is talking to me! The rock is talking to me!" screamed the farmer.

"So what's the fuss?" the fish answered. "Besides," the fishing pole added, "you shouldn't kick rocks." The farmer jumped, yelled, and went running to the king.

"My yam is talking to me! My dog is talking to me! The rock is talking to me!" screamed the farmer. "Then a fish talked to me and a fishing pole, too!"

The king listened to the farmer. Finally, he said, "This is a wild story. Go back to your work before I punish you for disturbing the peace." The farmer went away and the king shook his head. "What a silly story. Stories like this upset all the people."

"You're right," answered his throne. "Imagine, a talking yam!"

Name _____

What Did You Say? continued

Complete the chart for the story "The Talking Yam."

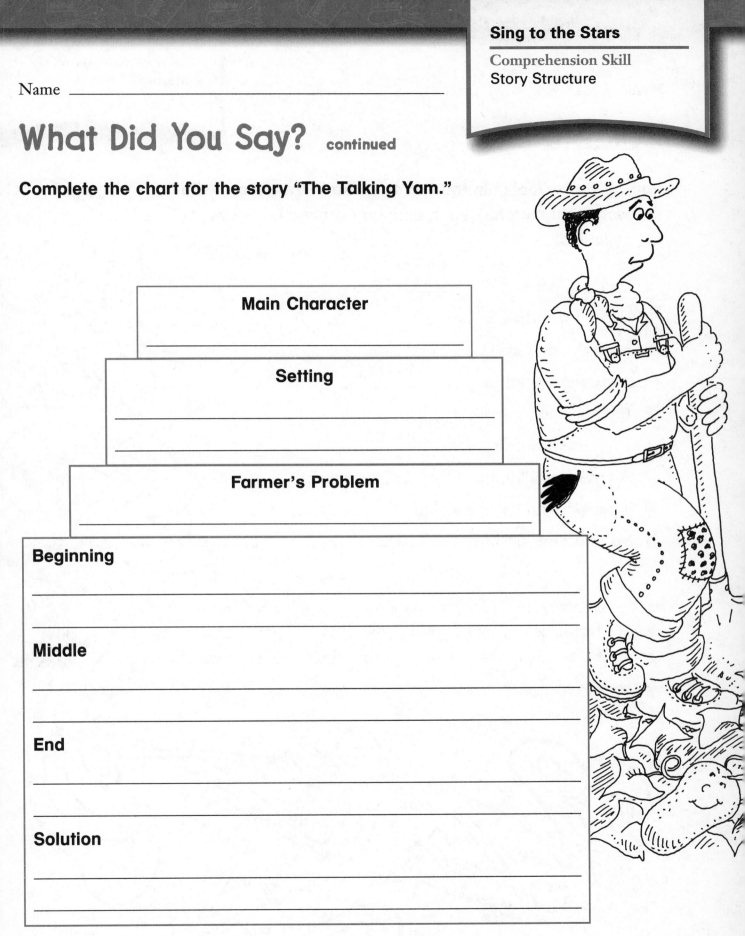

Main Character

_____

Setting

_____

_____

Farmer's Problem

_____

Beginning

_____

_____

Middle

_____

_____

End

_____

_____

Solution

_____

_____

_____

Name _____

Syllable Sort

Pair up the syllables in the box to make words, then write the word that matches each clue and draw a line between the syllables.

1. a tooth doctor _____

2. a tool for hitting nails _____

3. a windy snowstorm _____

4. a marriage ceremony _____

5. the opposite of before _____

6. a hat used to protect the head _____

7. A cricket is a kind of _____

8. a person who has great skill _____

9. Six and nine are both _____

10. having no mistakes _____

wed	fect	hel	mer	ding	den	in	per	zard	tist
sect	bers	ham	ter	af	num	pert	bliz	met	ex

Name _____

VCCV Pattern

Knowing how to divide a word into syllables can help you spell it. Remember these rules for dividing two-syllable words with the VCCV pattern:

► Divide most VCCV words between the consonants, whether the consonants are different or the same.

► Divide a VCCV word before the consonants if those consonants form a cluster.

► Divide a VCCV word after the consonants if those consonants spell one sound.

VC | CV	**pic | ture, at | tend**
V | CCV	**a | fraid**
VCC | V	**oth | er**

1. bottom
2. picture
3. other
4. attend
5. capture
6. common
7. danger
8. afraid
9. borrow
10. office
11. arrow
12. suppose
13. escape
14. whether
15. pillow
16. dinner
17. thirty
18. degree
19. allow
20. corner

Write each Spelling Word under the heading that shows where its syllables divide. Draw a line between its syllables.

VC | CV

_____

_____

_____

_____

_____

_____

_____

_____

_____

_____

V | CCV

_____

_____

VCC | V

_____

_____

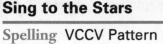

Name _____

Spelling Spree

Write the Spelling Word in each word below.

1. officer _____

2. uncommon _____

3. supposed _____

4. bottomless _____

5. swallow _____

6. borrower _____

7. pillowcase _____

Write the Spelling Word that answers each riddle.

8. You might find me inside a frame. Who am I?

9. I'm speeding cars and thin ice. Who am I?

10. Along with breakfast and lunch, I'm a winner. Who am I?

11. I have a point, and I'm very narrow. Who am I?

12. I'm smaller than forty and bigger than twenty. Who am I?

13. If I'm not one thing, I'm the _____.

14. I'm hot or cold, high or low. Who am I?

8. _____ 12. _____

9. _____ 13. _____

10. _____ 14. _____

11. _____

1. bottom
2. picture
3. other
4. attend
5. capture
6. common
7. danger
8. afraid
9. borrow
10. office
11. arrow
12. suppose
13. escape
14. whether
15. pillow
16. dinner
17. thirty
18. degree
19. allow
20. corner

Name _____

Proofreading and Writing

Proofreading Circle the six misspelled Spelling Words in this neighborhood flyer. Then write each word correctly.

Concert After Dark Series

You're invited to atend a concert in the park
every Saturday in August!

Ninety-degree temperatures got you down? Enjoy a concert and ekscape the summer heat. Come one, come all, wether young or old. Don't be afriad to leave work early. Invite your boss or bring a friend. Take the opportunity to capshur the sounds of summer to remember all winter long.

Concerts are held right around the korner in Davis Park.

1. bottom
2. picture
3. other
4. attend
5. capture
6. common
7. danger
8. afraid
9. borrow
10. office
11. arrow
12. suppose
13. escape
14. whether
15. pillow
16. dinner
17. thirty
18. degree
19. allow
20. corner

1. _____ 4. _____

2. _____ 5. _____

3. _____ 6. _____

➤ **Write a Character Sketch** Mr. Washington was kind and encouraging to Ephram. Were you surprised when Mr. Washington came and played at the concert? How would describe Mr. Washington to someone who hasn't read the story?

On a separate sheet of paper, describe the kind of person Mr. Washington was. Use Spelling Words from the list.

Name _____

All the Good News That's Fit to Print

Merry Times, the editor of the *Good News Gazette*, is having a problem with a new reporter, Peter Downhill. He wrote an article that uses many words with negative connotations. Help Merry replace each underlined word with one that has a more positive connotation. Write the new word on the line that has the same number.

Traffic along Maple Street today was horrible , all because
                                        1
of a family of   silly   geese. One driver described how traffic
                  2

 screeched safely to a halt when a stubborn mother goose and her
    3   4
family walked across the road. School children escaped their school
                                                    5
bus to watch. The bus driver explained that the   nosy   students
                                                     6
had never seen geese crossing a road. The students stood on the

sidewalk and screamed hello to the goose and her chicks. A police
                 7
officer stepped past the   mob   of people to   push   the geese
                            8   9
across the street. Everyone agreed that they would have an   odd
                                                              10
story to tell their families.

1. _____   6. _____

2. _____   7. _____

3. _____   8. _____

4. _____   9. _____

5. _____   10. _____

Name _____

Making Comparisons

**Write the correct comparing form of the adjective
in parentheses.**

1. Ephram thought this evening was _____
   than yesterday evening. (warm)

2. During the day, the streets were _____
   than they were at night. (noisy)

3. The _____ sounds of all come from
   a well-played violin. (sweet)

4. On stage, Ephram saw the _____ piano
   he had ever seen. (large)

5. Mr. Washington's fingers were _____
   than they had been before. (stiff)

6. As he thought about playing in public, Ephram felt
   _____ than when he played on the roof. (nervous)

7. The _____ moment of all came when Mr.
   Washington went up on stage with him. (happy)

8. One of the two singers on the program was
   _____ than the other. (thin)

Complete the chart with the correct form of the adjective.

Adjective	Compare 2	Compare 3 or more
hot	→ hotter	→
beautiful		most beautiful

Name _____

Comparing with Music

**Suppose Ephram kept a diary. Help him complete this diary
entry by writing the correct forms of the adjectives in the box.
Use -er, -est, more, or most.**

young	frightened	strong	nice
exciting	familiar	funny	wet

Playing in public yesterday was the _____

thing I have done in my life. When I went up on stage, someone

said I was the _____ person to play at a

concert there. I was a lot _____ than when I

play by myself on the roof. Grandma said that the sound of my

violin was _____ than she ever had heard it.

The _____ thing of all was getting Mr.

Washington to play the piano with me. I discovered that he was

once one of the _____ pianists in our city.

I won't forget this, either. I can't think of anything

_____ than feeling Shiloh's wet nose on my

elbow. That dog has the _____ nose of any

dog I know!

Name _____

Using Comparisons

Good writers are careful to use the correct forms of *good*
and *bad* when comparing two, three, or more.

**Read the following paragraph. Then rewrite it, replacing any
incorrect forms of *good* and *bad*.**

     Hot weather is more bad for a violin than cold weather. The
better temperature of all is around 72°F. One of the worse things
that can happen is for a violin string to break in the middle of a
performance. If the violin bow makes squeaky sounds, the better
thing of all to do is to rub resin on it. Some people think that the
cello has a more good sound than the violin. One thing for sure is
that flat notes sound worst than sharp notes. The baddest sound of
all is a squeaky violin. Personally, I think that the better music of all
is written for the violin.

_____

_____

_____

_____

_____

_____

_____

_____

_____

_____

Name _____

Writing a Message

Use this page to take a telephone *message*.

Date: _____ Time: _____

For: _____

From: _____

Phone Number: _____

Message: _____

_____

_____

_____

_____

_____

_____

_____

_____

Message taken by:

_____

276   Theme 4: **Problem Solvers**

Using Complete Information

When you take a message, always listen carefully and write the information exactly. Write down all the details. Do not leave anything out.

First "listen" to the following recordings left on a telephone answering machine. Then read the written messages that were taken. Make the written messages complete and exact by correcting any inaccuracies and adding any missing information.

1. Hey, Sam, it's Rick, on Sunday, at 5:00. Cheerleading practice has been changed from Monday and Wednesday to Tuesday and Thursday. Same place, the gym, same time, 3:15. I have to go to the library after practice. Call me, 555-1577.

Date: Sun. **Time:** 5:00
For: Sam **Caller:** Rick
Caller's number: 555-5177

Message: Cheerleading practice time change. Now it's Monday and Thursday. Same time and place. He has to go to the library. Call him.
Message taken by: Tom

2. Hi, Jason. It's me, Yasko, and it's Wednesday, 7:30. Can you bring the cake for the cheerleaders' party? Let me know by Friday. Oh, yeah, the party will be at Suzanne's house after the game on May 18, probably about 5 or 6:00. My number 556-3672. Bye now.

Date: Fri. **Time:** 7:30
For: Jason **Caller:** Yasko
Caller's number: 556-3672

Message: Can you bring the cake and plates for the cheerleaders' party? It's at Yasko's house, after the game on May 8, about 5 or 6:00. Let Yasko know by Fri.
Message taken by: Mom

Name _____

Vocabulary Items

Use the test-taking strategies and tips you have learned to help you answer vocabulary items. This practice will help you when you take this kind of test.

Read each sentence. Choose the word that means about the same as the underlined word. Fill in the circle for the correct answer at the bottom of the page.

1. The dragon's only <u>companions</u> were his severed tail, two empty shipping crates, and a jar of salted duck eggs.

   <u>Companions</u> means —

   A enemies   **C** friends

   B cousins   **D** pieces

2. Peter thought Chinatown seemed old and <u>alien</u> and strange.

   <u>Alien</u> means —

   F foreign   **H** unique

   G familiar   **J** exciting

3. Peter stroked the dragon's <u>tangled</u> whiskers and wondered how long it would take to unknot them.

   <u>Tangled</u> means —

   A straight   **C** curly

   B twisted   **D** short

4. Great Aunt told Peter that the dragons of her childhood received the <u>homage</u> of every living thing.

   <u>Homage</u> means —

   F interest   **H** honesty

   G respect   **J** anger

ANSWER ROWS   1 Ⓐ Ⓑ Ⓒ Ⓓ   3 Ⓐ Ⓑ Ⓒ Ⓓ

                2 Ⓕ Ⓖ Ⓗ Ⓙ   4 Ⓕ Ⓖ Ⓗ Ⓙ

Name _____

Vocabulary Items continued

5. Mr. Pang peered <u>suspiciously</u> over his newspaper as Peter walked up with the dragon.

   <u>Suspiciously</u> means —

   A approvingly   **C** angrily

   B happily   **D** distrustfully

6. Mr. Pang told Peter not to be <u>impatient</u> since repairing the dragon was a big job that would take quite a bit of time.

   <u>Impatient</u> means —

   F anxious   **H** upset

   G sorry   **J** disappointed

7. Peter learned to fly a fighting kite, which <u>entertained</u> his Great Aunt and her friends.

   <u>Entertained</u> means —

   A bothered   **C** amused

   B injured   **D** scared

8. The dragon looked <u>fierce</u> with its bold eyebrows, red cheeks, and sharp teeth.

   <u>Fierce</u> means—

   F gentle   **H** active

   G threatening   **J** silly

ANSWER ROWS   5 Ⓐ Ⓑ Ⓒ Ⓓ   7 Ⓐ Ⓑ Ⓒ Ⓓ

                 6 Ⓕ Ⓖ Ⓗ Ⓙ   8 Ⓕ Ⓖ Ⓗ Ⓙ

Name _____

Spelling Review

Write Spelling Words from the list on this page to answer the questions.

1–9. Which nine words have the final /ē/ sound?

1. _____   6. _____

2. _____   7. _____

3. _____   8. _____

4. _____   9. _____

5. _____

10–17. Which eight words have the /k/, /ng/, or /kw/ sound?

10. _____   14. _____

11. _____   15. _____

12. _____   16. _____

13. _____   17. _____

18–25. Which eight words have the final /j/, /ĭj/, or /s/ sound?

18. _____   22. _____

19. _____   23. _____

20. _____   24. _____

21. _____   25. _____

26–32. What letters are missing from each word below? Write each word.

26. of—   _____   30. sup—   _____

27. wheth—   _____   31. cor—   _____

28. af—   _____   32. beau—   _____

29. oth—   _____

Spelling Words

1. village
2. corner
3. office
4. sink
5. squirrel
6. alley
7. whether
8. ridge
9. mistake
10. afraid
11. question
12. other
13. lonely
14. attack
15. thirty
16. blanket
17. monkey
18. twice
19. chance
20. suppose
21. beauty
22. degree
23. crooked
24. honey
25. strange
26. glance
27. twenty
28. cottage
29. since
30. ready

Name _____

Spelling Spree

**Riddles Write the Spelling Word that answers each
question.**

Spelling Words

1. What is a place where people wash dishes?

   _____

2. What word sounds like *weather* and means "if"?

   _____

3. What animal eats nuts and chatters? _____

4. What is a long, narrow edge? _____

5. What is a narrow street? _____

6. What is the place where two lines, meet? _____

7. What kind of sentence are you reading? _____

8. What kind of animal is a baboon? _____

1. whether
2. afraid
3. ridge
4. alley
5. squirrel
6. degree
7. strange
8. sink
9. ready
10. question
11. twenty
12. corner
13. monkey
14. honey
15. chance

**Be a Poet Finish the rhymes by writing a Spelling Word in
each blank line. The Spelling Word should rhyme with the
underlined word.**

9. In their home on the <u>range</u>, those cows are so _____!

10. Don't be _____! That stranger is just the <u>maid</u>.

11. Hold the baseball bat <u>steady</u>. Then your swing will be _____.

12. We've had four cookies, and that should be <u>plenty</u>,

    But Jenny says no — she wants to have _____!

13. The temperature says it is just twenty-<u>three</u>.

    Maybe we should turn the heat up one _____!

14. Do we have enough <u>money</u> to buy that new kind of _____?

15. This is your last _____ to get up and <u>dance</u>.

Name _____

Proofreading and Writing

Proofreading **Circle the six misspelled Spelling Words in this plan. Then write each word correctly.**

This school year I will try to atak a new problem every day. I want to be reddy to do my best thinking. I will read each question at least twise. I won't just glanss at it. If I have to look at a problem thurty times before I solve it, I will. I suppoze this will be difficult, but I am prepared.

1. _____   4. _____

2. _____   5. _____

3. _____   6. _____

Speech, Speech **Use context clues to help you write the Spelling Word that belongs next to each number.**

In the 7. _____ of Pineville, there is a narrow,

8. _____ road near the pretty 9. _____ of the Wilson

family. It is a quiet and 10. _____ area with natural 11. _____. Some

people wanted to tear down the Wilson's house to widen the road. I said we

should try this 12. _____ idea: turn the area into a park. At first no one

liked the idea. I wanted to get into bed and pull a 13. _____ over my head!

Then I met with the mayor in her 14. _____. The mayor agreed that it

would be a 15. _____ to widen the road.

7. _____   10. _____   13. _____

8. _____   11. _____   14. _____

9. _____   12. _____   15. _____

Write a Persuasive Paragraph **Write a paragraph about a problem and how to solve it. Use the Spelling Review Words.**

Spelling Words

1. ready
2. mistake
3. crooked
4. glance
5. village
6. cottage
7. other
8. beauty
9. office
10. attack
11. twice
12. suppose
13. thirty
14. blanket
15. lonely

Theme 4: **Problem Solvers**   283

Name _____

Comparing Poems

Think about the elements of poetry. Choose three poems to compare and contrast. Then complete the chart below.

	_____ (title)	_____ (title)	_____ (title)
What kind of language is used in each poem?			
Does the poem express a feeling? If so, what feeling does it express?			
What images are in each poem?			

Tell which of these poems is your favorite and why.

_____

_____

_____

Name _____

May the Best Poems Win!

You are hosting an awards ceremony for poetry. Choose one of the poems from this theme to receive the Best Rhythm Award, another to get the Best Rhyme Prize, and a third for Best Imagery. Explain why each poem won that prize, giving an example from that poem.

Rhythm Award

Winning Poem: _____

Why: _____

_____

Example: _____

_____

Rhyme Prize

Winning Poem: _____

Why: _____

_____

Example: _____

_____

Best Imagery

Winning Poem: _____

Why: _____

_____

Example: _____

_____

Name _____

Heroes

Fill in the information to show what you think about heroes.

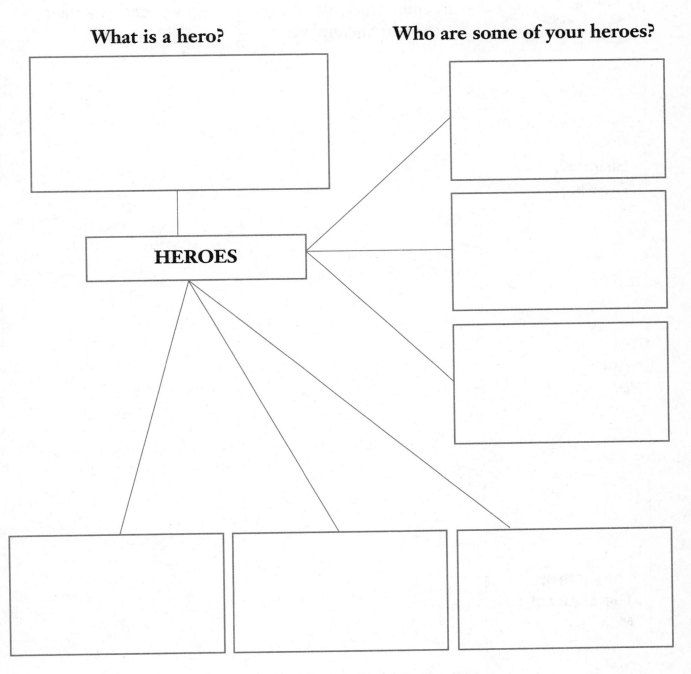

What is a hero?

Who are some of your heroes?

HEROES

What are some characteristics of a hero?

Name _____

Heroes

	Name the hero or heroes in each story. What are their achievements?	What qualities helped them achieve their goals?
Happy Birthday, Dr. King!		
Gloria Estefan		
Lou Gehrig: The Luckiest Man		

Name _____

Civil Rights Crossword

Complete the crossword puzzle using words from the vocabulary box.

Vocabulary

boycott   civil rights   fare   protest   stupendous

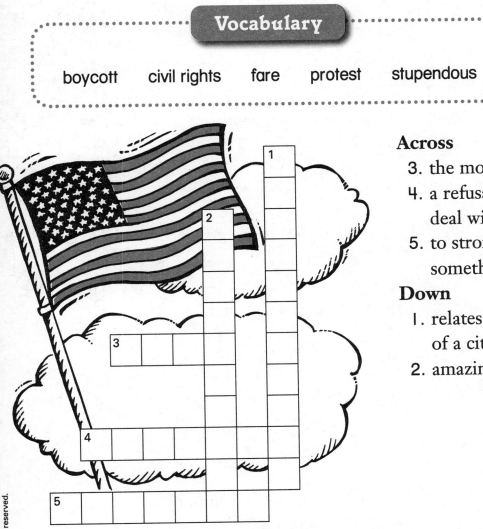

Across

3. the money paid to travel
4. a refusal to use, buy from, or deal with a company
5. to strongly object to something

Down

1. relates to the legal privileges of a citizen
2. amazing

Write a sentence using at least two of the vocabulary words.

_____

_____

Cause and Effect Chart

Cause	Effect
page 536 Jamal gets a note from the principal.	_____ _____ _____
page 539 _____ _____	Grandpa Joe gets angry at Jamal.
page 541 Jamal apologizes to Grandpa Joe for fighting. _____ _____	_____ _____ Rosa Parks got arrested.
page 542 African Americans heard about Rosa Parks's arrest.	_____ _____
page 544 _____ _____	Dr. King's birthday is honored and celebrated with a national holiday.
page 547 Dad explains to Jamal that Dr. King worked in peaceful ways.	_____ _____

Name _____

Knowing Dr. King

Read and answer the questions.

1. Why was Grandpa Joe so angry that Jamal got into a fight to sit in the back of the bus?

   _____

   _____

2. Which two famous African Americans did Jamal and Grandpa Joe talk about?

   _____

   _____

3. What did Jamal's father say about the way Dr. King made things happen?

   _____

   _____

   _____

4. What was the Montgomery Bus Boycott?

   _____

   _____

5. Dr. King become a leader of what movement?

   _____

   _____

6. What did Jamal decide to do for the Martin Luther King, Jr., assembly?

   _____

   _____

   _____

The Effects of Hard Work

Read the story below and then complete the chart on the next page.

The Family Business

Pedro never thought he would miss collecting old newspapers from his neighbors and recycling them. As a kid, he hated spending one Saturday every two weeks picking up the papers and taking them to the recycling center. The newspapers made him dirty. He missed playing games with his friends on those days. He especially didn't like working in the hot sun of the summer. He used to think there wasn't anything good about the job. He thought it was a waste of his time.

But now that he was moving with his family to a new neighborhood, he thought back on all the good things that happened because of the job. His sisters, who started the business, each saved enough money to pay for their own summer vacations to Europe. Pedro was able to buy a stereo for his room and send himself to summer camp.

"Hey, Pedro! Come in here please," his mother called from the kitchen. "Grampa's on the phone and he wants to say good-bye."

"Hello, Grampa! I was just thinking about the paper recycling business you convinced Anna and Katrina to begin. It sure brought us many good things."

"I'm glad to hear that, Pedro," his grandfather said. "It just goes to show you that all it takes is a good idea."

Name _____

The Effects of Hard Work

continued

Complete the chart below based on "The Family Business."

Cause	Effect
_____ _____ _____ _____ _____ _____ _____ _____	Pedro didn't like his recycling job.
His sisters saved enough money to go to Europe. He bought a stereo. He paid for summer camp.	_____ _____

Name _____

Searching for Prefixes and Suffixes

In the puzzle below, find and circle the hidden words in the box. Then recall what you know about prefixes and suffixes and write each word by its meaning.

wasteful	disinfect
unprepared	amazement
priceless	tasteless
measurement	emptiness
research	dishonest

T	V	P	R	I	C	E	L	E	S	S	B
F	J	G	M	G	B	S	R	E	S	E	S
M	E	A	S	U	R	E	M	E	N	T	T
Y	U	D	R	B	I	V	W	I	Y	A	O
U	D	I	S	H	O	N	E	S	T	S	N
N	R	I	E	W	E	K	K	N	Y	T	L
P	E	Q	S	M	A	O	L	N	U	E	I
R	S	U	M	I	P	S	Y	L	X	L	Z
E	E	Y	H	Y	N	T	T	M	A	E	J
P	A	M	O	F	K	F	I	E	K	S	R
A	R	D	P	I	B	R	E	N	F	S	T
R	C	M	S	P	F	N	E	C	E	U	M
E	H	P	L	H	H	K	A	H	T	S	L
D	A	M	A	Z	E	M	E	N	T	B	S

1. to get rid of germs

   _____

2. not ready

   _____

3. great surprise

   _____

4. careful study

   _____

5. nothingness

   _____

6. untruthful

   _____

7. without flavor

   _____

8. using more than is needed

   _____

9. size or amount

   _____

10. very valuable

   _____

Name _____

Words with a Prefix or a Suffix

A **prefix** is a word part added to the beginning of a base word. A **suffix** is a word part added to the end of a base word. Both prefixes and suffixes add meaning.

Prefixes: **re**build, **dis**like, **un**lucky

Suffixes: sick**ness**, treat**ment**, beauti**ful**, care**less**

► In the starred word *awful*, the *e* was dropped from the base word *awe* before the suffix *-ful* was added.

Write each Spelling Word under its prefix or suffix.

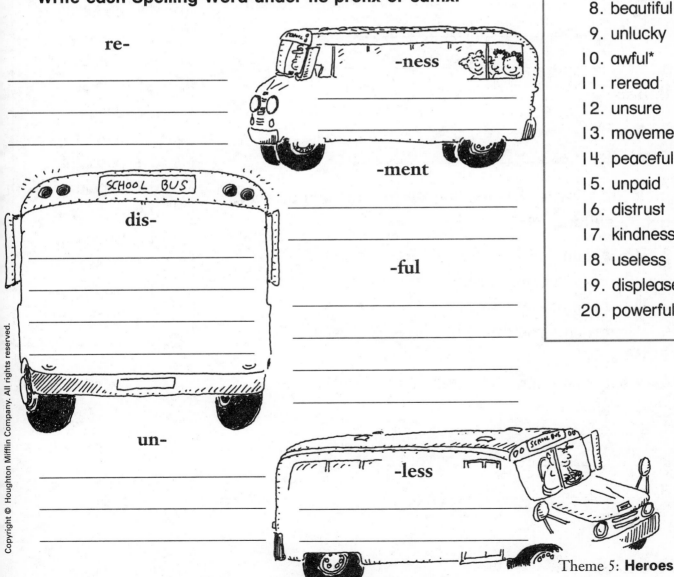

re-

_____

_____

_____

-ness

_____

_____

-ment

_____

_____

dis-

_____

_____

_____

-ful

_____

_____

_____

_____

un-

_____

_____

_____

-less

_____

_____

_____

Name _____

Spelling Spree

Finding Words **Each word below is hidden in a Spelling Word. Write the Spelling Word.**

Example: hop *hopeful*

1. ace _____
2. plea _____
3. eat _____
4. rust _____
5. are _____
6. owe _____
7. red _____
8. disco _____
9. aid _____
10. kin _____

Questions **Write the Spelling Word that best answers each question.**

11. What is an antonym for *health*?
12. What kind of object serves no purpose?
13. What is a milder word for *hate*?
14. What might you do if your house burns down?
15. What is a synonym for *terrible*?
16. What is another word for "unfortunate"?

11. _____   14. _____

12. _____   15. _____

13. _____   16. _____

Spelling Words

1. redo
2. treatment
3. rebuild
4. discolor
5. careless
6. dislike
7. sickness
8. beautiful
9. unlucky
10. awful*
11. reread
12. unsure
13. movement
14. peaceful
15. unpaid
16. distrust
17. kindness
18. useless
19. displease
20. powerful

Name _____

Proofreading and Writing

Proofreading Circle the four misspelled Spelling Words
in this book review. Then write each word correctly.

Are you unshure why we honor
Martin Luther King, Jr., with a holiday?
If so, get hold of a copy of *Happy Birthday,
Dr. King!* Jamal Wilson is the main
character of this beutiful but powerful
picture book. As Jamal learns about the
civil rights moovement, readers do, too.
Believe me, you won't read this book only
once. You'll rerread it many times!

1. _____   3. _____

2. _____   4. _____

Spelling Words

1. redo
2. treatment
3. rebuild
4. discolor
5. careless
6. dislike
7. sickness
8. beautiful
9. unlucky
10. awful*
11. reread
12. unsure
13. movement
14. peaceful
15. unpaid
16. distrust
17. kindness
18. useless
19. displease
20. powerful

Write Copy for a Book Jacket Many books have
jackets, paper covers that protect the hard covers. Book
jacket copy tells some details about the book. However, it
doesn't tell enough to spoil the book for readers.

**On a separate sheet of paper, write copy for a book
jacket for your favorite book. Tell only enough to make
readers want to read the book. Use Spelling Words from
the list.**

Crossword Prefixes

Name _____

Use the base words and prefixes in the box to make new words that match the clues. Enter the new words where they belong in the crossword puzzle.

Box: un- dis- re- / appear important changed like common pay cover respect done write

Across

2. The job isn't finished, so it is _____.
4. Something very different may be _____.
5. If you act rudely, you show _____.
6. When you give money back to people, you _____ them.
7. Something you lose may just seem to _____.

Down

1. If something doesn't matter much, it's _____.
3. It's no different than before, so it's _____.
4. Take your cap off and _____ your head.
7. If you don't care much for something you _____ it.
8. When you do your lesson over, you _____ it.

Name _____

Replacing Nouns with Pronouns

For each sentence below, write a subject pronoun to replace the word or words given in parentheses. Write your sentence on the lines provided.

1. (Jamal's mother) looks at the pink slip.

   _____

2. (Jamal) was in trouble now.

   _____

3. His mother asked Jamal, "Did (Jamal) get in trouble today?"

   _____

4. (Alisha) was not home yet.

   _____

5. (Jamal's classmates) are planning a celebration for Dr. King.

   _____

6. (Grandpa Joe) was angry with Jamal for fighting.

   _____

7. (Jamal) listened to Grandpa Joe's story about the boycott.

   _____

8. (Grandpa Joe and his wife) boycotted the buses.

   _____

Name _____

In Search of a Subject Pronoun

Suppose that Jamal's class is having a discussion about what to do for the Martin Luther King, Jr., celebration. Write a subject pronoun to replace the word or words in parentheses.

Mrs. Gordon: Jamal says that (Jamal) _____ thinks a skit would be a good idea.

Jamal: Yes, that way (the rest of the class and I) _____ could all have a part.

Albert: How about the subject of the skit? What will (the subject) _____ be?

Mrs. Gordon: Jamal says that (Jamal) _____ has an idea.

Jamal: Well, (Jamal) _____ thought that we could do a skit about two boys on a bus. (The two boys) _____ are arguing over an empty seat at the back of the bus.

Frieda: That skit sounds like a good idea. (The skit) _____ is about Mrs. Parks's fight for civil rights.

Margie: Mrs. Gordon, would (Mrs. Gordon) _____ direct the skit?

Mrs. Gordon: Yes, (Mrs. Gordon) _____ would be happy to do that.

Billy: Aminta should have a part. (Aminta) _____ can play the part of the bus driver.

Name _____

Sentence Combining with Subject Pronouns

When two sentences have different subjects but the same predicate, you can combine them into one sentence with a compound subject.

Read the sentences below. Then rewrite them, combining each pair of sentences into one sentence with a compound subject. Use the joining word in parentheses to write the new sentences.

1. She gave the bus driver money for a ticket. I gave the bus driver money for a ticket. (and)

   _____

2. You were there to hear the entire speech. They were there to hear the entire speech. (and)

   _____

3. She will recite part of the speech from memory. You will recite part of the speech from memory. (or)

   _____

4. They listened to the words carefully. I listened to the words carefully. (and)

   _____

5. She will prepare a report about Martin Luther King, Jr. I will prepare a report about Martin Luther King, Jr. (or)

   _____

Name _____

Writing an Information Paragraph

Use this graphic organizer to help you plan your information paragraph about a leader you admire. Tell why you admire this person, and what he or she did that is admirable, and why you chose this leader.

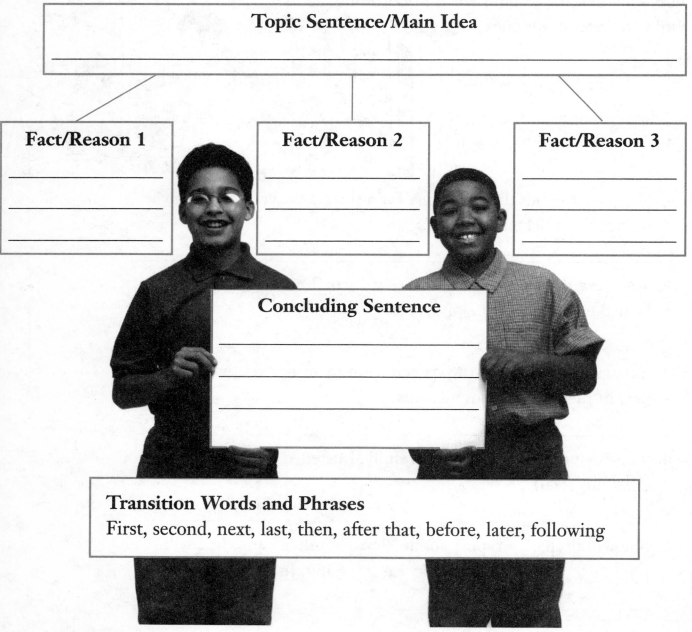

Topic Sentence/Main Idea

_____

Fact/Reason 1

_____
_____
_____

Fact/Reason 2

_____
_____
_____

Fact/Reason 3

_____
_____
_____

Concluding Sentence

_____
_____
_____

Transition Words and Phrases
First, second, next, last, then, after that, before, later, following

302   Theme 5: **Heroes**

Name _____

Using Facts

Good writers use facts to support the main idea of an information paragraph. To do so, they organize them in different ways.

► Writers use chronological order to put events in the order in which they happen.

► Writers use spatial order to describe how things look.

► Writers use the order of importance to organize facts from least to most important or from most to least important.

Read the following clusters of facts. Then decide on a main idea and use the facts to write a paragraph of information. Identify the kind of order you used.

1. On Tuesday, the math teacher gives us a mini-test.
   We have a history test on Wednesday.
   Monday afternoon, we have a special art class.
   Every Friday, there's a spelling quiz.

   _____

   _____

   _____

   _____

2. The third graders sang a medley of civil rights songs.
   Jamal's skit was the hit of the Dr. Martin Luther King, Jr., assembly.
   Everyone talked about it for weeks.
   The first graders recited Dr. King's "I Have a Dream" speech.

   _____

   _____

   _____

   _____

Name _____

Revising Your Personal Essay

Reread your personal essay. What do you need to make it better? Use this page to help you decide. Put a checkmark in the box for each sentence that describes your personal essay.

Rings the Bell!

☐ My essay has a beginning that will get my readers' attention.

☐ Each paragraph has a main idea, supported by details.

☐ It reads as if I were saying it to someone.

☐ I have a good conclusion that sums up my point.

☐ There are almost no mistakes.

Getting Stronger

☐ I could make the beginning more attention grabbing.

☐ My main ideas are there, but I need to add more details.

☐ It still could sound more like me.

☐ I need to add a stronger conclusion.

☐ There are a few mistakes.

Try Harder

☐ I need a better beginning.

☐ My main ideas aren't clear, and I need to add details.

☐ There is no conclusion.

☐ There are a lot of mistakes.

Name _____

Pronoun Reference

Pronouns are words that replace nouns. Write the word or words that the underlined pronoun refers to in each exercise.

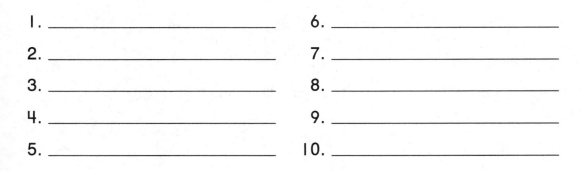

1. I would love to start my own magazine. <u>It</u> would be called *Cartoon.*

2. This magazine would be all cartoons. <u>They</u> would be on every page.

3. I would write all the articles for the magazine. My friend Jimmy would edit <u>them</u>.

4. "You write the articles," Jimmy says. "Let me edit <u>them</u>."

5. Jimmy and I love those old Bugs Bunny cartoons. We have made tapes of <u>them</u>.

6. We also love newspaper cartoons. Jimmy collects <u>them</u>.

7. We both really like *Peanuts* by Charles Schulz. <u>He</u> had his characters say such funny things.

8. My sister would like to interview Matt Groening. <u>She</u> thinks he is the best cartoonist of all.

9. Do you know who Matt Groening is? <u>He</u> is the creator of *The Simpsons.*

10. The characters on the show are based on real people. <u>They</u> have the same names as people in Groening's family.

1. _____   6. _____

2. _____   7. _____

3. _____   8. _____

4. _____   9. _____

5. _____   10. _____

Name _____

Spelling Words

Words Often Misspelled Look for familiar spelling patterns to help you remember how to spell the Spelling Words on this page. Think carefully about the parts that you find hard to spell in each word.

Write the missing letters in the Spelling Words below.

1. br ___ ___ ___ ___ t

2. en ___ ___ ___ ___

3. b ___ y

4. ___ ___ ess

5. Sat ___ ___ day

6. Jan ___ ___ ___ y

7. Feb ___ ___ ___ ___ y

8. favor ___ ___ ___

9. l ___ ing

10. t ___ ing

11. ___ round

12. swim ___ ing

13. h ___ ___ rd

14. a ___ ___ o

15. tr ___ ___ ___

Spelling Words

1. brought
2. enough
3. buy
4. guess
5. Saturday
6. January
7. February
8. favorite
9. lying
10. tying
11. around
12. swimming
13. heard
14. also
15. tried

Study List **On a separate piece of paper, write each Spelling Word. Check your spelling against the words on the list.**

Name _____

Spelling Spree

Opposites **Write a Spelling Word that means the opposite of the underlined words.**

1. I was <u>telling the truth</u> when I said that I knew how to fly a plane. _____

2. We went to the store to <u>sell</u> some groceries to get ready for the big storm. _____

3. She <u>didn't attempt</u> to call you to let you know what the homework was. _____

4. Isn't your <u>most disliked</u> singer playing a concert next month? _____

5. It was <u>nowhere near</u> ten o'clock when we finished watching the movie. _____

Spelling Words

1. brought
2. enough
3. buy
4. guess
5. Saturday
6. January
7. February
8. favorite
9. lying
10. tying
11. around
12. swimming
13. heard
14. also
15. tried

Crack the Code **Some Spelling Words have been written in the code below. Use the code to figure out each word. Then write the words correctly.**

CODE: u d m r s i q o b a c e f z v t y n p h
LETTER: a b c d e f g h i j l m n o r s t u w y

6. Aufnuvh   9. osuvr   12. sfznqo   15. qnstt
7. dvznqoy   10. yhbfq   13. uctz
8. tpbeebfq   11. Isdvnuvh   14. Tuynvruh

6. _____   10. _____   14. _____

7. _____   11. _____   15. _____

8. _____   12. _____

9. _____   13 _____

Proofreading and Writing

Proofreading Circle the four misspelled Spelling Words in this inscription on a statue. Then write each word correctly.

Name _____

This statue is in honor of the accomplishment of Elmer Fitzgerald on Saterday, February 21, 1920. On that day, he single-handedly caught enouf fish to feed his entire village for three months. Unfortunately, before the fish could be brot back to shore, they were all eaten by sharks. Elmer treid to drive the sharks off with his fishing pole, but there were just too many of them. At least, that's what Elmer told us.

1. brought
2. enough
3. buy
4. guess
5. Saturday
6. January
7. February
8. favorite
9. lying
10. tying
11. around
12. swimming
13. heard
14. also
15. tried

1. _____

2. _____

3. _____

4. _____

✏ Write a Round-Robin Story Get together in a small group with other students. Then write a story about a hero, with each of you writing one sentence at a time. Use a Spelling Word from the list in each sentence.

Name _____

Be a Recording Star!

Complete the sentences in this ad for a recording company.
Use each vocabulary word once.

Vocabulary

career	contract	demonstrated	eventually
specializes	tireless	worldwide	

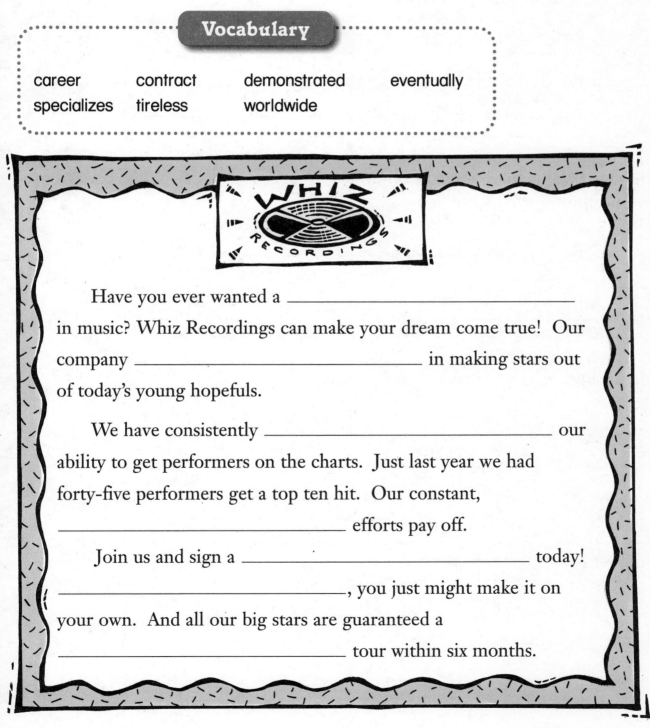

Have you ever wanted a _____
in music? Whiz Recordings can make your dream come true! Our

company _____ in making stars out

of today's young hopefuls.

We have consistently _____ our

ability to get performers on the charts. Just last year we had

forty-five performers get a top ten hit. Our constant,

_____ efforts pay off.

Join us and sign a _____ today!

_____, you just might make it on

your own. And all our big stars are guaranteed a

_____ tour within six months.

Name _____

Judgments Chart

Why Might Someone Call Gloria Estefan a "Hero"?

Chapter One: Escaping with Music

_____

_____

_____

**Chapter Two: Making Music with Emilio
and Chapter Three: Changes**

_____

_____

_____

Chapter Four: World Fame—and Tragedy

_____

_____

_____

Chapter Five: "Here for Each Other"

_____

_____

_____

Name _____

Music World

Help the reporter from *Music World* write an article on Gloria Estefan by answering his questions about the star. Use complete sentences.

I hear you have read a lot about Gloria Fajardo Estefan. Tell me something about her childhood, up to age 16.

_____

_____

_____

Tell me the story of how Gloria became a member of Emilio Estefan's band—and how they fell in love.

_____

_____

_____

In your opinion, what were Gloria's most important achievements before her accident in 1990? What are the most important things she has done since then?

Before the accident: _____

_____

_____

Since the accident: _____

_____

_____

What can a young person learn from Gloria Estefan?

_____

_____

_____

Name _____

Judge for Yourself

Read the story. Then complete the following page.

The Singing Cubs

My friends and I have a band that we call The Singing Cubs, and we're planning on entering the school talent show this year. I'm Bobby, the group's lead guitar player and singer. My friend Megan also plays the guitar, and Ralphie is our drummer.

The day before the talent show, the principal announced that all assignments had to be turned in first thing in the morning for those students participating in the show. We knew it would be a busy night.

Ralphie's parents decided they couldn't stand his messy room any longer. They said he needed to clean it up or no show. Then to make matters worse, my mother got sick and I had to help with dinnertime. I was so busy. I washed, carried, served, and washed again. Finally, dinner was over and I could begin my homework.

After dinner, I finished most of my homework. Then I called Megan because I needed help on my book report. She was also hard at work on her report. She needed help on it too. We talked a few things over and were soon ready to finish the reports on our own.

Then Ralphie called. He said, "There's no way I can get my room clean tonight. It's too messy." Both Megan and I went to Ralphie's house and worked hard on his room until it was spotless. Nothing could stand in our way now!

When it came time to perform the next day, we were exhausted but proud of ourselves. Mr. Major introduced us as "The Hard-Working Singing Cubs" and looked pleased with all that we had accomplished. Our parents were sitting in the front row, beaming with pride.

Name _____

Judge for Yourself continued

Complete this Judgments Chart for the story "The Singing Cubs."

Event	Response	Judgment
All talent show performers must hand in their homework early.		
Bobby's mom gets sick.		
Ralphie cannot participate unless he cleans his room.		
Bobby and Megan need some help on their book reports.		
The principal realizes how hard the children have been working to be in the talent show.		

Name _____

Musical Changes

Make music of your own by joining the words and endings. Write only one letter on each line. Remember, when a base word ends with *y*, change the *y* to *i* before adding *-es*, *-er*, *-ed*, or *-est*.

1. noisy + er

___ ___ ___ ___ ___ ___ ___
       7

2. marry + ed

___ ___ ___ ___ ___ ___ ___
        8

3. story + es

___ ___ ___ ___ ___ ___
       4

4. hungry + er

___ ___ ___ ___ ___ ___ ___
  6

5. country + es

___ ___ ___ ___ ___ ___ ___ ___ ___
  9

6. early + est

___ ___ ___ ___ ___ ___ ___
        3   1

7. family + es

___ ___ ___ ___ ___ ___ ___ ___
        5

8. worry + ed

___ ___ ___ ___ ___ ___ ___
  2

Solve the riddle by writing each numbered letter on the line with the matching number.

Riddle: What kind of music do shoes like to listen to?

___ ___ ___ ___   ___ ___ ___ ___ ___
1 2 3 4   5 6 7 8 9

Name _____

Changing Final *y* to *i*

If a word ends with a consonant and *y*, change the *y* to *i* when adding *-es*, *-ed*, *-er*, or *-est*.

city + es = cit**ies**   study + ed = stud**ied**

sunny + er = sunn**ier**   heavy + est = heav**iest**

Write each Spelling Word under its ending.

-es or -ed

_____

_____

_____

_____

_____

_____

_____

-er or -est

_____

_____

_____

_____

_____

_____

_____

_____

_____

_____

Spelling Words

1. sunnier
2. cloudier
3. windier
4. cities
5. heaviest
6. prettiest
7. studied
8. easier
9. noisier
10. families
11. ferries
12. crazier
13. funnier
14. earlier
15. copied
16. hobbies
17. angriest
18. emptied
19. worried
20. happiest

Spelling Spree

Meaning Match Write a Spelling Word that has each meaning and ending below.

1. do like + ed
2. making a lot of sound + er
3. having strong air movement + er
4. needing little effort + er
5. having great weight + est
6. full of sunshine + er
7. causing laughter + er

1 _____   5. _____

2. _____   6. _____

3. _____   7. _____

4. _____

Code Breaker Some Spelling Words are written in the code below. Figure out each word, and write it correctly.

8. 6-5-15-15-9-5-16   12. 5-11-14-17-9-5-4
9. 19-13-15-15-9-5-4   13. 1-12-7-15-9-5-16-17
10. 3-10-13-18-4-9-5-15 14. 16-17-18-4-9-5-4
11. 8-13-2-2-9-5-16   15. 3-15-1-20-9-5-15

8. _____   12. _____

9. _____   13. _____

10. _____   14. _____

11. _____   15. _____

CODE:	1	2	3	4	5	6	7	8	9	10	11	12	13	14	15	16	17	18	19	20
LETTER:	a	b	c	d	e	f	g	h	i	l	m	n	o	p	r	s	t	u	w	z

Spelling Words

1. sunnier
2. cloudier
3. windier
4. cities
5. heaviest
6. prettiest
7. studied
8. easier
9. noisier
10. families
11. ferries
12. crazier
13. funnier
14. earlier
15. copied
16. hobbies
17. angriest
18. emptied
19. worried
20. happiest

Name _____

Proofreading and Writing

Proofreading Circle the five misspelled Spelling Words in this poster ad. Then write each word correctly.

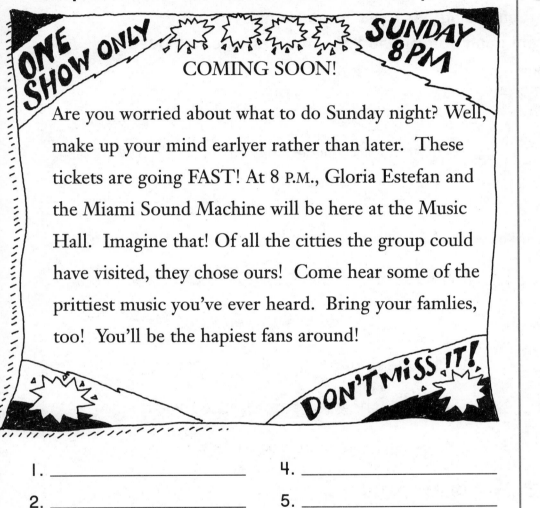

ONE SHOW ONLY

SUNDAY 8 PM

COMING SOON!

Are you worried about what to do Sunday night? Well, make up your mind earlyer rather than later. These tickets are going FAST! At 8 P.M., Gloria Estefan and the Miami Sound Machine will be here at the Music Hall. Imagine that! Of all the citties the group could have visited, they chose ours! Come hear some of the prittiest music you've ever heard. Bring your famlies, too! You'll be the hapiest fans around!

DON'T MISS IT!

1. _____ 4. _____

2. _____ 5. _____

3. _____

✏️ **Write Interview Questions** If you could interview Gloria Estefan, what questions would you ask her? Would you want to know more about her childhood? Would you ask why she chose to be a musician?

On a separate piece of paper, write a list of interview questions to ask Gloria Estefan. Use Spelling Words from the list.

Name _____

Sounds Like

Have you ever used a spelling checker on a computer? Then you know that it cannot tell the difference between two homophones.

Help Rosa by proofreading her letter to her aunt. Write the correct word from each pair on the line. The first one has been done for you.

Dear Tía Lara,

(Your You're) __You're__ not going to believe this, but I finally (won one)

_____ something! You (no know) _____ that I
　　　　1　　　　　　　　　　　　　　　　　　　　　　2

like to play basketball. Well, (there they're) _____ was a
　　　　　　　　　　　　　　　　　　　　　　　　3

contest to see who could get the most baskets in three minutes.

I (threw through) _____ more than anyone. I (new knew)
　　　　　　　　　　　4

_____ I had a good chance of winning. I practiced for
　　　5

(hours ours) _____ the week before. The (whole hole)
　　　　　　　　　6

_____ fourth grade took part, even the teachers. Our
　　　7

teacher, Mr. Barnes, (beet beat) _____ all the others.
　　　　　　　　　　　　　　　　　　　8

The coach asked if (weed we'd) _____ like to do it again,
　　　　　　　　　　　　　　　　9

and everyone said yes. So just (weight wait) _____
　　　　　　　　　　　　　　　　　　　　　　　　　10

until next month!

　　　　　　　　　　　　　　　　　Love,
　　　　　　　　　　　　　　　　　Rosa

Name _____

Writing with Object Pronouns

Complete the following paragraph by writing the correct pronoun to replace the noun in parentheses. Be careful! Some of the pronouns are subjects. Use the lines provided.

When Gloria's father went to Cuba, (her father) _____ was away for two years. Gloria and her mother did not know that (Gloria and her mother) _____ would be alone so long. Although Gloria did not speak English, she learned (English) _____ quickly. After her father came back from Cuba, (her father) _____ joined the U.S. Army. Her father became ill, and Gloria took care of (her father) _____. She listened to many songs and learned to sing (the songs) _____. Gloria wanted to be a professional singer but wasn't sure that (Gloria) _____ could sing well enough. At first, singing with a band was a weekend job for (Gloria) _____. Gloria was singing but still made time for her school courses. She did not want to neglect (the courses) _____. Gloria and Emilio decided that (Gloria and Emilio) _____ wanted to make music a full-time career.

Name _____

Object Pronouns

Emilio hired five workers to help him get ready for recording
sessions at a studio. You are one of them! Fill in the schedule
by writing your name on the line next to every *. Then use the
schedule to answer each question with a complete sentence.

	Monday	Tuesday	Friday
6:00 A.M. Set up instruments	* _____ Enrique	Helene * _____	* _____ Teisha
8:00 A.M. Tune guitars	* _____ Enrique	Helene Teisha	* _____ Helene
5:00 P.M. Pack up audio	Helene Teisha	* _____ Helene	* _____ Enrique
7:00 P.M. Pack instruments	* _____ Lynn	Enrique Helene	Lynn Teisha

1. If no one arrives Monday at 6:00 A.M., whom should Emilio call?

_____

2. Who is supposed to pack up instruments on Monday?

_____

3. Who is supposed to pack up the audio at 5:00 on Tuesday
   evening?

_____

4. Emilio gives a key to the workers who set the instruments up.
   To whom should he give the key Friday morning?

_____

5. E-mail messages are always sent to the workers who tune the
   guitars. To whom will they be sent on Friday?

_____

Name _____

Using Correct Pronouns

Letty and her friends belong to a music club at school. One day they were having a discussion about their favorite Latin CDs. Read the paragraph to find out which of Gloria Estefan's albums they like best. You will have to choose and write in the correct pronouns in the sentences, so read carefully.

Letty said that (her, she) _____ likes Gloria Estefan's songs and knows (they, them) _____ all by heart. Ricardo thinks the Miami Sound Machine is one of the best bands that (he, him) _____ has ever heard. Alicia says that even the group's earliest hits are favorites with (she, her) _____. Alicia likes "Dr. Beat" because (they, it) _____ has a Latin style but is in English. Letty has two favorite songs, and (they, them) _____ are in English too. Letty says that *Eyes of Innocence* is special for (she, her) _____. (We, Us) _____ all like Jonathan's collection because (he, him) _____ has a lot of Latin albums. Jonathan met Gloria at a concert and told (we, us) _____ about the performance.

Problem/Solution Paragraph

Use this graphic organizer to plan your problem-solution paragraph. Write about a problem you faced at school or at home, or about a problem you might face in the future. Tell about the pros and cons of possible solutions. Then tell what solution you decided on.

Topic Sentence/Problem Statement:

_____

_____

Possible Solution 1:

_____

_____

_____

Pros: _____

_____

_____

Cons: _____

_____

_____

Possible Solution 2:

_____

_____

_____

Pros: _____

_____

_____

Cons: _____

_____

_____

Concluding Sentence/Problem Solution Statement:

_____

_____

Name _____

Combining with Pronouns

Writers avoid repeating the same noun over and over by
replacing it with a pronoun.

Two sentences: The name of Emilio's band was **the Miami Latin Boys.**
                 The Miami Latin Boys soon changed the name.

One sentence: The name of Emilio's band was **the Miami Latin
                 Boys,** but **they** soon changed the name.

**Read each pair of sentences. Combine them by replacing a
noun with a pronoun in the second sentence. You may need
to add or delete some words from the sentences when you
combine them.**

1. Gloria got good grades in school.   Gloria made the honor roll.

   _____

   _____

2. The band played gigs on weekends.   School vacations gave the
   band a chance to play too.

   _____

   _____

3. Mrs. Fajardo was a kindergarten teacher in Cuba.   Mrs. Fajardo had to go
   back to school to get her American teaching degree.

   _____

   _____

4. Gloria's father had multiple sclerosis.   Gloria had to give Gloria's father
   constant care.

   _____

   _____

5. Gloria loved singing. Singing became her profession.

   _____

Name _____

Baseball Scramble

Unscramble the vocabulary words. Then unscramble the circled letters to solve the riddle.

Vocabulary

- consecutive
- fielding
- first baseman
- honor
- modest
- shortstop
- sportsmanship

SUTINECCOVE

__ __ __ __ ◯ __ ◯ __ __ __

Hint: means "following one right after the other"

ROHON ◯ __ __ __ __

Hint: means "to show special respect for"

SPOSTRANPIMSH

__ __ __ __ ◯ __ __ __ __ __ __ __

Hint: means "quality of someone who acts with dignity in difficult situations"

NEDILFIG __ __ __ ◯ __ __ __ __

Hint: means "to catch, stop, or pick up a baseball in play and throw it to the correct player"

SMOEDT __ __ __ ◯ __ __

Hint: means "having a quiet, humble view of oneself"

FRITS SEMBANA

__ __ __ __ __ ◯◯ __ __ __ __ __

Hint: means "the person who plays the position around first base"

SPOTTROSH __ ◯ __ ◯ __ __ __ __

Hint: means "the position in baseball between second and third bases"

What did the pitcher do?

__ __ __ __ __ w __ __ __ __ __ __ __ l __

Name _____

Fact and Opinion Chart

Statement	Fact or Opinion	How Can You Tell? Explain.
page 585 _____ _____	Fact	_____ _____
page 586 _____ _____	Fact	_____ _____
page 589 _____ _____	Opinion	_____ _____
page 590 _____ _____	Fact	_____ _____
page 594 _____ _____	Opinion	_____ _____
page 597 _____ _____	Opinion	_____ _____
page 598 _____ _____	Fact	_____ _____

Name _____

Lou Hits a Home Run

Start at home plate and round the bases. Add words to complete each sentence that tells about an important event in Lou Gehrig's life.

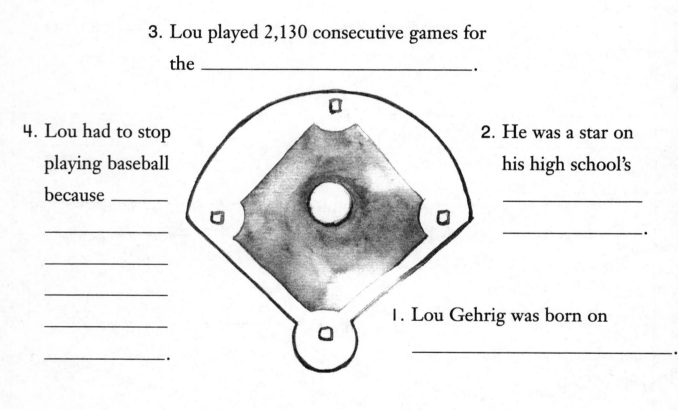

3. Lou played 2,130 consecutive games for

the _____.

4. Lou had to stop
playing baseball
because _____
_____
_____
_____
_____.

2. He was a star on
his high school's
_____
_____.

1. Lou Gehrig was born on
_____.

5. Lou was inducted into the _____

_____

in December 1939 and is remembered for

his _____

_____.

Check Your Facts

Read the story. Then complete the chart on the following page.

A Hero for All Seasons

Roberto Clemente is the greatest baseball player of all time. He had an incredible batting average—above .300 twelve out of the eighteen seasons he played. Having won four batting titles, twelve Gold Glove awards, and a Most Valuable Player award, he is certainly the best that ever played.

Besides being the best baseball player, Roberto Clemente was also a great man and a hero. In 1972, there was an earthquake in Nicaragua. On December 31 of that year, Clemente flew to Nicaragua to take supplies to the people. Almost immediately after takeoff, the plane crashed into the Caribbean Sea.

The best honors for Clemente came after he died. He was the first Latino voted into the Baseball Hall of Fame. In 1999, the city of Pittsburgh, where he played baseball, renamed a bridge after him—a bridge that leads to the city's beautiful new stadium.

No one summed up the life of Roberto Clemente as well as the baseball commissioner when, at Clemente's Hall of Fame award ceremony, he said, "He was so very great a man, as a leader and humanitarian, so very great an inspiration to the young and to all in baseball, especially to the proud people of his homeland, Puerto Rico." The commissioner further honored Clemente by creating a sportsmanship award in his name.

Name _____

Check Your Facts continued

Complete the chart below with facts and opinions from the story "A Hero for All Seasons."

Facts	Opinions
_____	_____
_____	_____
_____	_____
_____	_____
_____	_____
_____	_____
_____	_____
_____	_____
_____	_____
_____	_____
_____	_____
_____	
_____	
_____	
_____	
_____	

Name _____

Syllable Scores

As you read each sentence, pay careful attention to the underlined words. If the first vowel in a word has a long sound, circle the word. If the first vowel has a short sound, put a box around the word.

1. Lou Gehrig was a baseball player with amazing <u>talent</u>.

2. He was twice <u>chosen</u> as the American League's MVP.

3. Gehrig was a real <u>hero</u> because of the way he acted.

4. No matter how great he was, he was always a <u>modest</u> person.

5. When Gehrig stopped playing baseball, many people wanted to <u>honor</u> him.

6. It was only <u>proper</u> that Lou Gehrig know how people cared about him.

7. Thousands of fans wanted to say their <u>final</u> good-byes to Lou Gehrig.

8. No Yankee will ever again wear the number 4 on his <u>uniform</u>.

9. Lou Gehrig was <u>visibly</u> moved by the way the fans acted.

10. There will <u>never</u> be another baseball player quite like Lou Gehrig.

Count the number of words in boxes and enter the number in the box. Count the number of words in circles and enter the number in the circle below. Which team won?

	Hits	Runs
Home Team	10	☐
Visitors	7	○

Name _____

VCV Pattern

Divide a VCV word into syllables before the consonant if the first vowel sound is long or if the first syllable ends with a vowel sound. Divide a VCV word into syllables after the consonant if the first syllable has a short vowel sound followed by a consonant sound.

V|CV: **pi | lot**   VC|V: **vis | it**

Write each Spelling Word under the heading that tells where its syllables are divided.

V|CV

_____   _____

_____   _____

_____   _____

_____   _____

_____   _____

_____   _____

VC|V

_____   _____

_____   _____

Name _____

Spelling Spree

Hidden Words Write the Spelling Word that you find in each row of letters. Don't let the other words fool you!

Example: s k i o r a n g e p   *orange*

1. e a t u n a b i   _____
2. o r p r i s o n e t   _____
3. s t o p v i s i t r n   _____
4. p o s h u m a n d   _____
5. w o n e v e n t h   _____
6. i r k r e a s o n e   _____
7. b u s e v e n c e   _____
8. r i p a r e n t i c   _____
9. t o p e n i t h   _____
10. t i n e v e r e s   _____

Spelling Words

1. pilot
2. depend
3. visit
4. human
5. seven
6. chosen
7. paper
8. reason
9. become
10. parent
11. never
12. modern
13. tiny
14. tuna
15. event
16. fever
17. moment
18. prison
19. basic
20. open

Syllable Match Match the syllables at the top with the numbered syllables to write Spelling Words.

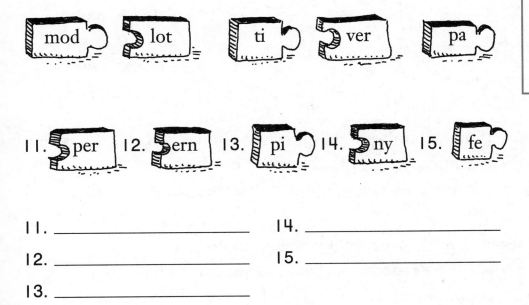

11. _____   14. _____
12. _____   15. _____
13. _____

Name _____

Proofreading and Writing

Proofreading Circle the five misspelled Spelling Words in these rules. Then write each word correctly.

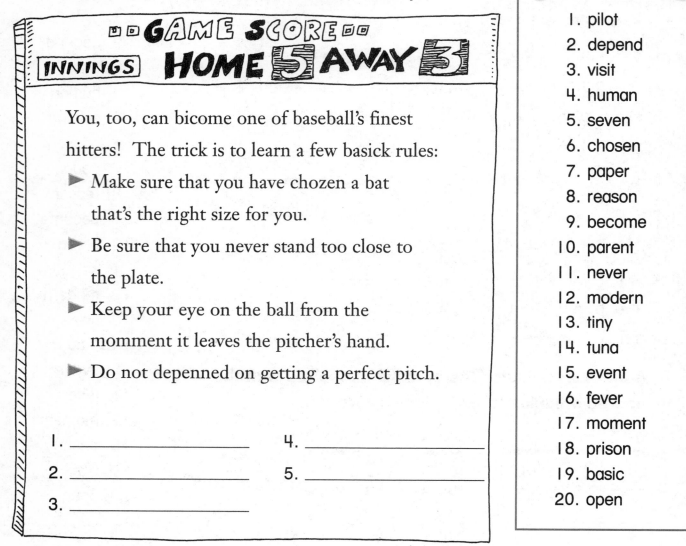

GAME SCORE

INNINGS **HOME 5 AWAY 3**

You, too, can bicome one of baseball's finest hitters! The trick is to learn a few basick rules:

► Make sure that you have chozen a bat that's the right size for you.

► Be sure that you never stand too close to the plate.

► Keep your eye on the ball from the momment it leaves the pitcher's hand.

► Do not depenned on getting a perfect pitch.

1. _____ 4. _____

2. _____ 5. _____

3. _____

Spelling Words

1. pilot
2. depend
3. visit
4. human
5. seven
6. chosen
7. paper
8. reason
9. become
10. parent
11. never
12. modern
13. tiny
14. tuna
15. event
16. fever
17. moment
18. prison
19. basic
20. open

━━━► **Write an Opinion** An **opinion** tells how you think or feel about something. For example, you might think that baseball is an exciting sport. On the other hand, you might feel that baseball is a slow, dull game.

On a separate piece of paper, write your opinion about a popular sport or game. Give reasons to back up your opinion. Use Spelling Words from the list.

Name _____

History of Base and Ball

Baseball is made up of two words, *base* and *ball*.

Read the sentences below. Write the number of the definition that shares the same word history as the underlined word or words.

base[1] *noun* **1.** The lowest part; bottom. **2.** A part used for support. **3.** The main part of something. **4.** One of the four corners of a baseball diamond. [Middle English, from Old French, from Latin *basis*, from Greek]

base[2] *adjective* **1.** Not honorable; shameful. **2.** Not of great value. [Middle English *bas*, low, from Old French, from Medieval Latin *bassus*]

ball[1] *noun* **1.** Something that is round. **2.** A round object used in a game or sport. **3.** A game, especially baseball, that is played with a ball. **4.** A baseball pitch that is not swung at by the batter and not thrown over home plate between the batter's knees and shoulders. [Middle English *bal*, probably from Old English *beall*]

ball[2] *noun* A formal social dance. [French *bal*, from Old French, from *baller*, to dance, from Late Latin *ballāre*, from Greek *ballizein*]

1. Our <u>basement</u> flooded during the storm.

   _____

2. The <u>base</u> word of hitter is hit. _____

3. She goes to <u>ballet</u> class every Saturday.

   _____

4. The <u>wedding</u> was held in a large ballroom.

   _____

5. Everyone in the <u>ballpark</u> cheered after the home run.

   _____

Name _____

Announcements with Possessives

Finish the baseball stadium announcer's greeting by completing the sentences with possessive pronouns.

Good afternoon, ladies and gentlemen. The Centerville Bombers are playing _____ fiftieth game of the season today. The players and the management hope you will enjoy _____ afternoon at the ballpark. We in the booth will do _____ best to make sure you do. Brenda Jones, the manager, has _____ work cut out for her. Larraine Gillespie at first base has hurt _____ foot. The center fielder and right fielder have misplaced _____ sunglasses. We hope they catch the fly balls out there. The pitcher thinks that the mitt she is using may not be _____. Carl Staub, the catcher, is now pulling on _____ face mask. We hope you have _____ scorecards ready. We have _____.

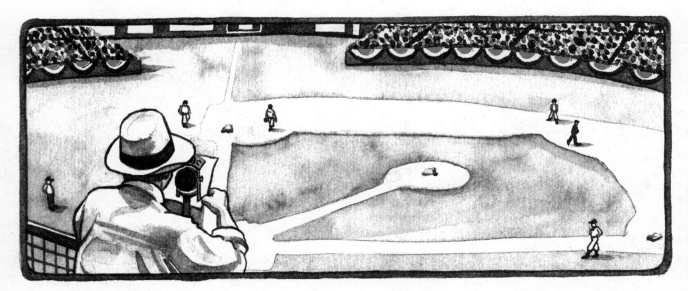

Name _____

Play Ball!

Here is a baseball game you can play. Fill in the missing possessive pronouns for the players in their positions on the field.

The center fielder knows the next job at bat will be _____ .

The left fielder is checking _____ mitt.

The second-base player moves to _____ left.

The first-base player looks at the pitcher and tosses the ball to _____ right.

The third-base player says the error was _____.

The pitcher thinks, "_____ arm is still good."

The manager tells a player, "You will get _____ time to bat."

The catcher and pitcher almost get _____ signals mixed.

Name _____

Watching Your *its* and *it's*

Good writers are careful to use the possessive pronoun *its* and the contraction *it's* correctly in sentences.

Read the paragraph below. On the blank lines, write either *its* or *it's*, depending on which is correct. Then rewrite the paragraph correctly on the lines provided.

_____ no secret that Lou Gehrig was one of the Yankees' best players. The team moved _____ home from Baltimore to New York in 1903. Some people say of 1903, "_____ a fateful year." _____ the same year in which Lou Gehrig was born. Even when he was younger, Lou was a talented player. _____ significant that playing on his high school baseball team, he was one of _____ stars. When Lou went to Columbia University, he was a good player on _____ baseball team, too. In one of the games there, a Yankee scout saw him play. _____ a fact of history that the Yankees signed him soon afterward.

_____

_____

_____

_____

_____

_____

_____

_____

Name _____

Planning a Magazine Article

Use this organizer to plan a magazine article about a sports hero or other person you admire.

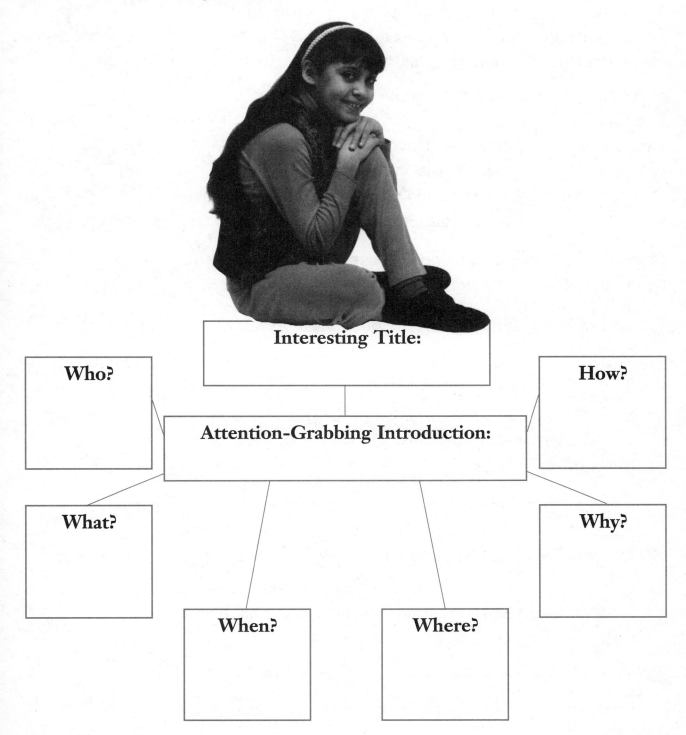

Interesting Title:

Who?

How?

Attention-Grabbing Introduction:

What?

Why?

When?

Where?

Name _____

Using Possessive Pronouns

Good writers combine sentences using possessive pronouns to improve their sentence.

► Writers use possessive pronouns to show ownership.

Singular Possessives: my, your, his, her, its

Plural Possessives: our, your, their

► Writers combine sentences using possessive pronouns to avoid repetition.

Two sentences: Doctors wanted to examine **Lou Gehrig**.
                 They ran tests on **Lou Gehrig's** condition.

One Sentence: Doctors wanted to examine **Lou Gehrig**, and they ran tests on **his** condition.

Combine the sentences using a possessive pronoun. You may need to delete or add words to combine the sentences.

1. Lou stayed with the Yankees. Lou's illness prevented him from playing.

   _____

   _____

2. Lou Gehrig spoke to the fans. He said, "Lou Gehrig's wife is a tower of strength."

   _____

   _____

3. Lou was losing weight. Lou's hair was turning gray.

   _____

4. Sixty thousand fans were in the stadium. Lou would never forget the fans' cheers.

   _____

   _____

Name _____

Writing an Answer to a Question

Use what you have learned about taking tests to help you write answers to questions about something you have read. This practice will help you when you take this kind of test.

Read these paragraphs from the selection *Happy Birthday, Dr. King!*

Grandpa Joe took a deep breath and began . . .

"A long time ago I was raising my family in Montgomery, Alabama. This is what used to happen when African Americans wanted to ride the city buses.

"First, we'd get on at the front of the bus, pay our fare, and get off. Then we'd get back on again at the rear of the bus. We didn't like it, but that's how things were. It was the law. Then one day, in 1955, a lady named Rosa Parks . . . "

"Rosa Parks," Jamal interrupted, "we read about her. She sat in the front of the bus and wouldn't give her seat to a white man, and she got arrested."

"But, Jamal, there is more to the story. When African Americans heard about her arrest, many of us stopped riding the buses. We wanted to protest her arrest and get the same rights that white people had. That was the Montgomery Bus Boycott. And the boycott worked. We finally won — without fighting."

Name _____

Writing an Answer to a Question continued

Now write your answer to each question.

1. Why was Rosa Parks arrested in 1955?

_____

_____

_____

_____

_____

2. Why did many African Americans stop riding the city buses when they heard that Rosa Parks had been arrested?

_____

_____

_____

_____

_____

3. What happened as a result of the Montgomery Bus Boycott?

_____

_____

_____

_____

_____

Name _____

Spelling Review

Write Spelling Words from the list on this page to answer the questions.

1–10. Which ten words have prefixes (*re-, dis-,* or *un-*) or suffixes (*-ment, -ful,* or *-less*)?

1. _____   6. _____

2. _____   7. _____

3. _____   8. _____

4. _____   9. _____

5. _____   10. _____

11–20. Which ten words have a base word that changes the final *y* to *i* when an ending is added?

11. _____   16. _____

12. _____   17. _____

13. _____   18. _____

14. _____   19. _____

15. _____   20. _____

21–30. Write the ten words with the VCV pattern that do not have prefixes, suffixes, or endings. Then draw a line between each syllable.

21. _____   26. _____

22. _____   27. _____

23. _____   28. _____

24. _____   29. _____

25. _____   30. _____

Spelling Words

1. parent
2. angriest
3. fever
4. powerful
5. visit
6. unsure
7. families
8. seven
9. crazier
10. displease
11. tuna
12. redo
13. kindness
14. cities
15. dislike
16. easier
17. never
18. paper
19. movement
20. reread
21. happiest
22. prison
23. become
24. peaceful
25. studied
26. reason
27. copied
28. earlier
29. useless
30. worried

Spelling Spree

Crossword Puzzle Write a Spelling Word in the puzzle
that means the same as each clue.

Spelling Words

1. movement
2. happiest
3. seven
4. earlier
5. dislike
6. cities
7. powerful
8. paper
9. tuna
10. prison
11. worried
12. angriest
13. peaceful
14. parent
15. studied

Across

1. not *warlike* but _____
3. I study now. You
   _____yesterday.
5. one, three, five, _____,
   nine
7. happy, happier, _____

Down

1. pencil and _____
2. towns and _____
4. the opposite of *like*
6. not *later* but
   _____

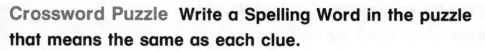

Context Clues Use a Spelling Word to finish each phrase.

9. not free but in _____

10. not carefree but _____

11. not the happiest but the
    _____

12. not weak but _____

13. not the child but the
    _____

14. not a salmon but a
    _____

15. not motionless but showing
    _____

Proofreading and Writing

Proofreading Circle the six misspelled Spelling Words in this essay. Then write each word correctly.

When we rereed stories about heroes, we find that they almost nevur attempt useles tasks. They often come from familys where honesty is important. Sometimes they are shown much kindnes by others. Sometimes they are unshur of themselves.

1. _____   4. _____

2. _____   5. _____

3. _____   6. _____

Description of a Hero Write Spelling Words to complete this description.

Every day Mrs. Mendez goes to 7. _____ a family nearby. The 8. _____ she does this is to help them. One day their baby had a high 9. _____. The parents kept getting 10. _____ with worry, but they didn't have a car. Mrs. Mendez took them to the doctor in her car, which was much 11. _____ and faster than riding the bus. Some neighbors have 12. _____ Mrs. Mendez's idea and are helping others. I hope to 13. _____ a neighborhood hero like Mrs. Mendez! Her actions never 14. _____ anyone. First I will help my sister 15. _____ her homework.

✏️ **Write a Letter On a separate sheet of paper, write a letter to a friend about a hero you admire. Use the Spelling Review Words.**

Spelling Words

1. redo
2. reread
3. unsure
4. useless
5. displease
6. kindness
7. easier
8. families
9. copied
10. crazier
11. visit
12. reason
13. become
14. never
15. fever

Name _____

Talking About Tales

Compare and contrast two of the pourquoi tales you just read by completing the chart below.

	Story #1 _____ (title)	Story #2 _____ (title)
How are the characters the same and different?		
How is the problem and solution the same and different?		
How is the language the same and different?		

Now tell which pourquoi tale is your favorite and why.

_____

_____

_____

_____

Name _____

Believe It or Not!

You are a news reporter for a local television station. Your program is called "Believe It or Not!" You have just found a very large turtle sleeping in the mud during winter. How will you explain it to your viewers? Tell them a pourquoi tale.

Write your notes below. Also, write questions you could ask the people — and animals — on the scene.

Name _____

Nature: Friend and Foe

How can nature be a friend? How can it be a foe?

Complete the word webs with words and phrases that describe spiders and thunderstorms, both as friends and as foes.

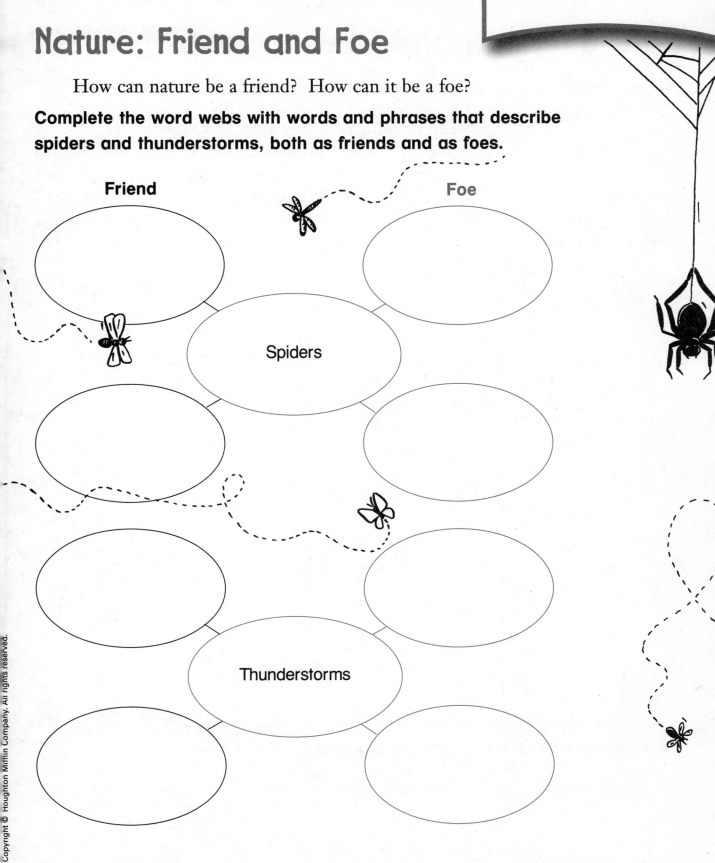

Friend

Foe

Spiders

Thunderstorms

Name _____

Nature: Friend and Foe

	Is nature shown as a friend or a foe? Explain.	What do you think this selection says about people's relationship with nature?
Salmon Summer		
Wildfires		
Skylark		

Tell how one selection changed the way you think of nature.

_____

_____

Name _____

Word Riddle

Write a word from the box that answers the riddle.

1. What do you call relatives from whom you have descended? _____

2. What do you call it when fish lay eggs and reproduce in a river? _____

3. What do you call a plentiful supply of something?

   _____

4. I am the fake bait that fishermen use to attract fish. What am I?

   _____

5. I'm the name for animals that feed on dead plants and animals. What am I?

   _____

Vocabulary

abundance
ancestors
lure
scavengers
spawn

Write a sentence using two words from the box.

_____

_____

Name _____

Directions Flow Chart

	Catching and Preparing Salmon to Eat	Hooking Halibut and Making Tamuuq
Materials Needed		
Steps	▽ ▽ ▽ separate fish ▽ ▽ ▽ hang outside ▽ ▽ ▽ The salmon is ready to eat.	▽ ▽ hang line overboard ▽ ▽ ▽ hold on and pull line in ▽ ▽ ▽ The tamuuq is ready to eat.

Name _____

Nothing But the Truth

Mark *T* if the statement is true and *F* if it is false. If the statement is false, rewrite it on a separate sheet of paper to make a true statement.

Statement	True or False?
1. Alex's favorite snack is smoked salmon.	1. _____
2. When he cleans fish for the smokehouse, Alex leaves the tails and skin on.	2. _____
3. Magpies and gulls are scavengers that eat fish scraps.	3. _____
4. Alex hangs smoked salmon in a closet to cure.	4. _____
5. Alex baits lobster traps with small salmon.	5. _____
6. When a crab is too big to keep, Alex throws it back.	6. _____
7. Alex fishes with a line and a silver lure.	7. _____
8. The fish head downstream to mate.	8. _____
9. To catch a halibut, Alex baits his hook with a salmon.	9. _____
10. To make tamuuq takes about ten hours.	10. _____

Name _____

Following Tradition

Read the story below and then answer the questions on the following page.

Thanksgiving with the Muslovs

It was the night before Thanksgiving and in the Muslov family that meant it was time to prepare the salmon. It was the way they had always celebrated, and this year was special for Leonin — he was finally old enough to help prepare the fish.

"Leo," his father called from the kitchen. "Go get the recipe box, will you?" Leonin got up from the living room floor where he was reading and quickly brought the recipe box into the kitchen. "Thank you, Leo. You ready? Okay. Read me the instructions, please."

"It says we need two to three pounds of salmon filets," Leo said carefully. "We need to place the salmon in a mixture of water, salt, sugar, garlic, and dill. The filets need to be coated with the mixture and then covered with plastic wrap. Then it says to leave them in the refrigerator overnight." Leo paused for a moment. "But Dad, we don't have any filets."

"You're right, but we do have whole salmon in the refrigerator. Your job is to cut off their heads and tails and pull out their insides. Then you have to carefully remove their bones so you're left with the biggest, most tender piece of meat. That's the filet."

It was at that moment that Leonin began to wonder why he had been so excited to help.

Name _____

Following Tradition continued

Complete the chart below and answer the questions based on "Thanksgiving with the Muslovs."

What ingredients and materials do you need?

What are the step-by-step directions for preparing the salmon?

_____

_____

_____

_____

_____

_____

_____

Why do you think the salmon is supposed to be left in the mixture overnight? What do you think would happen if it wasn't?

_____

_____

_____

Theme 6: **Nature: Friend and Foe**   353

Name _____

Seaworthy Syllables

Read this description of a well-known sea animal. Write the number below each underlined word next to the word's definition. Use a dictionary if you need help. Then use the clues in the description to identify the sea animal.

This animal may <u>inhabit</u> shallow parts of the ocean or live in deep
1
waters. It got its name because of the eight long arms sticking out of its
head. The <u>underside</u> of each arm has <u>powerful</u> sucker. These suckers
2$$3
can provide <u>enormous</u> suction to help the animal attach itself to rocks.
4
This sea creature has two eyes, one on each side of its head. These
eyes are <u>similar to</u> the eyes of human beings. This animal has many
5
enemies, including whales, seals, and even certain fish. To protect
itself against these <u>predators</u>, this animal hides itself by <u>discharging</u>
6$$7
a cloud of inky fluid. It may also escape by <u>rapidly</u> changing its
8
color to scare an enemy or blend with its surroundings.

_____ very large _____ quickly

_____ releasing _____ like

_____ live in _____ having great strength

_____ enemies _____ surface underneath

The name of this sea animal is: _____.

Name _____

Three-Syllable Words

To spell a three-syllable word, divide the word into syllables. Remember to look for familiar spelling patterns. Pay attention to the spelling of the unstressed syllables. Spell the word by syllables.

yes | ter | day   /yĕs′ tər dā/   **de | liv | er**   /dĭ lĭv′ ər/

Write each Spelling Word under the heading that tells which syllable is stressed.

First Syllable Stressed

_____
_____
_____
_____
_____
_____
_____
_____

Second Syllable Stressed

_____
_____
_____
_____
_____
_____

Spelling Words

1. deliver
2. favorite
3. camera
4. yesterday
5. tomorrow
6. important
7. together
8. victory
9. remember
10. library
11. enemy
12. animal
13. another
14. however
15. banana
16. alphabet
17. hospital
18. hamburger
19. carpenter
20. several

Theme 6: **Nature: Friend and Foe**   355

Spelling Spree

Questions Write a Spelling Word to answer each
question.

1. Which word names a fruit?
2. Who builds things?
3. What do you call a living organism that is not a plant?
4. What word names more than one?
5. What tastes great with ketchup?
6. Where do you go when you need an operation?
7. Where is the quietest place in town?
8. What do you need to make any word?
9. What day came just before today?
10. What word is the opposite of *friend*?

1. _____
2. _____
3. _____
4. _____
5. _____
6. _____
7. _____
8. _____
9. _____
10. _____

Word Search Write the Spelling Word
that is hidden in each sentence.

Example: The troop leaders always
r<u>un happy</u> meetings. *unhappy*

11. Are membership forms available for the
Girl Scouts?
12. I'd like to show everyone this video.
13. My mother made liver and bacon for dinner.
14. Which team was the victor yesterday?
15. The fire truck came racing down the street.

11. _____
12. _____
13. _____
14. _____
15. _____

Name _____

Proofreading and Writing

Proofreading Circle the five misspelled Spelling Words in this part of an e-mail message. Then write each word correctly.

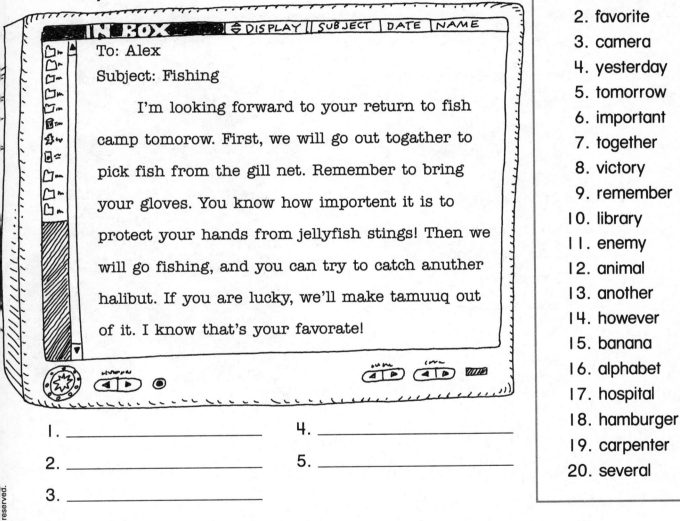

IN BOX | ⇕DISPLAY | SUBJECT | DATE | NAME

To: Alex

Subject: Fishing

I'm looking forward to your return to fish camp tomorow. First, we will go out togather to pick fish from the gill net. Remember to bring your gloves. You know how importent it is to protect your hands from jellyfish stings! Then we will go fishing, and you can try to catch anuther halibut. If you are lucky, we'll make tamuuq out of it. I know that's your favorate!

1. _____ 4. _____

2. _____ 5. _____

3. _____

Spelling Words

1. deliver
2. favorite
3. camera
4. yesterday
5. tomorrow
6. important
7. together
8. victory
9. remember
10. library
11. enemy
12. animal
13. another
14. however
15. banana
16. alphabet
17. hospital
18. hamburger
19. carpenter
20. several

Write Animal Facts Alex knew a lot about salmon. He could recognize the different kinds, and he knew about the life cycle of the salmon. What animal do you know facts about?

On a separate sheet of paper, write a paragraph of information about an animal that you find interesting. Make sure to tell why you find this animal interesting. Use Spelling Words from the list.

Name _____

Sensible Meanings

As you read each sentence, think about the meaning of the underlined word. Then find the numbered meaning in the box. Print that number on the line by the sentence.

> 1. Water mammal
> 2. To close tightly
> 3. To go separate ways
> 4. A role
> 5. To be in flight
> 6. Two-winged insect
> 7. To pay out money
> 8. To pass time

1. The family will <u>fly</u> from California to Alaska. ____

2. The <u>seal</u> dove into the water and caught a fish. ____

3. We always <u>spend</u> the summer at the beach. ____

4. Henry and Lou were such good friends that they hated to <u>part</u>. ____

5. Toby licked the envelope to <u>seal</u> it. ____

6. He got the <u>part</u> of the detective because of his fine acting. ____

7. Every time we open the door, another <u>fly</u> comes in. ____

8. Don't <u>spend</u> all your allowance at once. ____

Name _____

Riddles with Adverbs

**Read these riddles about the animals on Kodiak Island.
Underline the adverb in each riddle. On the line, write the
animal that the riddle is about.**

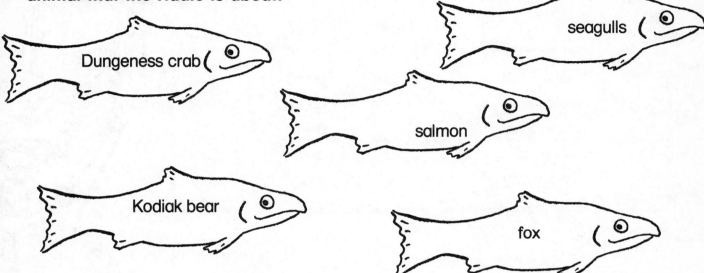

Dungeness crab

seagulls

salmon

Kodiak bear

fox

1. These animals swim alone into the river to catch their fish.

   _____

2. These fish swim upstream to spawn and die.

   _____

3. These birds swoop down to catch fish scraps.

   _____

4. This animal looks watchfully for food for her young pups.

   _____

5. This animal crawls backward on the sea bottom.

   _____

**On a separate sheet of paper, write two riddles of your own
about other things in the story. Use an adverb in each and
underline it. Draw a clue for each riddle.**

Name _____

Adverbs and Kodiak Island

The Fremson family members are taking a trip to Kodiak Island. Complete the sentences by writing adverbs that tell how, when, or where. The word in parentheses tells you what kind of adverb to use.

cheerfully	early
close	happily
curiously	quickly
outside	slowly
suddenly	soon

1. We leave _____ in the morning. (when)

2. Mother and Father put their coats on

   _____. (how)

3. _____, a taxi arrives. (how)

4. The family goes _____. (where)

5. The Fremsons _____ wave goodbye

   to their neighbors. (how)

6. The taxi moves _____ down the street.

   (how)

7. Brenda _____ sings a song. (how)

8. Marcus studies the map _____. (how)

9. _____ the taxi arrives at the airport.

   (when)

10. The taxi stops _____ to the entrance.

    (where)

Name _____

Writing with Adverbs

Adverbs add specific details to your sentences and make them more interesting.

Read the sentences, and then choose an adverb from the list below to expand each sentence. Write your sentences on the lines.

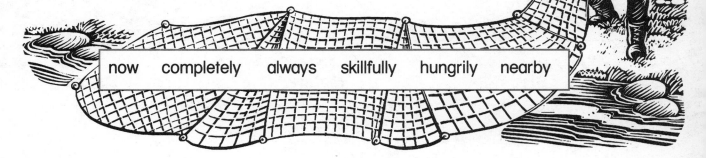

| now | completely | always | skillfully | hungrily | nearby |

1. Alex and his father fish in the neighborhood stream. (where)

   _____

2. At age nine, the boy can help his father fish with a net. (when)

   _____

3. The boy picks fish from the net. (how)

   _____

4. Alex wears gloves to protect his hands. (when)

   _____

5. Alex cuts the fish and hangs them up to dry. (how)

   _____

6. Alex and his brother Larry eat the smoked salmon. (how)

   _____

On another sheet of paper, write two of your own sentences about Alex. Use at least one adverb in each sentence. Underline the adverb.

Name _____

How-to Paragraph Planner

You can use this graphic organizer to help plan your how-to
paragraph. Then write an interesting topic sentence and
a closer that sums up the directions.

| Topic: How to _____ |||
Steps	Materials	Details

Topic Sentence:
_____
_____
Closing Sentence:
_____
_____

Name _____

Order Words and Phrases

Good writers use order words and phrases to tell the
sequence of steps and make instructions easy to follow.

Order words and phrases include **first, second, next, during,
while, now, then, later, after that, the next step,** and **finally.**

**Read each how-to paragraph. Rewrite the paragraph,
adding order words or phrases.**

1. Making an apple and peanut butter sandwich is easy. All you
   need is an apple, a knife, and a jar of peanut butter. You slice the
   apple into thin wedges. You spread every other apple slice with
   peanut butter. You put one clean slice and one peanut butter slice
   together to make a sandwich.

   _____

   _____

   _____

   _____

   _____

2. Eli makes his own trail mix. He needs a large plastic container,
   raisins, peanuts, chocolate chips, and half a dried apple. He puts
   the raisins, peanuts, and chocolate chips into the container. He
   cuts up the dried apple into small pieces. He adds the apple pieces
   to the mix. He puts the lid on the container and shakes it up.

   _____

   _____

   _____

   _____

   _____

   _____

Name _____

Revising Your Report

Reread your research report. How can you make it better? Use this page to help you decide. Put a checkmark in the box for each sentence that describes your research report.

Rings the Bell!

- [ ] I chose an interesting topic to research.
- [ ] I used an outline to help plan my report.
- [ ] I used reliable sources to find information on the topic.
- [ ] I took careful notes and used them to write my report.
- [ ] My paragraphs contain topic sentences and supporting facts.
- [ ] I used adverbs correctly.
- [ ] There are very few mistakes.

Getting Stronger

- [ ] I could make the topic sound more interesting to the reader.
- [ ] More sources might help me make sure I have the facts right.
- [ ] I need to follow my notes more closely.
- [ ] Some of my pronoun references are unclear.
- [ ] There are quite a few errors that need to be fixed.

Try Harder

- [ ] My topic isn't very interesting.
- [ ] I didn't use enough sources to find my facts.
- [ ] I didn't take careful notes on what I found out.
- [ ] Too many mistakes make the report hard to read.

Name _____

Using Adverbs Correctly

Underline the adverb that correctly completes each sentence.

1. I love watching (quiet/quietly) as rain comes down outside.

2. I like to hear the thunder boom (loud/loudly).

3. My cat, Molly, moves (careful/carefully) across the room.

4. The thunder is (real/really) loud.

5. Molly slinks (slow/slowly) under the couch.

6. The lightning flashes (bright/brightly) in the sky.

7. The room lights up (total/totally).

8. Molly meows (sad/sadly) from under the couch.

9. I reach under the couch to pet her (gentle/gently).

10. She hisses (anger, angrily), thinking I'm the
    thunder coming to get her.

Theme 6: **Nature: Friend and Foe**   365

Name _____

Spelling Words

Most of the Spelling Words on the list are homophones. Homophones are words that sound alike but have different meanings and spellings. When you write a homophone, be sure to spell the word that has the meaning you want.

Write the missing letters and apostrophes in the Spelling Words below.

1. their
2. there
3. they're
4. your
5. you're
6. its
7. it's
8. to
9. too
10. two
11. they
12. than
13. then
14. right
15. write

1. th ___ ___ r
2. th ___ r ___
3. th ___ ___ ___ ___ ___
4. y ___ ___ ___
5. you ___ ___ ___
6. it ___
7. it ___ ___
8. t ___

9. t ___ ___
10. t ___ ___
11. th ___ ___
12. th ___ n
13. th ___ n
14. r ___ ___ ___ ___
15. ___ rite

Study List On a separate sheet of paper, write each Spelling Word. Check your spelling against the words on the list.

Name _____

Spelling Spree

Homophone Blanks The blanks in each of the following sentences can be filled with homophones from the Spelling Word list. Write the words in the correct order.

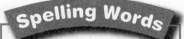
Spelling Words

1-3. It's _____ o'clock now, so it's probably
   1

   _____ late _____ go out for lunch.
      2   3

4-5. So _____ telling me that's not _____ car?
         4   5

6-7. I heard _____ unusual to see a snake during the
              6

   time it sheds _____ skin.
                  7

8-9. When you address the letter, be sure to _____
                                              8

   the _____ zip code.
        9

1. their
2. there
3. they're
4. your
5. you're
6. its
7. it's
8. to
9. too
10. two
11. they
12. than
13. then
14. right
15. write

Th- Clues Use the clues to write these *th-* Spelling Words.

10. If someone asks you the question "where?" you can use this word to answer.

11. This word is used to compare (more _____, less _____).

12. This contraction can be used to tell what others are doing.

13. This is a word for something that belongs to others.

14. This is a word you can use to talk about a group of people.

15. This word can be used to put a story in the right order.

10. _____   13. _____

11. _____   14. _____

12. _____   15. _____

Theme 6: **Nature: Friend and Foe**   367

Reading-Writing
Workshop

Frequently Misspelled Words

Proofreading and Writing

Proofreading Circle the five misspelled words in this storm warning. Then write each word correctly.

Spelling Words

1. their
2. there
3. they're
4. your
5. you're
6. its
7. it's
8. to
9. too
10. two
11. they
12. than
13. then
14. right
15. write

The National Weather Service has issued a tornado warning for our viewing area. So far, too tornadoes have already touched down, and they're saying that more could hit before this storm passes. If you are out in you're car, try to find shelter as quickly as you can. Get off the road right now even if the sky looks okay to you—better to be safe then sorry. Do the rite thing and go somewhere safe. We'll keep you posted on this storm until its over.

_____

_____

_____

_____

_____

✏ **Write a Poem** On a separate piece of paper, write a short poem about nature in its role of friend, foe, or both. Use Spelling Words from the list.

Name _____

Fire Words

Choose the meaning that best fits the underlined vocabulary word as it is used in the sentence. Write the letter of your answer on the line.

1. Forest fires seem to occur in <u>cycles</u>. _____
   A. hilly areas   C. repeating periods of time
   B. circles   D. dry areas

2. If that liquid is <u>flammable</u>, keep it away from the fire. _____
   A. able to be set on fire   C. hot
   B. excitable   D. oily and thick

3. The burning <u>ember</u> perhaps caused the fire. _____
   A. yellow rock   C. red rock
       found on a beach
   B. piece of glowing   D. fountain
       wood or coal

4. The firefighters fought the blaze <u>aggressively</u> and bravely. _____
   A. from the air   C. in great fear
   B. forcefully   D. with axes and knives

5. The fire <u>consumed</u> almost all the trees and bushes in the area. _____
   A. blew down   C. protected
   B. held in   D. burned up

6. Some of the trees were <u>charred</u> but not burned completely. _____
   A. burned slightly   C. reduced to ashes
   B. scratched   D. dry

7. Eventually the tops of the trees were <u>ablaze</u>. _____
   A. bright green and in bloom   C. falling to earth
   B. in flames   D. saved from fire

8. After a fire, plant life will soon <u>renew</u> itself. _____
   A. relax   C. bring new life to
   B destroy   D. take away some of

Name _____

Topic, Main Idea, and Supporting Details Chart

Topic: _____

page 662 Main Idea _____ **Supporting Details** _____ _____ _____	**page 664 Main Idea** _____ _____ **Supporting Details** _____ Most animals flee from fires. _____ _____
page 672 Main Idea Wildfires are good for bugs and animals. **Supporting Details** _____ _____ _____ _____	**page 674 Main Idea** _____ _____ **Supporting Details** _____ _____ Small animals run away or hide. _____

370   Theme 6: **Nature: Friend and Foe**

Name _____

A Fire Gone Wild

Complete each sentence with information from the selection _Wildfires_.

1. The selection mainly deals with the hot, dry summer
   of _____.

2. On June 23, a _____ started
   a fire in Yellowstone National Park.

3. Officials previously had allowed such fires to burn themselves
   out unless _____.

4. Officials changed their mind when more fires
   _____.

5. Hundreds of _____ were sent to
   battle and stop the fires.

6. On August 19, the wind blew _____
   a mile away and started new fires.

7. August 20, known as _____, saw
   an area more than twice the size of Chicago burning.

8. _____, not humans, saved the day
   and finally ended the fires.

9. Yellowstone could now start the process of
   _____.

10. New _____ began
    to appear and thrive in the charred woods.

Name _____

What's the Big Idea?

Read the story. Then complete the chart about the topic, main idea, and supporting details on the following page.

Bye-Bye Beaches?

Along both coasts of America, land is being eroded away by the nonstop crashing of ocean waves. During big storms, especially hurricanes, there are pictures on newscasts and in newspapers showing large chunks of earth falling and sliding into the sea. Houses are seen collapsing into the ocean. It's a frightening sight, yet people continue to build homes on the water's edge.

What should these people do about the problem of erosion? Should they build walls to keep the water away? Should they pile up sand into huge mounds that look like dunes? Should they build their homes up high on stilts?

Of course, a problem is who should pay to help keep the water from damaging the land. Many people who own homes on the water believe that the government should pay since it owns much of the coastline. Others believe it is the homeowners' problem, so they should fix it. Some people even want nothing done, believing the beaches should not have houses on them in the first place. They would be happy if all the houses were washed away.

Whatever side you stand on, our beaches need to be protected before they disappear.

Name _____

What's the Big Idea? continued

Complete the chart below about topic, main idea, and supporting details based on "Bye-Bye Beaches?" from the previous page.

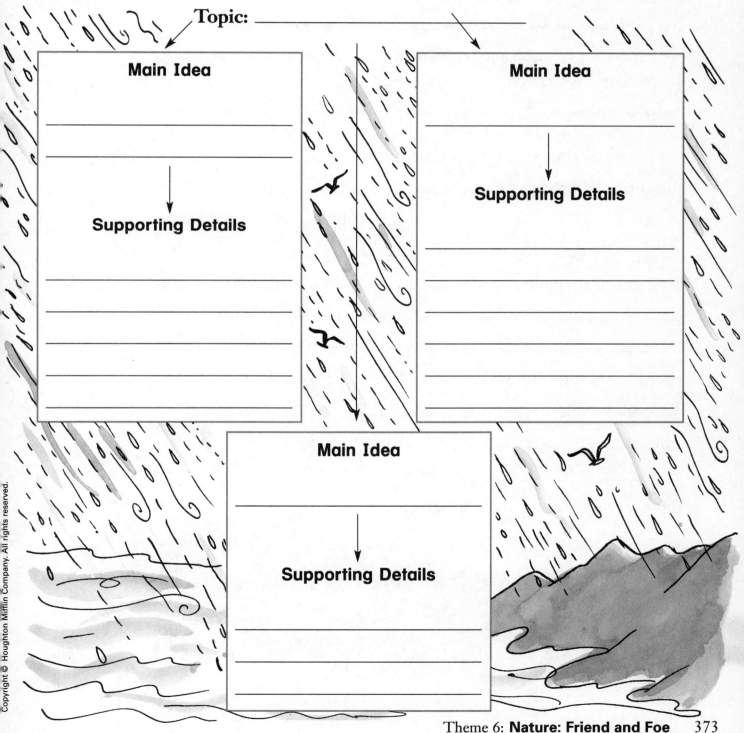

Topic: _____

Main Idea

_____

_____

↓

Supporting Details

_____

_____

_____

_____

Main Idea

_____

↓

Supporting Details

_____

_____

_____

Main Idea

_____

↓

Supporting Details

_____

_____

_____

Theme 6: **Nature: Friend and Foe** 373

Sleepy Suffixes

Use what you know about suffixes to help you complete this TV advertisement with words from the box. If you need help, use a dictionary.

hopeless	invention	loveliness	decision	sleepless
restless	action	happiness	darkness	solution

Are you tired of _____ nights spent tossing and turning in the _____? If so, we've got the _____ to your problem. With the Sleep-o-matic you'll never have another _____ night again! Plug in this marvelous _____ and end the _____ struggle to fall asleep. The _____ of a new morning will amaze you after a good night's rest. Instead of feeling tired all the time, your days will be filled with energy and _____! The _____ is easy. Take _____ now! Call 1-800-555-REST and order your new Sleep-o-matic today!

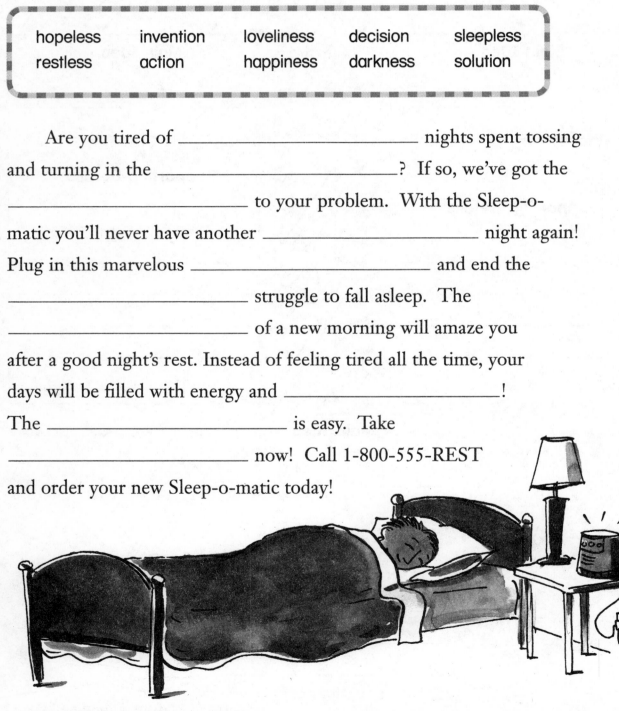

374   Theme 6: **Nature: Friend and Foe**

Name _____

Unusual Spellings

Some words have sounds with unusual spelling patterns. The spellings of these words have to be remembered.

Write the Spelling Words. Underline the unusual spelling patterns.

Spelling Words

1. health
2. blood
3. type
4. against
5. receive
6. flood
7. month
8. magazine
9. guess
10. women
11. guide
12. style
13. wealth
14. guilt
15. says
16. guard
17. wonder
18. guest
19. gasoline
20. neither

_____   _____

_____   _____

_____   _____

_____   _____

_____   _____

_____   _____

_____   _____

_____   _____

_____   _____

_____   _____

Name _____

Spelling Spree

Sentence Fillers **Write the Spelling Word that best completes each sentence.**

> **Example**: The naughty puppy chewed my left _____!
> *shoe*

1. Be my _____ and help yourself to the food.
2. If you can't find a book, read a _____.
3. The thief admitted his _____.
4. First came the rain, then came the _____.
5. I _____ what I'll be when I grow up.
6. The millionaire accumulated his _____ through hard work.
7. I _____ a letter from my pen pal every month.

1. _____   5. _____
2. _____   6. _____
3. _____   7. _____
4. _____

Words in Words **Write the Spelling Word in each word below.**

> **Example**: forehead   *head*

8. lifeguard _____
9. bloodshed _____
10. essays _____
11. bimonthly _____
12. guesswork _____
13. typewriter _____
14. freestyle

Spelling Words

1. health
2. blood
3. type
4. against
5. receive
6. flood
7. month
8. magazine
9. guess
10. women
11. guide
12. style
13. wealth
14. guilt
15. says
16. guard
17. wonder
18. guest
19. gasoline
20. neither

Name _____

Proofreading and Writing

Proofreading Circle the six misspelled Spelling Words in this notice. Then write each word correctly.

State Forestry Service Warning!

To gard against wildfires, tend your campfires carefully. Put out cooking fires completely, and bury the ashes. Remember, niether matches nor pocket lighters should be used carelessly. Never bring gasaline to a campsite! All men, wemen, and children must follow the rules of safe camping. Your helth and safety depend on it. Pick up our guid on the use of fire in the state forest at the nearest ranger station.

1. health
2. blood
3. type
4. against
5. receive
6. flood
7. month
8. magazine
9. guess
10. women
11. guide
12. style
13. wealth
14. guilt
15. says
16. guard
17. wonder
18. guest
19. gasoline
20. neither

1. _____   4. _____

2. _____   5. _____

3. _____   6. _____

Write a Safety Poster Everyone must be careful in the woods, for one's own safety and for the protection of the forest. Think of some safety rules or tips for hikers and campers.

On a separate piece of paper, write and decorate a poster about safety in the woods. Use Spelling Words from the list.

Name _____

How Are They Related?

Think about the relationship between the first two items in the analogies below. Write the word that best completes the analogy.

1. **Ankle** is to **wrist** as **knee** is to _____.
   toe   calf   elbow

2. **Right** is to **correct** as **wrong** is to _____.
   grade   incorrect   friend

3. **Seed** is to **sprout** as **child** is to _____.
   grow   play   eat

4. **Ash** is to **burning** as **water** is to _____.
   flame   melting   cold

5. **Pine** is to **tree** as daisy is to _____.
   flower   elm   rose

6. **Writer** is to **poem** as **painter** is to _____.
   paint   sculpture   picture

7. **Softball** is to **sports** as **jazz** is to _____.
   saxophone   music   country

8. **Hard** is to **soft** as **cruel** is to _____.
   friend   enemy   kind

9. **Baby** is to **adult** as **fawn** is to _____.
   deer   lion   pack

10. **Egg** is to **dozen** as **milk** is to _____.
    chocolate   gallon   cow

Name _____

Writing with Adverbs

Write the correct form of the adverb given in parentheses to complete each statement.

1. After a forest fire, young plants grow

   _____ of all. (quickly)

2. The Yellowstone National Park fire of 1988 burned some areas

   _____ than others. (completely)

3. Animals die in a forest fire _____

   than you might think. (rarely)

4. Some blazes spread _____ than a

   person can run. (fast)

5. Matches are the cause of fires _____

   than some other things. (frequently)

6. The _____ firefighters get to a fire,

   the sooner it can be controlled. (soon)

7. Fire spreads through the treetops

   _____ than it does on the ground.

   (easily)

8. In a fire, energy is released _____ as

   heat and light. (instantly)

9. Fires start from natural causes _____

   than from other causes. (often)

10. Big wildfires burn _____ of all when

    small fires are not allowed to burn. (intensely)

Name _____

Writing with Adverbs

Write the correct form of the adverb in parentheses to complete each statement.

1. After a fire, the owl finds food
   _____ in open areas. (easily)

2. The bison gets to eat new grass
   _____. (often)

3. The woodpecker finds insects _____
   of all in dead bark. (quickly)

4. The tree swallow can build a nest _____
   in a dead tree than in a live one. (rapidly)

5. The deer walks away from a burnout
   _____ than other animals. (soon)

6. The elk finds grass _____ to a fire
   than deer do. (close)

7. The fire beetle lays eggs _____ of all
   in burnt logs. (successfully)

8. The hawk can see food _____ of all
   after a fire. (clearly)

Name _____

Writing with Comparisons

Using *good* and *well* Good writers are careful to use
good and *well* correctly in their sentences.

**Fill in the blanks with either *good* or *well*. Then rewrite
each sentence correctly on the line below it.**

1. I hope everyone learns the lessons of wildfires _____.

   _____

2. Fire can sometimes be a _____ thing.

   _____

3. Scavengers eat _____ after a fire.

   _____

4. Birds eat many _____ meals of insects.

   _____

5. Rodents find _____ hiding places under rocks.

   _____

6. Other small animals do _____ in burrows.

   _____

7. Some pine cones open only as a result of a _____, hot fire.

   _____

8. It is _____ for them when fire burns away the resin.

   _____

9. Plants without diseases look _____ when checked.

   _____

10. Some of these photos of the fire of 1988 are very _____.

    _____

Learning Log Entry

Select three examples of your own writing. Write a paragraph commenting on your writing. Then fill in the Learning Log entry.

Learning Log

What I Learned:	My Goals:
_____	_____
_____	_____
_____	_____
_____	_____
_____	_____
_____	_____
_____	
_____	
_____	
_____	
_____	
_____	

Name _____

Elaborating with Adverbs

Good writers improve their sentences by using **adverbs** to tell more. Adverbs can describe verbs, by telling *how* or *when* an action occurs.

How	When
rapidly	always
quietly	sometimes
quickly	once
noisily	anytime
slowly	now
happily	then
dangerously	again

Complete the sentences by filling each blank with an adverb that answers the question in parentheses.

1. Wet wood burns _____ because water keeps air from reaching the fire. (how?)

2. _____, in 1988, fire and smoke in Yellowstone Park drove thousands of tourists away. (when?)

3. Gale-force winds can _____ drive burning embers to start new fires. (how?)

4. Nature adjusts _____ to changes, finding new life in a burnt forest. (how?)

5. New meadows grow _____ where once there was scorched earth. (when?)

Name _____

Prairie Scene

Choose the word from the vocabulary list that makes the most sense in the sentence. Write the word on the line provided.

1. Among the animals on the Great Plains, the _____ dog protects itself by burrowing in the ground.

2. When no rain falls for a long time, the land suffers from a _____.

3. Sometimes people get so hot in the summer they faint and _____ to the ground.

4. Horses on a farm often are kept from wandering by enclosing them in a _____.

5. At one time, the only way people could hear music that wasn't live was to play records on a _____.

6. A _____ is a kind of wolf that lives on the prairie.

Name _____

Inferences Chart

Page 690

Details About Anna	_____
	_____
	+
What I Know	_____
	_____
	=
Inference	_____

Page 692

Details About Papa's Feelings Toward Sarah	_____
	+
What I Know	_____
	_____
	=
Inference	_____

Page 700

Details About Sarah and Papa and the Fire	_____
	_____
	+
What I Know	_____
	_____
	=
Inference	_____

Name _____

The Reasons for Their Actions

Complete the chart below. Fill in the empty boxes to show who does what in *Skylark*, and why. Some boxes have been filled in for you.

Who	What They Do	Why?
page 690: Papa	gets his rifle	to shoot a coyote that is drinking from a bucket at the farm
page 692:	stops Papa from shooting	she feels sorry for the coyote, who only wants water, as the family does
pages 693–695: Papa, Anna, and Caleb		because it is her birthday, and they hope it will cheer her up
page 699: Matthew, Maggie, and their children	leave their farm	
page 699:	has a dream about her family playing in lots of water	because she is wishing very hard that the drought will end
page 700: Caleb	runs to get Moonbeam	
page 703: Sarah	shakes her head twice	
page 703:	plans to stay on the farm while the rest of the family goes to Maine	someone needs to take care of the animals and rebuild the farm.

Reading Between the Lines

**Read the story below. Then answer the questions about the
story on the following page.**

The Long Wait

Lucy came into the cottage in only her stocking feet. She had
left her boots and coat on the porch. She began to warm her hands
and feet by the fire when she noticed her brother, Seth, sitting at
the kitchen table with a wool blanket wrapped around him, peeling
small potatoes for supper.

Seth turned toward Lucy and asked, "How are Starlight and
the cows? Did they get enough food?"

"They're doing as well as can be expected," Lucy said. "Starlight's
having a bit of trouble breathing again, but she'll be fine."

"You worried about Mama and Pa yet?" Seth asked.

"Nah, not really. They'll be home soon. They only went into
town for a few supplies and the wagon ought to be working okay.
The snow isn't falling as hard anymore."

"I just hope they will be here soon," Seth said. "I don't like it
when our family is apart."

"I know what you mean, Seth. I know what you mean."

Name _____

Reading Between the Lines continued

Answer the following questions based on your reading of "The Long Wait."

How would you describe Lucy?

Details		**What You Know**
_____		_____
_____	+	_____
_____		_____
_____		_____
_____		_____

Inference
_____

How would you describe Seth?

Details		**What You Know**
_____		_____
_____	+	_____
_____		_____
_____		_____
_____		_____

Inference
_____

Name _____

Root Out the Roots

> *graph* means "to write, draw, or record"
> *tract* means "to draw or pull"

**Write the root *graph* or *tract* to complete each word.
Then write the word to complete each sentence.**

1. something that draws attention away:

   dis _____ ion

   The birthday party was a wonderful _____

   from the troubles caused by the drought.

2. pleasing, drawing attention: at _____ ive

   Papa looked _____ in his clean shirt and vest.

3. a written story of a person's life: bio _____ y

   Anna's gift was a _____ about Sarah's life.

4. a division of writing that contains sentences on a single idea:

   para _____

   Sarah read the first _____ aloud.

5. an image recorded by a camera: photo _____

   Anna wished she had a _____ of the party.

**Now write two sentences of your own. In one sentence,
use a word with the root *graph*. In the other, use a word
with the root *tract*.**

_____

_____

_____

Name _____

Silent Consonants

Some words have consonants that are not pronounced. These consonants are called "silent" consonants. The spellings of words with silent consonants have to be remembered.

kneel   clim**b**   cal**f**   **w**rinkle   **h**onest

Write each Spelling Word under the heading that shows its silent consonant.

1. knight
2. soften
3. honor
4. kneel
5. climb
6. wrinkle
7. limb
8. handsome
9. answer
10. calf
11. listen
12. calm
13. knit
14. often
15. palm
16. thumb
17. wrist
18. lamb
19. knob
20. honest

/n/ Spelled *kn*

_____
_____
_____
_____

/r/ Spelled *wr*

_____
_____

/ŏ/ Spelled *ho*

_____
_____

/m/ Spelled *mb*

_____
_____
_____
_____

Silent *l*

_____
_____
_____

Silent *t*

_____
_____
_____

Silent *d*

_____

Silent *w*

_____

Name _____

Spelling Spree

Opposites Write a Spelling Word that means the opposite of each word or group of words below.

Example: right   *wrong*

1. question   _____
2. excited   _____
3. harden   _____
4. rarely   _____
5. descend   _____
6. back of the hand _____
7. ugly   _____

Word Addition Write a Spelling Word by adding the beginning of the first word to the middle and end of the second word.

Example: top + walk   *talk*

8. know + slob
9. hope + finest
10. write + twinkle
11. knee + light
12. they + crumb
13. wrap + mist
14. list + comb
15. knot + wheel

Spelling Words

1. knight
2. soften
3. honor
4. kneel
5. climb
6. wrinkle
7. limb
8. handsome
9. answer
10. calf
11. listen
12. calm
13. knit
14. often
15. palm
16. thumb
17. wrist
18. lamb
19. knob
20. honest

8. _____   12. _____
9. _____   13. _____
10. _____   14. _____
11. _____   15. _____

Theme 6: **Nature: Friend and Foe**   391

Name _____

Proofreading and Writing

Proofreading **Circle the five misspelled Spelling Words in this journal entry. Then write each word correctly.**

May 9 — I love to lisen to the birds at dawn. Their songs are so happy. They make me hopeful that rain is on the way. As I lay in bed I thought about the new caff born last night. It's strong like its mother. I have the honer of owning not one but three baby animals! This spring a tiny lame was born to my sheep, and Star's colt gets friskier every day. He will be a handsome horse. I have to go now. Before I do my chores, Mother wants me to help her nit a sweater for our friend's baby.

1. _____

2. _____

3. _____

4. _____

5. _____

Spelling Words

1. knight
2. soften
3. honor
4. kneel
5. climb
6. wrinkle
7. limb
8. handsome
9. answer
10. calf
11. listen
12. calm
13. knit
14. often
15. palm
16. thumb
17. wrist
18. lamb
19. knob
20. honest

✏️ **Write a Weather Report** Prairie families were dependent on the weather for their livelihood. Too little rain would cause the crops to die, but too much rain could result in flash floods. Blizzards and tornadoes were also common on the prairies.

On a separate sheet of paper, write a weather report for a family living on the prairie in the 1800s. Be sure to include details that you think would be useful for a family back then to know. Use Spelling Words from the list.

Name _____

Nouns, Verbs, and Adjectives

Use each word below in a sentence. Make sure to use the word as the part of speech given.

1. stream (v.) _____

   _____

2. post (v.) _____

   _____

3. post (n.) _____

   _____

4. catch (n.) _____

   _____

5. fire (v.) _____

   _____

Read the sentences below. Tell the part of speech for the underlined word.

6. Sarah walked to the <u>window</u> to look out too. _____

7. Caleb's hair was brushed <u>smooth</u>. _____

8. We will <u>write</u> letters. _____

9. Sometimes it was hard to <u>adapt</u> to prairie life. _____

10. A thin <u>coyote</u> was drinking water out of the pail. _____

Name _____

Prepositions and Prepositional Phrases

Complete these directions to the farm by using prepositions from the list. You will use some words more than once.

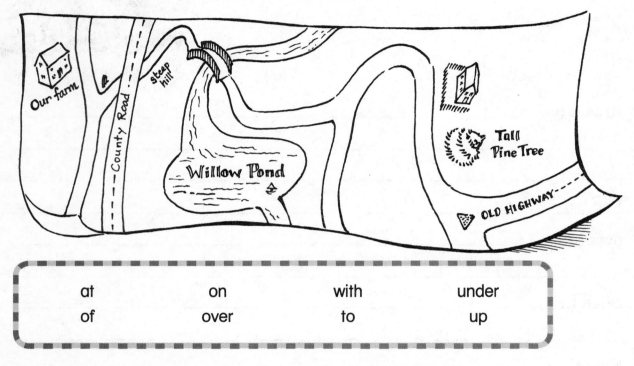

at	on	with	under
of	over	to	up

When you get _____ the Old Highway, turn right.

Soon you will see _____ your right a tree we call the Tall

Pine Tree. Next, you will see a house _____ a picket

fence. Then drive carefully _____ the curvy road until

you turn right again. When the road straightens, you will have a

lovely view _____ Willow Pond. The road turns right

and passes _____ a bridge and _____ a steep

hill. Next you will drive _____ the County Road. Turn

right immediately _____ the stop sign, and you will be

_____ our farm.

Name _____

Completing with Prepositions

**Read the sentences. Underline the prepositions in each
sentence. Then list each prepositional phrase on the lines
provided under each sentence.**

1. The horse paddock is across the driveway from the barn.

   _____

2. The chicken coop is near the vegetable garden.

   _____

3. The farmhouse is at the end of the driveway.

   _____

4. The barn is between the farmhouse and the horse paddock.

   _____

5. The vegetable garden is beside the farmhouse.

   _____

Name _____

Using Prepositions

Good writers use prepositional phrases to add specific details to their writing.

Read the paragraph below. Then rewrite it, adding prepositional phrases to the sentences on the lines provided. Use phrases from the list.

> on the phonograph   on the porch
> to the music   out her window
> down the stairs   to her
> in the yard   with a cloth
> of food and drinks

Wagons were pulling up _____. Sarah heard the noise outside and looked _____. Papa saw her running _____. A table had been set _____. It was full _____. Papa carried a large object covered _____. Sarah appeared _____. Everyone turned _____ and sang "Happy Birthday." Papa uncovered the large object. It was a phonograph! Then Anna handed Papa a record. He put a needle _____, and soon everyone was dancing _____.

Name _____

Planning a Speech

Use this graphic organizer to help you plan your speech. Write notes for a speech about something that happened to you or something you feel strongly about. Then write your speech on another sheet of paper.

Title: _____

Opening sentence: _____

_____

Event 1: _____

   details: _____

_____

_____

Event 2: _____

   details: _____

_____

_____

_____

Event 3: _____

   details: _____

_____

_____

_____

Concluding sentence: _____

Name _____

Prepositional Phrases

Good writers combine sentences to make their writing
smoother. Sometimes combining sentences with
prepositions helps avoid repetition.

Two sentences: Papa looked **up the stairs.**
Papa looked **at Sarah.**
One sentence: Papa looked **up the stairs at Sarah.**
Two sentences: Maggie liked the pink roses.
The roses were **on the dress.**
One sentence: Maggie liked the pink roses **on the dress.**

**Combine each set of sentences. You may need to
add, delete, or change words to combine
the sentences.**

1. Sarah and Papa danced. They danced on the lawn.

_____

2. They could not live without water. The water was in the well.

_____

3. Anna fell asleep. The time was about midnight.

_____

4. Sarah wiped the tears. The tears were from her eyes.

_____

5. The party was a great success. The party was for Sarah's
birthday.

_____

Name _____

Writing an Opinion Essay

Use what you have learned about taking tests to help you write an essay that tells your opinion about a topic. This practice will help you when you take this kind of test.

Fires can happen in all forests. In _Wildfires_, you read about the ways wildfires help the forest. Write an essay explaining why you think fire helps or hurts the forest.

_____

_____

_____

_____

_____

_____

_____

_____

_____

_____

_____

_____

_____

_____

_____

_____

_____

_____

_____

Name _____

Writing an Opinion Essay continued

Read your essay. Check to be sure that

► the opening introduces your topic in an interesting way

► each paragraph has a topic sentence that tells the main idea

► your reasons are strong and are supported with details

► your conclusion sums up the important points

► there are few mistakes in capitalization, punctuation, grammar, and spelling

Now pick one way to improve your essay. Make your changes below.

Name _____

Spelling Review

Write Spelling Words from the list on this page to answer the questions.

1–11. Which eleven words have three syllables?

1. _____   7. _____

2. _____   8. _____

3. _____   9. _____

4. _____   10. _____

5. _____   11. _____

6. _____

12–21. Which ten words have silent consonants?

12. _____   17. _____

13. _____   18. _____

14. _____   19. _____

15. _____   20. _____

16. _____   21. _____

22–30. Which nine remaining words have an unusual
       spelling of a short or long vowel sound or the
       consonant sound /g/?

22. _____   27. _____

23. _____   28. _____

24. _____   29. _____

25. _____   30. _____

26. _____

Spelling Words

1. listen
2. favorite
3. style
4. library
5. honor
6. deliver
7. knight
8. gasoline
9. alphabet
10. calf
11. however
12. climb
13. handsome
14. another
15. women
16. guard
17. banana
18. neither
19. kneel
20. soften
21. against
22. says
23. remember
24. blood
25. thumb
26. wrist
27. camera
28. health
29. animal
30. wonder

Name _____

Spelling Spree

Analogies Write a Spelling Word that completes each analogy.

1. **Dog** is to **puppy** as **cow** is to _____.

2. **Taste** is to **apple** as _____ is to **music**.

3. **Stand** is to **feet** as _____ is to **knees**.

4. **Electricity** is to **refrigerator** as _____ is to **automobile**.

5. **Pump** is to **water** as **heart** is to _____.

6. **Go** is to **come** as **forget** is to _____.

7. **Heard** is to **hears** as **said** is to

_____.

8. **Wade** is to **stream** as _____ is to **mountain**.

Phrase Filler Complete each phrase by writing a Spelling Word.

9. a furry little _____

10. my _____ color

11. to _____ why

12. an attractive hair _____

13. a _____ full of books

14. a _____ and film

15. _____ day of rain

Spelling Words

1. wonder
2. favorite
3. another
4. blood
5. remember
6. camera
7. says
8. calf
9. animal
10. listen
11. climb
12. gasoline
13. library
14. style
15. kneel

Name _____

Proofreading and Writing

Proofreading Circle the six misspelled Spelling Words in this scientist's log. Then write each word correctly.

September 12 Today Julia fell, sprained her rist, and hurt her thum. Then we saw three monkeys share a bannana. Nature can be both friend and foe. At night one of us is always on gard. When I keep watch, I lean agianst a tree. Luckily, niether wild nor tame beasts have bothered us.

Spelling Words

1. honor
2. deliver
3. knight
4. alphabet
5. however
6. handsome
7. women
8. guard
9. banana
10. neither
11. soften
12. against
13. thumb
14. wrist
15. health

1. _____   4. _____

2. _____   5. _____

3. _____   6. _____

Help the Announcer **Write Spelling Words in the blanks to complete this TV commercial.**

Attention men and 7. _____! Do us the 8. _____ of watching *Nature Knows*. See a wild and 9. _____ lion play and a huge elephant eat. Watch a baboon 10. _____ a gift to his girlfriend. Study an entire 11. _____ of animals from ape to zebra. Seeing cuddly tiger cubs will 12. _____ your views about fierce cats. All animals are important; 13. _____, many are in trouble. Their 14. _____ is endangered. Be a 15. _____ in shining armor and help save these animals. Watch our show to find out how.

7. _____   10. _____   13. _____

8. _____   11. _____   14. _____

9. _____   12. _____   15. _____

✏️ **Write a Description** **On a separate sheet of paper, describe a scientific trip you would like to take. Use Spelling Review Words.**

Student Handbook

Contents

How to Study a Word

1. LOOK at the word.
► What does the word mean?
► What letters are in the word?
► Name and touch each letter.

2. SAY the word.
► Listen for the consonant sounds.
► Listen for the vowel sounds.

3. THINK about the word.
► How is each sound spelled?
► Close your eyes and picture the word.
► What familiar spelling patterns do you see?
► Did you see any prefixes, suffixes, or other word parts?

4. WRITE the word.
► Think about the sounds and the letters.
► Form the letters correctly.

5. CHECK the spelling.
► Did you spell the word the same way it is spelled in your word list?
► If you did not spell the word correctly, write the word again.

again
all right
a lot
also
always
another
anyone
anything
anyway
around

beautiful
because
before
believe
brought
build
buy

cannot
can't
caught
choose
chose
clothes
coming
could
cousin

didn't
different
divide
don't

eighth
enough
every
everybody
everyone
excite

family
favorite
February
finally
first
friend

getting
girl
goes
going
guess

happened
haven't
heard
height
here

I'd
I'll
I'm
instead
into
its
it's

January

knew
know

let's
letter
little
loose
lose
lying

might
millimeter
minute
morning
myself

ninety

o'clock
off
once
other
our

people
pretty
probably

quit
quite

really
received
right

said
Saturday
school
someone
stopped
stretch
suppose
sure
swimming

than
that's
their
then
there
there's
they
they're
thought
through
to
tongue
tonight
too
tried
truly

two
tying

until
usually

very

weird
we're
where
while
whole
won't
world
would
wouldn't
write
writing

your
you're

Grandfather's Journey

The /ĭ/, /ī/, /ŏ/, /ō/ Sounds

/ĭ/ → st**i**ll
/ī/ → cr**ime**, fl**igh**t, gr**i**nd
/ŏ/ → sh**o**ck
/ō/ → wr**ote**, c**oa**st, sn**ow**, g**o**ld

Spelling Words

1. snow
2. grind
3. still
4. coast
5. odd
6. crime
7. gold
8. wrote
9. flight
10. build
11. broke
12. blind
13. folk
14. grown
15. shock
16. ripe
17. coal
18. inch
19. sigh
20. built

Challenge Words

1. remind
2. approach
3. rigid
4. recognize
5. continent

My Study List
Add your own spelling words on the back. ➡

Journeys
Reading-Writing Workshop

Look for familiar spelling patterns in these words to help you remember their spellings.

Spelling Words

1. cannot
2. can't
3. don't
4. haven't
5. won't
6. wouldn't
7. I'd
8. I'll
9. let's
10. we're
11. I'm
12. didn't
13. o'clock
14. that's
15. there's

Challenge Words

1. minute
2. stretch
3. instead
4. ninety
5. divide

My Study List
Add your own spelling words on the back. ➡

Akiak

The /ă/, /ā/, /ĕ/, and /ē/ Sounds

/ă/ → p**a**st
/ā/ → s**a**fe, g**ai**n, gr**ay**
/ĕ/ → k**e**pt
/ē/ → r**ea**ch, sw**ee**t

Spelling Words

1. gain
2. cream
3. sweet
4. safe
5. past
6. reach
7. kept
8. gray
9. field
10. break
11. east
12. shape
13. steep
14. pray
15. pain
16. glass
17. west
18. cheap
19. steak
20. chief

Challenge Words

1. graceful
2. descent
3. athletic
4. knead
5. activity

My Study List
Add your own spelling words on the back. ➡

Take-Home Word List

Name _____

My Study List

1. _____
2. _____
3. _____
4. _____
5. _____
6. _____
7. _____
8. _____
9. _____
10. _____

Review Words

1. need
2. last
3. stage
4. left
5. paint

How to Study a Word

Look at the word.
Say the word.
Think about the word.
Write the word.
Check the spelling.

Take-Home Word List

Name _____

My Study List

1. _____
2. _____
3. _____
4. _____
5. _____
6. _____
7. _____
8. _____
9. _____
10. _____

How to Study a Word

Look at the word.
Say the word.
Think about the word.
Write the word.
Check the spelling.

Take-Home Word List

Name _____

My Study List

1. _____
2. _____
3. _____
4. _____
5. _____
6. _____
7. _____
8. _____
9. _____
10. _____

Review Words

1. drop
2. mix
3. smoke
4. sight
5. know

How to Study a Word

Look at the word.
Say the word.
Think about the word.
Write the word.
Check the spelling.

Journeys
Spelling Review

Spelling Words

1. safe	16. few
2. kept	17. trunk
3. gray	18. steal
4. grown	19. weight
5. wrote	20. meat
6. blind	21. past
7. suit	22. reach
8. crumb	23. coast
9. wait	24. odd
10. creak	25. sigh
11. steep	26. true
12. gain	27. tube
13. still	28. steel
14. gold	29. creek
15. crime	30. meet

**See the back for
Challenge Words.**

My Study List
Add your own
spelling words
on the back. ➡

By the Shores of
Silver Lake

Homophones
Homophones are words
that sound alike but have
different spellings and
meanings.

Spelling Words

1. steel	11. beet
2. steal	12. beat
3. lead	13. meet
4. led	14. meat
5. wait	15. peek
6. weight	16. peak
7. wear	17. deer
8. ware	18. dear
9. creak	19. ring
10. creek	20. wring

Challenge Words

1. pour
2. pore
3. vain
4. vein
5. vane

My Study List
Add your own
spelling words
on the back. ➡

Finding the *Titanic*

**The /ŭ/, /yo͞o/, and
/o͞o/ Sounds**

/ŭ/	➡	br**u**sh
/yo͞o/	➡	t**u**be, f**ew**,
and /o͞o/		tr**ue**, j**ui**ce

Spelling Words

1. brush	11. suit
2. juice	12. pump
3. fruit	13. due
4. tube	14. dull
5. lunch	15. tune
6. crumb	16. blew
7. few	17. trunk
8. true	18. sum
9. truth	19. glue
10. done	20. threw

Challenge Words

1. newscast
2. commute
3. continue
4. attitude
5. slumber

My Study List
Add your own
spelling words
on the back. ➡

Name _____

My Study List

1. _____
2. _____
3. _____
4. _____
5. _____
6. _____
7. _____
8. _____
9. _____
10. _____

Review Words

1. chew
2. blue
3. rub
4. shut
5. June

How to Study a Word

Look at the word.
Say the word.
Think about the word.
Write the word.
Check the spelling.

412

Name _____

My Study List

1. _____
2. _____
3. _____
4. _____
5. _____
6. _____
7. _____
8. _____
9. _____
10. _____

Review Words

1. its
2. it's
3. there
4. their
5. they're

How to Study a Word

Look at the word.
Say the word.
Think about the word.
Write the word.
Check the spelling.

412

Name _____

My Study List

1. _____
2. _____
3. _____
4. _____
5. _____
6. _____
7. _____
8. _____
9. _____
10. _____

Challenge Words

1. descent
2. graceful
3. rigid
4. newscast
5. knead
6. remind
7. continue
8. pour
9. slumber
10. pore

How to Study a Word

Look at the word.
Say the word.
Think about the word.
Write the word.
Check the spelling.

412

Tanya's Reunion

The /ōō/ and /ŏŏ/ Sounds

/ōō/ ➡ t**oo**l
/ŏŏ/ ➡ w**oo**d, p**u**t

Spelling Words

1. wood
2. brook
3. tool
4. put
5. wool
6. push
7. full
8. roof
9. group
10. prove
11. stood
12. stool
13. hook
14. smooth
15. shoot
16. bush
17. fool
18. pull
19. soup
20. move

Challenge Words

1. soot
2. marooned
3. pudding
4. cocoon
5. superb

My Study List
Add your own spelling words on the back. ➡

American Stories
Reading-Writing Workshop

Look for familiar spelling patterns in these words to help you remember their spellings.

Spelling Words

1. a lot
2. other
3. another
4. anyone
5. every
6. someone
7. myself
8. family
9. friend
10. people
11. again
12. anything
13. anyway
14. everyone
15. first

Challenge Words

1. beautiful
2. clothes
3. cousin
4. everybody
5. weird

My Study List
Add your own spelling words on the back. ➡

Tomás and the
Library Lady

The /ou/ and /ô/ Sounds

/ou/ ➡ h**ow**l, p**ou**nd
/ô/ ➡ j**aw**, c**au**se, **al**ways

Spelling Words

1. pound
2. howl
3. jaw
4. bounce
5. cause
6. always
7. shout
8. aloud
9. south
10. couple
11. drawn
12. scout
13. false
14. proud
15. frown
16. sauce
17. gown
18. couch
19. dawn
20. mount

Challenge Words

1. gnaw
2. prowl
3. pounce
4. doubt
5. scrawny

My Study List
Add your own spelling words on the back. ➡

Name _____

My Study List

1. _____
2. _____
3. _____
4. _____
5. _____
6. _____
7. _____
8. _____
9. _____
10. _____

Review Words

1. walk
2. lawn
3. loud
4. sound
5. clown

How to Study a Word

Look at the word.
Say the word.
Think about the word.
Write the word.
Check the spelling.

Name _____

My Study List

1. _____
2. _____
3. _____
4. _____
5. _____
6. _____
7. _____
8. _____
9. _____
10. _____

How to Study a Word

Look at the word.
Say the word.
Think about the word.
Write the word.
Check the spelling.

Name _____

My Study List

1. _____
2. _____
3. _____
4. _____
5. _____
6. _____
7. _____
8. _____
9. _____
10. _____

Review Words

1. cook
2. spoon
3. shook
4. school
5. tooth

How to Study a Word

Look at the word.
Say the word.
Think about the word.
Write the word.
Check the spelling.

American Stories Spelling Review

Spelling Words

1. howl
2. false
3. sauce
4. put
5. roof
6. hardly
7. dairy
8. charge
9. dirty
10. world
11. bounce
12. couch
13. wood
14. push
15. pull
16. year
17. alarm
18. horse
19. curl
20. return
21. jaw
22. dawn
23. tool
24. full
25. gear
26. spare
27. cheer
28. chore
29. heard
30. search

See the back for Challenge Words.

My Study List
Add your own spelling words on the back. ➡

415

A Very Important Day

The /ôr/, /ûr/, and /y͞oor/ Sounds

/ôr/ ➡ h**or**se, ch**ore**
/ûr/ ➡ f**ir**m, c**ur**ve, l**ear**n, w**or**m
/y͞oor/ ➡ p**ure**

Spelling Words

1. horse
2. chore
3. firm
4. learn
5. dirty
6. curve
7. world
8. pure
9. board
10. course
11. heard
12. return
13. cure
14. score
15. worm
16. thirteen
17. worn
18. curl
19. shirt
20. search

Challenge Words

1. thoroughbred
2. fortunate
3. hurdle
4. foreign
5. earnest

My Study List
Add your own spelling words on the back. ➡

415

Boss of the Plains

The /îr/, /är/, and /âr/ Sounds

/îr/ ➡ g**ear**, ch**eer**
/är/ ➡ sh**ar**p
/âr/ ➡ st**are**, h**air**y

Spelling Words

1. gear
2. spear
3. sharp
4. stare
5. alarm
6. cheer
7. square
8. hairy
9. heart
10. weird
11. starve
12. charm
13. beard
14. hardly
15. spare
16. stairs
17. year
18. charge
19. dairy
20. scarce

Challenge Words

1. pioneer
2. awareness
3. startle
4. marvel
5. weary

My Study List
Add your own spelling words on the back. ➡

415

Name _____

My Study List

1. _____
2. _____
3. _____
4. _____
5. _____
6. _____
7. _____
8. _____
9. _____
10. _____

Review Words

1. air
2. near
3. large
4. scare
5. chair

How to Study a Word

Look at the word.
Say the word.
Think about the word.
Write the word.
Check the spelling.

Name _____

My Study List

1. _____
2. _____
3. _____
4. _____
5. _____
6. _____
7. _____
8. _____
9. _____
10. _____

Review Words

1. first
2. hurt
3. work
4. third
5. storm

How to Study a Word

Look at the word.
Say the word.
Think about the word.
Write the word.
Check the spelling.

Name _____

My Study List

1. _____
2. _____
3. _____
4. _____
5. _____
6. _____
7. _____
8. _____
9. _____
10. _____

Challenge Words

1. pounce
2. pudding
3. cocoon
4. awareness
5. fortunate
6. scrawny
7. marooned
8. pioneer
9. marvel
10. earnest

How to Study a Word

Look at the word.
Say the word.
Think about the word.
Write the word.
Check the spelling.

Cendrillon

Final /ər/, /l/, or /əl/

/ər/ ➡ weath**er**, harb**or**, sug**ar**

/l/ ➡ mod**el**, fin**al**,

or /əl/ middl**e**

Spelling Words

1. harbor
2. final
3. middle
4. weather
5. labor
6. model
7. chapter
8. special
9. sugar
10. bottle
11. medal
12. collar
13. proper
14. towel
15. beggar
16. battle
17. trouble
18. shower
19. uncle
20. doctor

Challenge Words

1. shoulder
2. decimal
3. trifle
4. solar
5. cancel

My Study List
Add your own spelling words on the back. ➡

That's Amazing!
Reading-Writing Workshop

Look for familiar spelling patterns in these words to help you remember their spellings.

Spelling Words

1. tonight
2. whole
3. while
4. could
5. world
6. writing
7. build
8. school
9. finished
10. morning
11. coming
12. stopped
13. getting
14. goes
15. going

Challenge Words

1. happened
2. received
3. believe
4. quit
5. quite

My Study List
Add your own spelling words on the back. ➡

The Stranger

Compound Words
A compound word may be written as one word, as two words joined by a hyphen, or as two separate words.

Spelling Words

1. railroad
2. airport
3. seat belt
4. everywhere
5. homesick
6. understand
7. background
8. anything
9. ninety-nine
10. already
11. fireplace
12. ourselves
13. all right
14. forever
15. breakfast
16. whenever
17. everything
18. meanwhile
19. afternoon
20. make-believe

Challenge Words

1. landmark
2. nationwide
3. postscript
4. motorcycle
5. handkerchief

My Study List
Add your own spelling words on the back. ➡

Take-Home Word List

Take-Home Word List

Take-Home Word List

Name _____

Name _____

Name _____

My Study List

1. _____
2. _____
3. _____
4. _____
5. _____
6. _____
7. _____
8. _____
9. _____
10. _____

Review Words

1. inside
2. outside
3. birthday
4. baseball
5. sometimes

My Study List

1. _____
2. _____
3. _____
4. _____
5. _____
6. _____
7. _____
8. _____
9. _____
10. _____

My Study List

1. _____
2. _____
3. _____
4. _____
5. _____
6. _____
7. _____
8. _____
9. _____
10. _____

Review Words

1. neighbor
2. little
3. dollar
4. daughter
5. circle

How to Study a Word

Look at the word.
Say the word.
Think about the word.
Write the word.
Check the spelling.

How to Study a Word

Look at the word.
Say the word.
Think about the word.
Write the word.
Check the spelling.

How to Study a Word

Look at the word.
Say the word.
Think about the word.
Write the word.
Check the spelling.

My Name Is María Isabel

The /k/, /ng/, and /kw/ Sounds

/k/ → shar**k**, atta**ck**, publi**c**

/ng/ → si**n**k

/kw/ → **qu**estion

Spelling Words

1. shark
2. attack
3. risk
4. public
5. sink
6. question
7. electric
8. jacket
9. blank
10. ache
11. crooked
12. drink
13. topic
14. track
15. blanket
16. struck
17. mistake
18. junk
19. squirrel
20. stomach

Challenge Words

1. aquatic
2. comic
3. tropical
4. speckled
5. peculiar

That's Amazing!
Spelling Review

Spelling Words

1. railroad
2. homesick
3. anything
4. seat belt
5. battle
6. beggar
7. doctor
8. smelling
9. pleasing
10. dimmed
11. airport
12. understand
13. ninety-nine
14. final
15. trouble
16. towel
17. medal
18. striped
19. skipped
20. checking
21. all right
22. make-believe
23. whenever
24. proper
25. uncle
26. weather
27. raced
28. snapping
29. hiking
30. fainted

See the back for Challenge Words.

Heat Wave!

Words with *-ed* or *-ing*

race + **ed** = rac**ed**

land + **ed** = land**ed**

snap + **ing** = sna**pping**

Spelling Words

1. dancing
2. skipped
3. hiking
4. flipped
5. snapping
6. raced
7. landed
8. pleasing
9. checking
10. dared
11. dimmed
12. rubbing
13. striped
14. wasting
15. traced
16. stripped
17. tanning
18. smelling
19. phoning
20. fainted

Challenge Words

1. breathing
2. tiring
3. urged
4. scrubbed
5. striving

My Study List
Add your own spelling words on the back. ➡

My Study List
Add your own spelling words on the back. ➡

My Study List
Add your own spelling words on the back. ➡

Name _____

My Study List

1. _____
2. _____
3. _____
4. _____
5. _____
6. _____
7. _____
8. _____
9. _____
10. _____

Review Words

1. cared
2. joking
3. tapping
4. wrapped
5. fixing

How to Study a Word

Look at the word.
Say the word.
Think about the word.
Write the word.
Check the spelling.

420

Name _____

My Study List

1. _____
2. _____
3. _____
4. _____
5. _____
6. _____
7. _____
8. _____
9. _____
10. _____

Challenge Words

1. handkerchief   6. postscript
2. motorcycle   7. shoulder
3. decimal   8. cancel
4. scrubbed   9. breathing
5. striving   10. urged

How to Study a Word

Look at the word.
Say the word.
Think about the word.
Write the word.
Check the spelling.

420

Name _____

My Study List

1. _____
2. _____
3. _____
4. _____
5. _____
6. _____
7. _____
8. _____
9. _____
10. _____

Review Words

1. quick
2. luck
3. picnic
4. basket
5. sock

How to Study a Word

Look at the word.
Say the word.
Think about the word.
Write the word.
Check the spelling.

420

The Last Dragon

Final /j/ and /s/
/j/ ➡ bri**dge**, stran**ge**
/ĭj/ ➡ villa**ge**
/s/ ➡ fen**ce**

Spelling Words

1. village
2. cottage
3. bridge
4. fence
5. strange
6. chance
7. twice
8. cage
9. change
10. carriage
11. glance
12. ridge
13. manage
14. damage
15. since
16. marriage
17. edge
18. lodge
19. cabbage
20. dodge

Challenge Words

1. fleece
2. fragrance
3. homage
4. fringe
5. excellence

My Study List
Add your own
spelling words
on the back. ➡

421

Marven of the Great North Woods

Final /ē/
Final /ē/ ➡ beaut**y**, hon**ey**

Spelling Words

1. beauty
2. ugly
3. lazy
4. marry
5. ready
6. sorry
7. empty
8. honey
9. valley
10. movie
11. duty
12. hungry
13. lonely
14. alley
15. body
16. twenty
17. turkey
18. hockey
19. fifty
20. monkey

Challenge Words

1. fiery
2. envy
3. mercy
4. chimney
5. imaginary

My Study List
Add your own
spelling words
on the back. ➡

421

Problem Solvers
Reading-Writing Workshop

Look for familiar spelling patterns in these words to help you remember their spellings.

Spelling Words

1. sure
2. here
3. knew
4. might
5. pretty
6. really
7. very
8. where
9. little
10. until
11. into
12. off
13. said
14. our
15. letter

Challenge Words

1. finally
2. different
3. excite
4. truly
5. suppose

My Study List
Add your own
spelling words
on the back. ➡

421

Name _____

My Study List

1. _____
2. _____
3. _____
4. _____
5. _____
6. _____
7. _____
8. _____
9. _____
10. _____

How to Study a Word

Look at the word.
Say the word.
Think about the word.
Write the word.
Check the spelling.

422

Name _____

My Study List

1. _____
2. _____
3. _____
4. _____
5. _____
6. _____
7. _____
8. _____
9. _____
10. _____

Review Words

1. pretty
2. sadly
3. friendly
4. city
5. slowly

How to Study a Word

Look at the word.
Say the word.
Think about the word.
Write the word.
Check the spelling.

422

Name _____

My Study List

1. _____
2. _____
3. _____
4. _____
5. _____
6. _____
7. _____
8. _____
9. _____
10. _____

Review Words

1. nice
2. place
3. huge
4. judge
5. page

How to Study a Word

Look at the word.
Say the word.
Think about the word.
Write the word.
Check the spelling.

422

Happy Birthday, Dr. King!

Words with a Prefix or a Suffix

re + paint = **re**paint
dis + like = **dis**like
un + lucky = **un**lucky
un + pack = **un**pack
sick**ness**   treat**ment**
beauti**ful**   care**less**

Spelling Words

1. redo
2. treatment
3. rebuild
4. discolor
5. careless
6. dislike
7. sickness
8. beautiful
9. unlucky
10. awful
11. reread
12. unsure
13. movement
14. peaceful
15. unpaid
16. distrust
17. kindness
18. useless
19. displease
20. powerful

Challenge Words

1. unusual
2. rearrange
3. appointment
4. discontinue
5. resourceful

My Study List

Add your own spelling words on the back. ➡

Problem Solvers
Spelling Review

Spelling Words

1. sink
2. squirrel
3. question
4. twenty
5. alley
6. twice
7. chance
8. glance
9. thirty
10. afraid
11. blanket
12. crooked
13. honey
14. monkey
15. ready
16. cottage
17. since
18. other
19. corner
20. office
21. mistake
22. attack
23. lonely
24. beauty
25. strange
26. ridge
27. village
28. suppose
29. degree
30. whether

See the back for Challenge Words.

My Study List

Add your own spelling words on the back. ➡

Sing to the Stars

VCCV Pattern

VC | CV :   **dan|ger**,
              at|tend,
              din|ner
V | CCV :   **a|fraid**
VCC | V :   **rock|et**

Spelling Words

1. bottom
2. picture
3. other
4. attend
5. capture
6. common
7. danger
8. afraid
9. borrow
10. office
11. arrow
12. suppose
13. escape
14. whether
15. pillow
16. dinner
17. thirty
18. degree
19. allow
20. corner

Challenge Words

1. method
2. concert
3. narrate
4. abrupt
5. challenge

My Study List

Add your own spelling words on the back. ➡

Name _____

My Study List

1. _____
2. _____
3. _____
4. _____
5. _____
6. _____
7. _____
8. _____
9. _____
10. _____

Review Words

1. between
2. lesson
3. enjoy
4. happen
5. teacher

How to Study a Word

Look at the word.
Say the word.
Think about the word.
Write the word.
Check the spelling.

Name _____

My Study List

1. _____
2. _____
3. _____
4. _____
5. _____
6. _____
7. _____
8. _____
9. _____
10. _____

Challenge Words

1. comic   6. tropical
2. aquatic   7. chimney
3. imaginary   8. fiery
4. homage   9. fleece
5. concert   10. narrate

How to Study a Word

Look at the word.
Say the word.
Think about the word.
Write the word.
Check the spelling.

Name _____

My Study List

1. _____
2. _____
3. _____
4. _____
5. _____
6. _____
7. _____
8. _____
9. _____
10. _____

Review Words

1. hopeful
2. remake
3. rewrite
4. useful
5. unfair

How to Study a Word

Look at the word.
Say the word.
Think about the word.
Write the word.
Check the spelling.

Lou Gehrig

VCV Pattern
V | CV : **pi | lot,**
           mo | ment
VC | V : **vis | it,**
           par | ent

Spelling Words

1. pilot
2. depend
3. visit
4. human
5. seven
6. chosen
7. paper
8. reason
9. become
10. parent
11. never
12. modern
13. tiny
14. tuna
15. event
16. fever
17. moment
18. prison
19. basic
20. open

Challenge Words

1. alert
2. license
3. select
4. radar
5. feature

My Study List
Add your own
spelling words
on the back. ➡

Gloria Estefan

Changing Final *y* to *i*
city   + es = cit**ies**
study + ed = stud**ied**
sunny + er = sunn**ier**
heavy + est = heav**iest**

Spelling Words

1. sunnier
2. cloudier
3. windier
4. cities
5. heaviest
6. prettiest
7. studied
8. easier
9. noisier
10. families
11. ferries
12. crazier
13. funnier
14. earlier
15. copied
16. hobbies
17. angriest
18. emptied
19. worried
20. happiest

Challenge Words

1. iciest
2. hazier
3. breezier
4. companies
5. qualities

My Study List
Add your own
spelling words
on the back. ➡

Heroes
Reading-Writing Workshop

Look for familiar spelling
patterns in these words
to help you remember
their spellings.

Spelling Words

1. brought
2. enough
3. buy
4. guess
5. Saturday
6. January
7. February
8. favorite
9. lying
10. tying
11. around
12. swimming
13. heard
14. also
15. tried

Challenge Words

1. choose
2. chose
3. loose
4. lose
5. millimeter

My Study List
Add your own
spelling words
on the back. ➡

Take-Home Word List

Take-Home Word List

Take-Home Word List

Name _____

Name _____

Name _____

My Study List

1. _____
2. _____
3. _____
4. _____
5. _____
6. _____
7. _____
8. _____
9. _____
10. _____

My Study List

1. _____
2. _____
3. _____
4. _____
5. _____
6. _____
7. _____
8. _____
9. _____
10. _____

My Study List

1. _____
2. _____
3. _____
4. _____
5. _____
6. _____
7. _____
8. _____
9. _____
10. _____

Review Words

1. hurried
2. stories
3. carried
4. pennies
5. babies

Review Words

1. before
2. travel
3. orange
4. ever
5. begin

How to Study a Word

Look at the word.
Say the word.
Think about the word.
Write the word.
Check the spelling.

How to Study a Word

Look at the word.
Say the word.
Think about the word.
Write the word.
Check the spelling.

How to Study a Word

Look at the word.
Say the word.
Think about the word.
Write the word.
Check the spelling.

Nature: Friend and Foe
Reading-Writing Workshop

Look for familiar spelling patterns in these words to help you remember their spellings.

Spelling Words

1. their
2. there
3. they're
4. your
5. you're
6. its
7. it's
8. to
9. too
10. two
11. they
12. than
13. then
14. right
15. write

Challenge Words

1. all right
2. usually
3. eighth
4. height
5. tongue

My Study List
Add your own spelling words on the back. ➡

Salmon Summer

Three-Syllable Words
yes | ter | day ➡
   /yĕs′ tər dā/
de | liv | er ➡
   /dĭ lĭv′ ər/

Spelling Words

1. deliver
2. favorite
3. camera
4. yesterday
5. tomorrow
6. important
7. together
8. victory
9. remember
10. library
11. enemy
12. animal
13. another
14. however
15. banana
16. alphabet
17. hospital
18. hamburger
19. carpenter
20. several

Challenge Words

1. interview
2. article
3. halibut
4. edition
5. photograph

My Study List
Add your own spelling words on the back. ➡

Heroes
Spelling Review

Spelling Words

1. redo
2. unsure
3. useless
4. kindness
5. easier
6. copied
7. crazier
8. seven
9. become
10. fever
11. dislike
12. movement
13. displease
14. cities
15. families
16. worried
17. angriest
18. paper
19. parent
20. prison
21. reread
22. peaceful
23. powerful
24. studied
25. earlier
26. happiest
27. visit
28. reason
29. never
30. tuna

See the back for Challenge Words.

My Study List
Add your own spelling words on the back. ➡

Take-Home Word List

Take-Home Word List

Take-Home Word List

Name _____

My Study List

1. _____
2. _____
3. _____
4. _____
5. _____
6. _____
7. _____
8. _____
9. _____
10. _____

Name _____

My Study List

1. _____
2. _____
3. _____
4. _____
5. _____
6. _____
7. _____
8. _____
9. _____
10. _____

Name _____

My Study List

1. _____
2. _____
3. _____
4. _____
5. _____
6. _____
7. _____
8. _____
9. _____
10. _____

Challenge Words

1. unusual
2. resourceful
3. breezier
4. select
5. radar
6. discontinue
7. companies
8. iciest
9. alert
10. license

Review Words

1. grandmother
2. grandfather
3. October
4. November
5. unhappy

How to Study a Word

Look at the word.
Say the word.
Think about the word.
Write the word.
Check the spelling.

How to Study a Word

Look at the word.
Say the word.
Think about the word.
Write the word.
Check the spelling.

How to Study a Word

Look at the word.
Say the word.
Think about the word.
Write the word.
Check the spelling.

Nature: Friend and Foe Spelling Review

Spelling Words

1. favorite	16. blood
2. camera	17. women
3. banana	18. listen
4. remember	19. honor
5. neither	20. kneel
6. against	21. another
7. wonder	22. library
8. climb	23. deliver
9. thumb	24. says
10. calf	25. gasoline
11. animal	26. style
12. however	27. soften
13. alphabet	28. wrist
14. health	29. handsome
15. guard	30. knight

See the back for Challenge Words.

My Study List
Add your own spelling words on the back. ➡

Skylark

Silent Consonants
Some words have a consonant that is not pronounced.

kneel clim**b** cal**f**
wrinkle **h**onest

Spelling Words

1. knight	11. listen
2. soften	12. calm
3. honor	13. knit
4. kneel	14. often
5. climb	15. palm
6. wrinkle	16. thumb
7. limb	17. wrist
8. handsome	18. lamb
9. answer	19. knob
10. calf	20. honest

Challenge Words

1. drought
2. knoll
3. heir
4. debt
5. wrestle

My Study List
Add your own spelling words on the back. ➡

Wildfires

Unusual Spellings

/ĕ/ ➡	h**ea**lth, ag**ai**nst, s**ay**s
/ĭ/ ➡	w**o**men
/ŭ/ ➡	bl**oo**d, m**o**nth
/ē/ ➡	rec**ei**ve, mag**a**z**i**ne
/ī/ ➡	t**y**pe
/g/ ➡	**gu**ess

Spelling Words

1. health	11. guide
2. blood	12. style
3. type	13. wealth
4. against	14. guilt
5. receive	15. says
6. flood	16. guard
7. month	17. wonder
8. magazine	18. guest
9. guess	19. gasoline
10. women	20. neither

Challenge Words

1. vaccine
2. quarantine
3. guarantee
4. threaten
5. rhyme

My Study List
Add your own spelling words on the back. ➡

Name _____

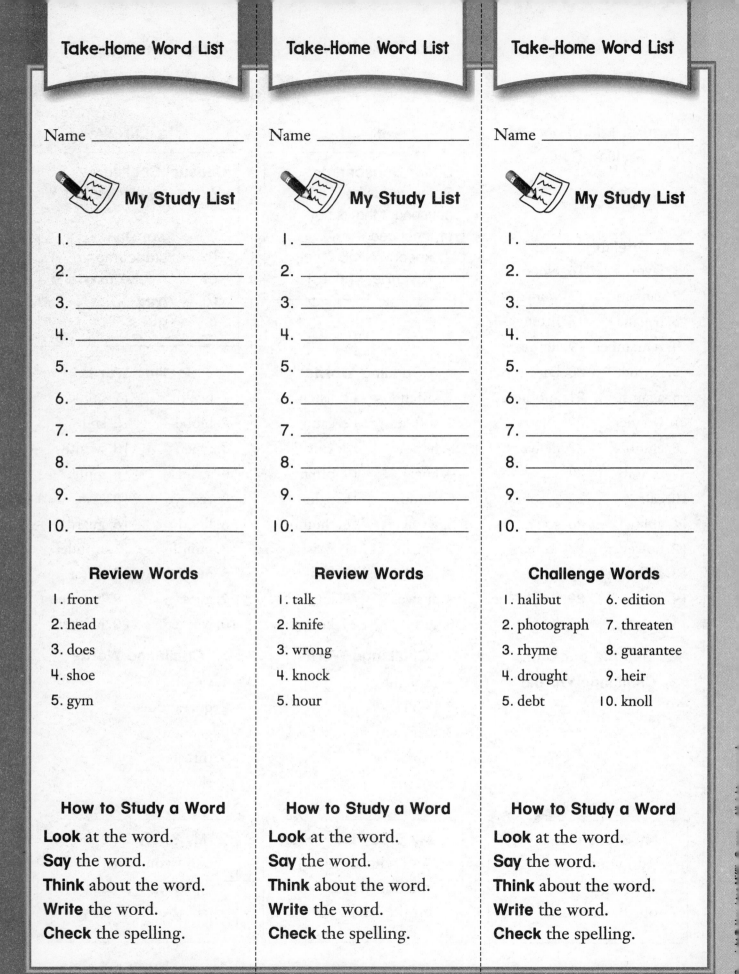

My Study List

1. _____
2. _____
3. _____
4. _____
5. _____
6. _____
7. _____
8. _____
9. _____
10. _____

Review Words

1. front
2. head
3. does
4. shoe
5. gym

How to Study a Word

Look at the word.
Say the word.
Think about the word.
Write the word.
Check the spelling.

Name _____

My Study List

1. _____
2. _____
3. _____
4. _____
5. _____
6. _____
7. _____
8. _____
9. _____
10. _____

Review Words

1. talk
2. knife
3. wrong
4. knock
5. hour

How to Study a Word

Look at the word.
Say the word.
Think about the word.
Write the word.
Check the spelling.

Name _____

My Study List

1. _____
2. _____
3. _____
4. _____
5. _____
6. _____
7. _____
8. _____
9. _____
10. _____

Challenge Words

1. halibut
2. photograph
3. rhyme
4. drought
5. debt
6. edition
7. threaten
8. guarantee
9. heir
10. knoll

How to Study a Word

Look at the word.
Say the word.
Think about the word.
Write the word.
Check the spelling.

Problem Words

Words	Rules	Examples
are our	*Are* is a verb. *Our* is a possessive pronoun.	<u>Are</u> these gloves yours? This is <u>our</u> car.
doesn't don't	Use *doesn't* with singular nouns, *he*, *she*, and *it*. Use *don't* with plural nouns, *I*, *you*, *we*, and *they*.	Dad <u>doesn't</u> swim. We <u>don't</u> swim.
good well	Use the adjective *good* to describe nouns. Use the adverb *well* to describe verbs.	The weather looks <u>good</u>. She sings <u>well</u>.
its it's	*Its* is a possessive pronoun. *It's* is a contraction of *it is*.	The dog wagged <u>its</u> tail. <u>It's</u> cold today.
set sit	*Set* means "to put." *Sit* means "to rest or stay in one place."	<u>Set</u> the vase on the table. Please <u>sit</u> in this chair.
their there they're	*Their* means "belonging to them." *There* means "at or in that place." *They're* is a contraction of *they are*.	<u>Their</u> coats are on the bed. Is Carlos <u>there</u>? <u>They're</u> going to the store.
two to too	*Two* is a number *To* means "toward." *Too* means "also" or "more than enough."	I bought <u>two</u> shirts. A cat ran <u>to</u> the tree. Can we go <u>too</u>? I ate <u>too</u> many peas.
your you're	*Your* is a possessive pronoun. *You're* is a contraction of *you are*.	Are these <u>your</u> glasses? <u>You're</u> late again!

Read each question below. Then check your paper. Correct any mistakes you find. After you have corrected them, put a check mark in the box next to the question.

☐   1. Did I indent each paragraph?

☐   2. Does each sentence tell one complete thought?

☐   3. Do I have any run-on sentences?

☐   4. Did I spell all words correctly?

☐   5. Did I use capital letters correctly?

☐   6. Did I use punctuation marks correctly?

☐   7. Did I use commas and apostrophes correctly?

☐   8. Did I spell all the words the right way?

Is there anything else you should look for? Make your own proofreading checklist.

☐ _____

☐ _____

☐ _____

☐ _____

☐ _____

☐ _____

☐ _____

Proofreading Marks

Mark	Explanation	Examples
¶	Begin a new paragraph. Indent the paragraph.	¶We went to an air show last Saturday. Eight jets flew across the sky in the shape of V's, X's, and diamonds.
∧	Add letters, words, or sentences.	The leaves were red ^and^ orange.
ꝉ	Take out words, sentences, and punctuation marks. Correct spelling.	The sky is bright ~~blew~~ blue. Huge clouds, move quickly.
/	Change a capital letter to a small letter.	The F/ireflies blinked in the dark.
≡	Change a small letter to a capital letter.	New York city is exciting.